The British and French in the Atlantic 1650–1800

The British and French in the Atlantic 1650–1800 provides a comprehensive history of this complex period and explores the contrasting worlds of the British and the French empires as they strove to develop new societies in the Americas.

Charting the volatile relationship between the British and French, this book examines the approaches that both empires took as they attempted to realise their ambitions of exploration, conquest, and settlement, and highlights the similarities as well as the differences between them. Both empires faced slave revolts, internal rebellion, and revolution, as well as frequent wars against one another, which came to dominate the Atlantic world and which culminated in the eventual failure of both empires in North America: the French following the end of the Seven Years' War in 1763 and the British 20 years later in the war against American independence.

Delving into key themes, such as exploration and settlement, the creation of societies, inequality and exploitation, conflict and violence, trade and slavery, and featuring a range of documents to enable a deeper insight into the relationship between the colonising Europeans and Native Americans, *The British and French in the Atlantic 1650–1800* is ideal for students of the Atlantic World, early modern Britain and France, and colonial America.

Gwenda Morgan, formerly Reader in American History and American Studies at the University of Sunderland, is now Honorary Research Fellow at the University of Durham. She has published on law and society in colonial America and the young republic, a monograph on Richmond County, Virginia, and *The Debate on the American Revolution* (2007).

Together they have published *Eighteenth-Century Criminal Transportation: The Formation of the Criminal Atlantic* (2003) and *Banishment in the Early Atlantic World: Convicts, Rebels and Slaves* (2013).

Peter Rushton is Professor of Historical Sociology at the University of Sunderland. He has published widely on aspects of the personal and social relations of early modern England, from witchcraft and welfare, to problems of marriage and family life.

Introduction to the series

History is the narrative constructed by historians from traces left by the past. Historical enquiry is often driven by contemporary issues and, in consequence, historical narratives are constantly reconsidered, reconstructed, and reshaped. The fact that different historians have different perspectives on issues means that there is often controversy and no universally agreed version of past events. *Seminar Studies* was designed to bridge the gap between current research and debate, and the broad, popular general surveys that often date rapidly.

The volumes in the series are written by historians who are not only familiar with the latest research and current debates concerning their topic but who have themselves contributed to our understanding of the subject. The books are intended to provide the reader with a clear introduction to a major topic in history. They provide both a narrative of events and a critical analysis of contemporary interpretations. They include the kinds of tools generally omitted from specialist monographs: a chronology of events, a glossary of terms, and brief biographies of 'who's who'. They also include bibliographical essays in order to guide students to the literature on various aspects of the subject. Students and teachers alike will find that the selection of documents will stimulate the discussion and offer insight into the raw materials used by historians in their attempt to understand the past.

Clive Emsley and Gordon Martel
Series Editors

The British and French in the Atlantic 1650–1800

Comparisons and Contrasts

Gwenda Morgan and Peter Rushton

LONDON AND NEW YORK

First published 2019
by Routledge
2 Park Square, Milton Park, Abingdon, Oxon OX14 4RN

and by Routledge
52 Vanderbilt Avenue, New York, NY 10017

Routledge is an imprint of the Taylor & Francis Group, an informa business

© 2019 Gwenda Morgan and Peter Rushton

The right of Gwenda Morgan and Peter Rushton to be identified as authors of this work has been asserted by them in accordance with sections 77 and 78 of the Copyright, Designs and Patents Act 1988.

All rights reserved. No part of this book may be reprinted or reproduced or utilised in any form or by any electronic, mechanical, or other means, now known or hereafter invented, including photocopying and recording, or in any information storage or retrieval system, without permission in writing from the publishers.

Trademark notice: Product or corporate names may be trademarks or registered trademarks, and are used only for identification and explanation without intent to infringe.

British Library Cataloguing-in-Publication Data
A catalogue record for this book is available from the British Library

Library of Congress Cataloging-in-Publication Data
Names: Morgan, Gwenda, author. | Rushton, Peter, author.
Title: The British and French in the Atlantic 1650–1800 :
  comparisons and contrasts / Gwenda Morgan and Peter Rushton.
Description: Abingdon, Oxon ; New York, NY : Routledge, 2019. |
  Series: Seminar studies | Includes bibliographical references and
  index.
Identifiers: LCCN 2018056455| ISBN 9781138657571 (hardback :
  alk. paper) | ISBN 9781138657588 (pbk. : alk. paper) |
  ISBN 9780429202643 (ebk.)
Subjects: LCSH: America—History—To 1810. | America—
  Discovery and exploration—British. | America—Discovery
  and exploration—French. | America—Colonization. | Great
  Britain—Colonies—America. | France—Colonies—America. |
  British—America—History—17th century. | British—America—
  History—18th century. | French—America—History—17th century. |
  French—America—History—18th century. | Great Britain—History,
  Naval—17th century. | Great Britain—History, Naval—18th
  century. | France—History, Naval—17th century. | France—History,
  Naval—18th century. | Great Britain—History, Military—17th
  century. | Great Britain—History, Military—18th century. | France—
  History, Military—17th century. | France—History, Military—18th
  century. | Atlantic Ocean Region—History—17th century. | Atlantic
  Ocean Region—History—18th century.
Classification: LCC E18.82 .M67 2019 | DDC 970.02—dc23
LC record available at https://lccn.loc.gov/2018056455

ISBN: 978-1-138-65757-1 (hbk)
ISBN: 978-1-138-65758-8 (pbk)
ISBN: 978-0-429-20264-3 (ebk)

Typeset in Sabon
by Apex CoVantage, LLC

Contents

List of maps	vii
Chronology	viii
Who's who	x
Note on terminology	xii
Maps	xiii

1 Introduction   1
    1.1 National, colonial, and Atlantic histories 5
    1.2 Patterns of contrast 8
    1.3 Sources and narratives 9

2 Exploration and settlement   11
    2.1 Exploration 14
    2.2 Maps and cultural misunderstandings 17
    2.3 Documented examples 19

3 New societies   22
    3.1 Migration 22
       3.1a Varieties of migrant 22
       3.1b Numbers 24
    3.2 Native encounters 28
    3.3 New societies, new economies 38
       3.3a Slave societies 46
       3.3b Servants and convicts 51
    3.4 Conclusion: New World, new societies 58

4 Wars across the Atlantic   60
    4.1 The Second Anglo-Dutch War (1665–1667) 63
    4.2 King William's War (1688–1697) or the Nine Years' War 64

    4.3 Queen Anne's War/the War of the Spanish Succession (1702–1713) 66
    4.4 The War of Jenkins' Ear/War of the Austrian Succession (King George's War) (1739–1748) 67
    4.5 The Seven Years' War/French and Indian War (1754–1763) 69

5   Resistance, rebellions, and revolutions   76
    5.1 Resistance 77
    5.2 Runaways: servants and slaves 'stealing themselves' 78
    5.3 Rebellions 81
    5.4 Slave conspiracies, real or imagined? 84
    5.5 White rebellions/rebellious whites 91
    5.6 Revolutions 95

6   Conclusion   107

Documents   111
Glossary   128
Further reading   130
References   133
Index   145

Maps

1	The Caribbean in the late seventeenth century	xiii
2	New France in the seventeenth century	xiv
3	North America in 1750	xv
4	Britain's 13 colonies	xvi

Chronology

1585	Roanoke (island off present-day North Carolina) – the first attempt at an English colony in America
1607	Jamestown (Virginia) founded by the British
1608	French settlement, 'Nouvelle France' – Quebec founded
1620	British Plymouth Colony established
1627	British Barbados settlement established
1628	Massachusetts Bay founded
1632	Maryland charter granted
1633	Charter for South Carolina granted by Charles I
1636	Pequot War, Massachusetts
1653	North Carolina founded
1655	Jamaica taken from the Spanish by the British
1675–76	King Philip's War (Massachusetts)
1681	Charter for Pennsylvania granted by Charles II to William Penn
1682	French Louisiana, named and controlled by the French until 1762
1688–97	King William's War or the Nine Years' War
1702–13	Queen Anne's War/the War of the Spanish Succession
1704	Louis's case (Paris), African slavery declared illegal in France
1718	New Orleans founded by the French
1733	Georgia founded by General James Oglethorpe
1736	Antigua Rebellion
1738	Jamaican authorities sign a peace treaty with the maroons: end of First Maroon War
1739–48	War of Jenkins' Ear and War of the Austrian Succession/King George's Succession
1741	New York conspiracy
1755–63	French and Indian War
1755	Braddock's defeat
1755	Acadians expelled by the British from Nova Scotia
1756–63	Seven Years' War
1759	Battle of Quebec, death of General Wolfe and Marquis de Montcalm

1760–61	Tacky's Rebellion, Jamaica
1763	Louisiana surrendered by the French under the Treaty of Paris that ended the Seven Years' War, the land east of the Mississippi to the British and to the west to the Spanish
1769–73	First Carib War, St. Vincent
1772	James Somerset case: African slavery in effect declared illegal in Britain – slaves could not be taken out of the country into a state of slavery
1776	Declaration of Independence of the United States
1776–83	American War for Independence
1777	British surrender at Saratoga under General John Burgoyne
1781	British commander Lord Cornwallis surrendered at Yorktown to combined forces of General George Washington and the French commander, Rochambeau
1783	US independence
1791	Haitian Revolution
1793	War between Britain and France
1795–96	Second Carib War, St. Vincent
1795–96	Grenada, Fédon's Rebellion suppressed
1795–96	Second Maroon War, and expulsion of the Trelawny maroons from Jamaica to Nova Scotia and then West Africa

Who's who

Nathaniel Bacon (1647–1676): English settler in Virginia, leader of the protest and 'rebellion' against Governor Sir William Berkeley; the rebellion collapsed after his death from disease

General Edward Braddock (1695–1755): killed in action against the French and Indians

Robert Cavelier de La Salle (1643–1687): explorer of territory from the Great Lakes to what he called Louisiana. He claimed all the land around the Mississippi for France. He was killed in what is now Texas, when his men mutinied during an unsuccessful search for the mouth of the Mississippi

Louis Dumont (Jean-François-Benjamin Dumont de Montigny) (1696–1760): soldier in Louisiana, author of *Memoires de Louisiane*

Bryan Edwards (1743–1800): English politician and writer in defence of slavery

Julien Fédon (?–1796): Grenada rebel, executed 1796

Richard Hakluyt (c.1552–1616): writer and geographer who advocated colonisation, and played a key part in setting up the Virginia Company; his *Discourse concerning Western Planting* (1584) was a major influence on the policies of both Elizabeth I and James I with regard to colonies

Louis Hennepin (1625–1701(+)): explorer and writer

Charles Lee (1732–1782): officer in the British army in America in the Seven Years' War, general under George Washington in the US Continental army

Jacob Leisler (c.1640–May 16, 1691): German emigrant to New York who staged first a protest and then a coup against the royal rule of James II in 1689 and was executed for rebellion. The British Parliament later granted him a posthumous pardon

Richard Ligon (c.1585–1662): emigrant and first historian of Barbados

Marquis de Montcalm (1712–1759): commander, French forces in the Seven Years' War, killed at Quebec

General James Oglethorpe (1696–1785): founder of Georgia, 1736

William Penn (1644–1718): Quaker founder of Pennsylvania

Jean-Baptiste Donatien de Vimeur, Comte de Rochambeau (1725–1807): commander of 7,000 French troops who joined George Washington at Yorktown in 1781

Charles de Rochefort (1605–1683): historian and writer

Admiral, Sir George Rodney (1718–1792): victor at the Battle of the Saintes, 1782

John Smith (1580–1631): early Virginian leader

Admiral Edward Vernon (1684–1757): commander at the capture of Porto Bello, 1739

Baron Friedrich Wilhelm von Steuben (1730–1794): major general in the United States army in the War for Independence, appointed by George Washington as inspector-general, and credited with introducing discipline and system into the drilling of American troops and the planning and design of military encampments

George Washington (1732–1799): Commander in Chief of the United States army, 1776–1783, later first President of the United States

General James Wolfe (1727–1759): commander of British forces in Canada in the Seven Years' War, killed at Quebec

Note on terminology

The title of this book speaks of Britain and the British, yet for the seventeenth century the colonial project was essentially 'English' in direction and culture but with many Irish and a few Scots involved. Nevertheless, we have used 'British' and 'Britain' throughout with regard to the colonies for the sake of clarity, and confined 'English' to those pieces of legislation or other institutions which were found only there, and not in Scotland; for example, the Poor Law, which was an English measure.

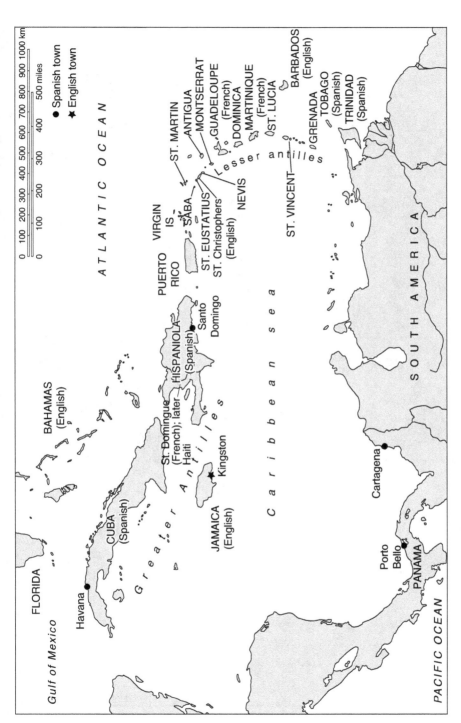

Map 0.1 The Caribbean in the late seventeenth century

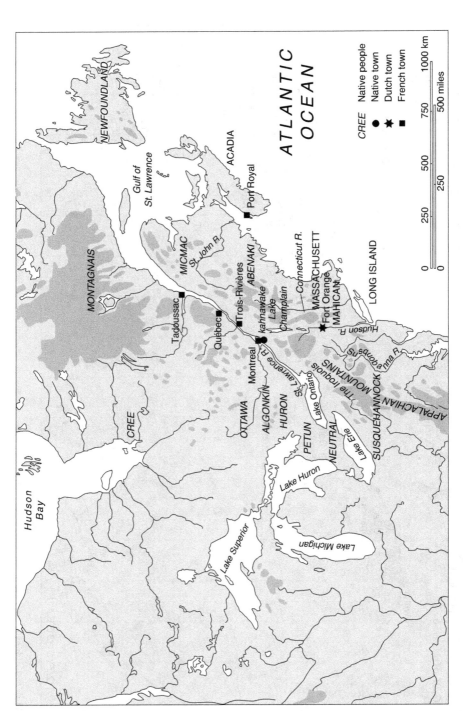

Map 0.2 New France in the seventeenth century

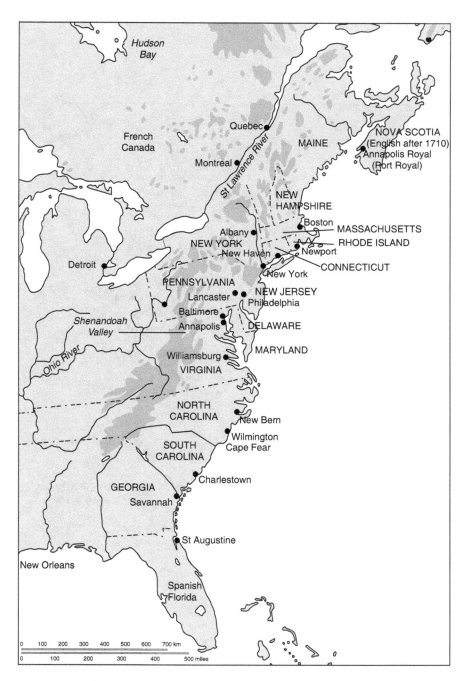

Map 0.3 North America in 1750

Map 0.4 Britain's 13 colonies

1 Introduction

1.1 National, colonial, and Atlantic histories
1.2 Patterns of contrast
1.3 Sources and narratives

This book examines the similarities and differences – the comparisons and contrasts – between two empires which rose together in the seventeenth century and faced defeat and loss in the eighteenth. In many ways the ambitions and the problems of the British and French empires were similar, but in terms of exploration, conquest, settlement, and relationships with natives there were many differences. Both produced slave societies in the Caribbean and North America and engaged in the transatlantic slave trade, but Britain, as the dominant mercantile power, was far more engaged in the shipping of Africans to the Americas. Patterns of white society in North America outside the areas of the slave plantations differed greatly, with contrasting economies and cultures: among the British colonies alone there were major differences between those (as in New England) which were driven by religious motivations and the rest. Both empires faced difficulties in controlling their colonies, particularly in the light of settlers' hunger for land, and everywhere expansion depended on defeating native peoples and clearing space for further settlement. The two empires watched each other with a mixture of respect and mistrust, which spilled over into frequent wars. The different aspects of the 150 years between 1650 and 1800 of struggle, competition, and change form the core of this book. The structure of the book is designed to discuss the key themes of the formation and development of these empires – exploration, the settlement and creation of new societies, the conflicts between the two European military powers, and finally the forms of internal resistance, rebellion, and revolution that the colonies produced. Each chapter can be read separately, if the reader wishes, and in any particular order, but in some ways they take different facets of the transatlantic empires, from start to finish, and can be understood as connected in significant ways. The experience of war, for example, both with natives and the European enemies, shaped the attitudes of these new societies. Their internal relationships, of exploitation (such as slavery) and resistance, affected their stability, but also determined much of the nature of their relationship with the metropolitan authorities in Europe. The slave colonies were among the most profitable aspects of both empires, and valued because of that alone. Yet imperial pride also mattered to some extent: loss of territory and prestige in their far-flung empires affected the political legitimacy of governments pledged to defend them. The book ends in rebellion and revolution, which shattered both empires but did not prevent them from continuing expansion elsewhere for at least another century. The sources for this diverse history are very varied, and this book cannot include all of them. Nevertheless, the documents have been chosen to illustrate the kinds of information available and they include extracts from personal diaries and memoirs, political statements, newspaper reports and advertisements, and official colonial records of the time.

In terms of the direction of the origins and development of the two empires, historians have usually been keen to explore the differences in the political driving forces, the kinds of colony and colonial government, the economic ambitions, and the forms of European settlement (types of settler, in effect) of the two empires. Some have emphasised the role of central government in France in initiating, managing, and supporting colonisation and expansion. By contrast, the venture companies, religiously motivated foundations, and settlements of the British empire may have needed initial licensing from the London authorities, but thereafter were left to their own devices for many aspects of their development. The British empire has been called an empire created by accident – in 1883 J.R. Seeley, in a collection significantly called *The Expansion of England*, remarked that 'we seem, as it were, to have conquered and peopled half the world in a fit of absence of mind', yet this was somewhat of an exaggeration. The government in London generated a huge amount of paper in monitoring and watching over the colonies (now published in the huge volumes of the *State Papers Colonial*). The system of governors created a method of monitoring and reporting on colonies and their problems, but many features of the British colonies, such as their legislation and legal systems, were left to local bodies such as legislative councils and elected assemblies. The resulting social and cultural diversity has influenced North American society ever since. It is worth noticing that the two empires did not develop in isolation: increasingly they came into competition and outright conflict by the end of the seventeenth century. They were both neighbours and rivals.

Europeans were on the move in the early modern period, both westwards across the Atlantic and eastwards to Siberia. Military conquest, settlement, problematic relations with native people, and the creation of significantly different, new societies characterised all of them (Pagden, 1990; Seed 1995). Every imperial nation had its own traditions when it came to taking and holding territories. Stamping their own names on places on maps and renaming rivers and mountains after famous Europeans (map-makers and explorers particularly) were common devices, and we now have the Hudson River in America and Mount Everest in Nepal as a result. Wherever natives had to be accepted as legitimate inhabitants, their names survived – mid-Atlantic rivers such as the Potomac and the Susquehanna are examples. Between the invaders and the natives there were often rituals of claim-making by the Europeans – 'the Spanish read out formal declarations of conquest and spelled out the terms of native submission. The English preferred to establish claims through action; they fenced in fields and sowed seeds to prove their 'title' (Kivelson, 2007: 37). After first contact there were complex forms of relationships with natives, except where disease virtually wiped them out, as in many Caribbean islands. The colonial period in Atlantic history was long and complex, with different phases from initial encounters between Europeans and natives to the final independence of many colonies as postcolonial states. In retrospect there is a tendency to assume that the final outcomes were an inevitable product of the period from 1492 onwards, but the history of rivalry and conflict between the British and French empires in the 150 years after 1650 shows how uncertain and unpredictable were the results. Both imperial ventures ended in failure, with the French losing their North American colonies in the Seven Years' War (1756–1763), and the British almost all of North America 20 years later with the independence of the United States. Despite many contrasts, the British and French shared many problems and difficulties; of exploration and settlement, negotiating with native peoples – or overwhelming them – and establishing economically secure colonies from the Arctic to the equator. They both established slave colonies in the Caribbean and southern areas of North America and participated in the largest forcible migration in history, the slave trade. Yet the colonies where white people settled and came to dominate differed widely, with only the British colonies attracting hundreds of thousands of determined settlers and creating an economic base independent from that of the home country.

Most scholars argue that the early period of European engagement, from the late fifteenth to the late eighteenth centuries, formed a distinctive phase in this story. Thomas Benjamin argues:

> It makes sense to differentiate the early Atlantic from our contemporary Atlantic. That earlier Atlantic was tied together in ways that were unique to that age and that no longer exist. Transatlantic empires, the slave trade and a commodities trade made possible by African slaves in New World plantations were just some of the most important connections. In that earlier Atlantic, unlike our Atlantic today, West Africa, South America, and the Caribbean were particularly important to the functioning of the international economy and the struggles between the great powers.
>
> (Benjamin, 2009: xxvi)

Not only was this world interconnected in ways that no longer exist, but the forms of imperial action and native reactions involved a high level of violence. Not for nothing did Bernard Bailyn call the seventeenth-century English 'peopling' of North America, defined by him as a 'conflict of civilisations', *The Barbarous Years* (Bailyn, 2012).

The experiences of the British and French in the Atlantic, from Africa to the Caribbean and North America, have many parallels as well as differences. Attempting to integrate these into a coherent picture, historians have been provoked to adopt many different kinds of perspectives and methods. Working within and occasionally beyond their native cultures, scholars have produced different kinds of history; of settlers, slaves, traders, natives, and invaders. Increasingly the focus has been not on the national histories of groups of colonies from one country, but on the Atlantic itself as a centre of many European, Native American, and African peoples' engagements with a wider world they had, between them, had a hand in making.

The 'expansion of Europe' sounds harmless enough and was once the framework for much history teaching of the period from the late fifteenth to the nineteenth centuries. Yet its Eurocentric approach, concentrating on the economic dynamics and inventiveness of only one part of the world, now seems self-obsessed or even racist in its denial of the actions and reactions of Africans, Asians, and Americans in the early modern period. In some ways, looking outwards from Europe, the approach made sense, if only because some countries had already begun a path to expansion – through reconquest of Islamic areas in Spain in the Middle Ages, by discovery and exploitation of the nearest Atlantic islands off the African coast by Portugal in the fifteenth century, and by the practice of 'plantation' in Ireland by the newly joined kingdoms of Scotland and England in the early seventeenth. These processes were easily transferred across the Atlantic. These countries were therefore keenly aware of the role of conquest in their own history (Canny, 1978: 7). So, to talk of 'British overseas enterprise' or the 'European opportunity' (or even of the 'global opportunity') offers some explanatory potential for understanding how what was once a cultural and economic backwater – the Atlantic coastal states of Europe – came to circulate around the globe and dominate the processes of overseas colonisation. Certainly, some explanation is needed for the concomitant failures of sophisticated states of the Ottoman, Mughal, or Chinese empires to match the Europeans (Marshall and Low, 1998; Bentley, 1997). The expansion perspective also allowed more conventional histories of imperial rivalries between England and Spain, or Britain and the Netherlands or France.

Yet this cannot provide the whole story of the Atlantic or even of British and French experiences. The impact of Europeans on Africans and Native Americans, and their influence on Europe, offers many different stories – of people and their movements, of diseases, of economic goods including new foods and crops, and of ideas.

1.1 National, colonial, and Atlantic histories

The key point to note, firstly, is that no place or people in the North Atlantic remained isolated or cut off from the others during the period 1650–1800. The establishment of exploratory settlements from the late sixteenth century onwards led both Britain and France to take part in complex forms of competition with each other and other rival powers, particularly the Spanish. In addition, trade with Native Americans in the western, and Africans in the eastern, side of the Atlantic was vital to the overall economic processes of the Atlantic and its imperial powers. In an attempt to integrate these different peoples and places, historians have developed a number of approaches which can loosely be called 'Atlantic history'. The starting point was the recognition of the 'triangular trade' at the height of the slave trade, with goods going to Africa in exchange for slaves, who were shipped across the ocean to the plantations, whose products were exported to the European centres of power. Initially this seemed a narrow and specialised process, but, beginning after the Second World War with scholars such as Bernard Bailyn in America, a broader Atlantic approach was developed, heavily influenced by the social and political feelings of Atlantic unity during the Cold War. Bailyn has sketched the context of its origins while also being critical of some of the conceptual weaknesses (Bailyn, 2005: 11–18). Some have examined this confusion of ideas and approaches and expressed scepticism about the possibilities of fulfilling the aim of an integrated history under such a vaguely defined banner. With time, however, scholars began to speak of the Atlantic *world*, or, in a more focused manner, of specific aspects of the Atlantic: the black Atlantic, the red Atlantic, the green Atlantic, the *criminal* Atlantic or the Atlantic proletariat (Gilroy, 1993; Linebaugh and Rediker, 2000; Morgan and Rushton, 2004). The 'world' concept was more ambitious, while the proliferation of smaller 'Atlantics' may reflect more focused and less sweeping approaches. The latter's success can be seen in some of the environmental and, particularly, economic history. DuPlessis' history of the many aspects of textile trading in the Atlantic is a fine model of what a concentrated focus can achieve within a general recognition of what the author calls the 'material Atlantic' (DuPlessis, 2016).

What does it mean, then, to write an Atlantic history? For one thing it involves recognition of the interconnections and relationships of many kinds; economic, cultural, and political. These connections crossed 'national' boundaries created by European empires which attempted to force their colonies to trade only with the 'mother country': the result was that smuggling between the different empires, for example, was endemic from the Caribbean to the Arctic. Second, it takes a broad view of as many factors as possible – and requires integration. As Bailyn has argued: 'The main stimulus to the proliferation of studies in and references to Atlantic history has been the explanatory power and suggestive implications created by the vision of the Atlantic region as a coherent whole' (Bailyn and Denaults, 2009: 2).

At the same time it recognises substantial differences and contrasts. 'One cannot accurately depict an "Atlantic World" without evaluating how all the Atlantic basin's peoples interacted, counteracted, and reacted to aims, behaviours, and decisions by others' (Falola and Roberts, 2008: x–xi). This differentiation takes into account that each aspect of these interrelationships had its own characteristics and dynamics: the concepts of the 'black' or 'criminal' Atlantics are to that extent justified by their systematic integration of both sides of the ocean.

The concept of an Atlantic 'world' by contrast – a single model – is perhaps the ideal rather than the reality of recent historiography: as Falola and Roberts point out, the use of the upper case 'w' in 'the Atlantic World' indicates a challenging project of grasping the complexity comprehensively in one go (Falola and Roberts, 2008: ix). Certainly, it would have been an odd conception to contemporaries in the seventeenth or eighteenth centuries. As the idea has been growing among Anglophone historians (less so among French scholars), some have reacted against the project and argued that this is simply a step too far, ironically providing too *narrow* a focus: 'virtually everywhere one looks in the Atlantic world in the early modern period, one finds other worlds impinging on and often shaping developments' (Coclanis, 2006: 728), above all those of Asia and its many valuable products such as porcelain or, more troublesome to patriotic revolutionary Americans, tea. Yet within those limits of the Atlantic basin, the focus can be very rewarding. As two early protagonists of the approach suggested:

> Atlantic history is an analytic construct and an explicit category of historical analysis that historians have devised to help them organise the study of some of the most important developments of the early modern era: the emergence in the fifteenth century and the subsequent growth of the Atlantic basin as a site for demographic, economic, social, cultural, and other forms of exchange among and within the four continents surrounding the Atlantic Ocean – Europe, Africa, South America, and North America – and all the islands adjacent to those continents and in that ocean.
>
> (Greene and Morgan, 2009: 3)

It may offer opportunities to integrate what were once separate areas of study: 'more recent exponents of Atlantic history, with a measure of missionary fervour, have increasingly begun to think of Atlantic history not merely as a perspective, but as a full-blown *field* of study with the potential to encompass older fields such as European, American, African, or Latin American history, and the imperial and national histories such continental classifications have traditionally assumed' (Greene and Morgan, 2009: 3–4). Above all, Atlantic approaches are as inclusive as possible, moving attention to the peripheries, the remote places on the margins, and the peoples there. 'So Atlantic history means a whole new cast of characters, people who may not appear in national stories, but who were the most important actors in creating a new historical reality' (Kupperman, 2012: 2).

In effect, 'Atlantic history' is a perspective that appreciates that no participant nation, group, culture, or economy remained the same once they had engaged with the broader Atlantic world. However much the British or French may have thought of the Americas as distant and alien, the home countries, their patterns of consumption and finance, war and politics, or their sense of their place in the world, could not remain untouched. The Atlantic's complexity is revealed by apparently specialist questions, as demonstrated by DuPlessis' study of cloth and clothing in his book *The Material Atlantic*: choices of desirable materials depended on different priorities and values held by natives and settlers, men and women, free or unfree. Those with the least choice, slaves and indentured servants, endured what John Styles has called 'involuntary consumption' (DuPlessis, 2016: 127), the result of a process of imposition that in fact began with many of them being stripped of their own clothing and enduring it being replaced by the clothes of their owners and employers. For the free, there were many choices to be made and the patterns of supply and demand of clothing, and variations in taste and design, embraced Europe, Africa, and the Americas. While examining the diversity of these related activities and cultures, this more integrative approach has the consequence of also allowing much broader generalisations about the common trends and experiences in different parts of the Atlantic. For example, Spanish conquest led to the enslavement of natives through forced labour (the *encomienda* system), and Native American slaves were also part of the British and French trading and raiding systems. In the areas of intensive plantation agriculture, however, enslaved Africans became the main workforce, whether the colonies were British, French, or Portuguese (Kupperman, 2012: 45). Servitude – of whites for shorter periods, of Africans for life (and for the lives of all their descendants) – became fundamental in certain areas on the western side of the Atlantic until the late eighteenth or even into the nineteenth centuries. Atlantic approaches should therefore attempt to integrate or draw together the differences, even if that involves allowing the 'methodological pluralism that characterises the new generation of Atlantic scholarship'. The individual need not be neglected. On the contrary. The Atlantic system 'is often conceived as a complex web of abstract economic and social structures. Its geographic width and chronological depth are such that individuals and their beliefs can appear almost irrelevant. Yet it is often individual lives that most clearly show the ways in which the Atlantic system altered local cultural and economic systems' (Coffman et al., 2015: 9, 125; Skidmore-Hess, 2013: 123–140).

This book relies on these different levels of viewing the Atlantic relationships and experiences, from the broad patterns of national and international trade and migration, forced labour, and economic change, to the personal narratives of individuals caught up in these processes.

1.2 Patterns of contrast

There were many similarities between the British and French intrusion into the Americas. Both countries had failed in the sixteenth century to establish a toe hold, and both managed to set down fragile roots only after 1600. Like the Spanish, Portuguese, and Dutch, the British and French states adopted an indirect method of funding such ventures, allowing individuals and groups in various types of 'proprietary' organisations to undertake the expensive and dangerous work of exploration and settlement. Despite their radically different political systems, both countries licensed private interests to establish their colonies. In the British case this resulted in a varied collection of proprietors responsible for colonies founded upon a contrasting set of legal charters. All colonies had the assemblies or legislatures required to generate their own laws and regulations. They were not exactly left to their own devices, but were never taken over directly by central government, as were the French colonies in the eighteenth century. Yet like France are often misleadingly seen as absolute, and therefore very centralised, states (Duindam, 2010). As L.H. Roper and B. Van Ruymbeke remark, 'early modern Western European states may have lurched towards centralisation. Yet, their governments remained dependent on a patchwork of officialdom—justices of the peace, councils, *audiencias, conseils*—to maintain order in localities. Proprietorships—whether captaincies, seigneuries, or corporations or some other device—constituted the only points of contact available to deal with the acknowledged problems of distance and ocean travel in attempting to administer transatlantic interests' (Roper and Van Ruymbeke, 2007: 13). Farming out the development of colonies, the seventeenth-century governments of France and Britain left the form of that development to a hodgepodge of organisations. Each attempted to entice Europeans to migrate and risk everything on the other side of the Atlantic, and from the first there were forms of *forced* migration to populate the colonies. 'Huge numbers of people migrated westward across the Atlantic in the centuries after 1492. Millions were enslaved and had no choice about either embarkation or destination. The others were free, but a very high proportion of the free migrants felt some compulsion in the choices they made. . . . The Americas offered opportunity to some, and the fortunate were able to make good on that promise. The logic of colonisation and plantation agriculture seemed to demand the forcible enlistment of unwilling labour' (Kupperman 2012: 44). The French Ministry of the Marine took more direct control of colonial matters eventually, providing its own military forces and supporting ventures such as warfare against native peoples and fortifying settlements and strongpoints. The British, too, as warfare with France became frequent, found themselves devoting more and more resources to their transatlantic possessions.

As to the settlers themselves, some were forced migrants, some reluctant but determined, and others inspired by dreams of freedom. The latter dominated in some contexts where religious motivation inspired people to migrate, particularly to New England. Alison Games (1997: 56, data for 1635) notes that 'the people travelling to New England came from all over [England]', largely channelled through the port of London. In French Canada, by contrast, Jesuit and Ursuline missionaries, together with elements of the French armed forces, shaped the pattern of settlements and could never attract such large numbers. Yet it was the British who tended to expel their own people to the colonies. The London authorities repeatedly forced people into migration, emptying carceral institutions into ships to Virginia in its early days, pardoning and transporting convicted criminals, or encouraging parishes to send their orphaned children. A century later, in 1718, mass transportation of criminals was instituted by a new statute, with the purpose of the 'better peopling' of the colonies. Though they did banish people, the French never attempted anything on that scale and the population of French settlers remained tiny compared with the settlers in the British colonies.

1.3 Sources and narratives

Inevitably history hinges upon stories as well as explanations. We can, therefore, draw upon personal accounts and experiences which, at the individual level, seem very similar: parallel lives, so to speak. Some speak through the accounts of others, particularly natives who had no writing though were able to represent their territories, peoples, and their histories in other ways, such as symbolically important maps. They were not entirely 'peoples without history', to coin a phrase about those Europeans encountered in many places around the world (Wolf, 2010). Colonial peoples represented themselves in many ways, but cultural production, particularly forms of print culture, was unevenly distributed. Literate colonies such as New England had a flourishing printing industry almost from the beginning. By the 1740s nearly all the British North American colonies had their own newspapers to supplement the production of pamphlets, notices, proclamations, and memoirs. Many religious and political disputes, and accounts of wars, captivity, crime, and confession were represented in publications by the Anglophone colonial printers. French colonies never manifested this level of independent production.

Accounts of colonial events were published in Europe, some annually such as the *Jesuit Relations* from French Canada, and there was a ready market for stories of exploration and descriptions of exotic wildlife and natives. Less attention was paid to the Caribbean after the initial period of seventeenth-century settlement, where local printed accounts were fewer. But in London and Paris the colonies figured regularly in all forms of print, from Aphra Behn's plays to Defoe's fictional Moll Flanders, and many accounts of the discovery and settlement of the colonies were published. Newspapers regularly reported Atlantic news, and personal accounts, always advertised as based on 'authentic' experience, were popular. Transported criminals, even former slaves, published their memoirs in London to an appreciative audience. Above all, the colonies generated vast quantities of paper in the official archives. One common feature of British and French Atlantic colonialism was the steadily expanding volume of correspondence, reports, and orders to and from the governors and administrators of the colonies. Only a selection of these can be chosen to illustrate the processes, personal narratives, and changes in the development of British and French Atlantic colonialism.

2 Exploration and settlement

2.1 Exploration
2.2 Maps and cultural misunderstandings
2.3 Documented examples

Cod, not gold or curiosity, first drove the French and English across the Atlantic, to exploit the rich fishing grounds of the Newfoundland Banks. By the early sixteenth century fishermen from several north-western French (mostly Breton) and western English ports, such as Bideford in Devon, were spending months off the coast of North America and bringing back fish to European markets. This familiarity with the navigation and coastline of the north-east, however, was not extended southwards for nearly another half-century. By the mid-seventeenth century, after the sixteenth-century experiments by both countries, in Surinam (South America) by the French and Roanoke (modern-day North Carolina) by the English, had failed, there were established outposts in both the Caribbean and North America. Moreover, there was a lively printing industry reporting on the character of the colonies, their natural environment, and native inhabitants. Within a few years of their establishment, histories were written of the colonies and their achievements. Marc Lescarbot wrote his *Histoire de Nouvelle France* in 1612, when the French had barely a toehold on North America, and the structure of his study, distinguishing 'natural' from 'moral' history, was followed a few years later by Charles de Rochefort, the second edition of whose *Histoire Naturelle et Morale des Iles Antilles de L'Amerique* of 1661 was swiftly translated into English (de Rochefort, 1666). By that time there were extensive French holdings in the Caribbean and many accounts of the colonies, their native peoples, and their language. De Rochefort was particularly keen to distinguish the way the British and French treated Native Americans, compared with the supposed policy of savagery and genocide adopted by the Spanish: they had not followed 'the inhumane and barbarous maximes of the Spaniards, nor after their example unmercifully exterminated the originary Inhabitants of the Country', he claimed (p. 158). Like other authors, he spent a great deal of text describing the physical character of the 'Antilles' (the common French term for the Caribbean) and the climatic variations to be experienced there, noting that the high temperatures were not really greater than those experienced in France. In some ways these accounts were both advertisements and invitations for a wider public to be attracted to the colonies, as well as a confirmation of their prosperity and general success. De Rochefort, for example, had to admit that the islands could not be used for cultivating wheat but, thankfully for a Frenchman, noted that vines flourished in that climate (Vol.1, p. 5). He provides a survey of each of the islands, its resources such as fauna and flora, and the uses to which the land could probably be put. This may have been the first comprehensive survey of the West Indies as a whole available in English, all the more valuable since it covered all the islands irrespective of the colonial authority involved. Some of these French accounts derived from the author's many years' experience in the Caribbean, though there have been doubts as to how long, or indeed whether, de Rochefort himself was in the West Indies (Harrigan, 2012: 117, note 6.).

The first, and for a long time the most important, British settlement in the Caribbean was in Barbados: by the 1640s there were 37,000 English people on the island, and the early experiments with tobacco had been replaced by investment in sugar cane (Benjamin, 2009: 256–257). At that point it acquired its first historian in Richard Ligon, whose *A True and Exact History of the Island of Barbados* (1657) provided audiences with a picture of the progress of the local economy and society. It was also a personal odyssey for him, driven into exile by the failure of the king's armies in the civil wars: by 1647, he said, he had felt like a 'stranger in my owne country' after the 'riot' of civil war destroyed his property (p. 1), and had accordingly taken ship for the Caribbean. In this he was copying his brother, who by then had gone to Virginia. Ligon's purpose in publishing his account, he said, was to describe the 'beauties and riches of that place', and, on the way, his voyage taking in Madeira, Las Palmas, and the Cape Verde Islands before crossing the Atlantic; he described the flying fish, birds, sharks, and other interesting phenomena such as unfamiliar constellations of stars. At Cape Verde he dined with a local gentleman and commented on the beauty and style of an African woman he met afterwards, described as a 'Padre's (priest's) Mistress' (pp. 12–13, 17). Ligon arrived in Barbados shortly after a joint revolt by African slaves and white servants, and in his analysis of local conditions was critical of the cruelty of plantation owners and masters who had driven them to desperation. His vivid travelogue and detailed account of Barbados, as well as his personal testimony concerning the individual landowners and their methods of management, were a unique revelation of conditions in a British colony (in fact, English at that time). His map was the first detailed plan of Barbados and marked the individual plantations and their owners as well as the road system. He recorded that 10,000 acres in the south of the island belonged to the 'Merchants of London' (a 1629 company of mostly Puritan merchants who had extensive interests in the islands, and had settled the smaller and more vulnerable Providence). The map is illustrated with many vignettes, of two camels and, implausibly, a naked, apparently crowned, native with a long bow, reminiscent of John White's engravings of Virginia natives. Most strikingly, he fills the blank at the north end of the island with a picture of a clearly European horseman chasing two scantily clad runaways, possibly slaves, and firing his pistol at them (p. 4). In his first impressions he noted the setting of the plantations visible from out at sea, rising one above another from the sea shore to the higher land in the interior, all apparently facing seawards. He had intended to go on to Antigua but for various reasons stayed in Barbados, noting that the place was already developed and, he observed, it was best to arrive with capital assets for, if you had money, it was better to buy a ready-equipped plantation there than try to establish one from scratch. The impression he gives is of a well-developed and flourishing colony.

This type of publication was very important in shaping popular consciousness of the colonies in Europe: they established the fascinating image of exotic plants and species and the potential for European settlement. Ligon's writings are justly famous for being one of the first critical accounts of colonial exploitation to appear in print. The image of whites in 'slavery' has remained one of the misleading impressions of their experiences (see Chapter 3). Nevertheless, it is important to stress how much colonial expansion and print culture went together almost from the time of Columbus, and published accounts of the colonies remained popular through to the nineteenth century. Some were travel narratives, while others were closer to adventure stories. This was particularly true even of the reluctant explorers such as convicted criminals: one of the earliest personal accounts of the West Indies was by Mary Carleton, a fraudster known as the 'German Princess', who was transported to Jamaica in 1671. Her brief account makes the newly acquired colony (taken in 1655) seem a natural destination for criminals (some of whom she had known in London, she claimed), and her supposed letter home to her fellow criminals in London's Newgate Gaol may be the first of its kind. Even if the accounts were written for her, they are one of the few – and the earliest – to centre on a woman's experience. Later these would be spun together into Daniel Defoe's deliberately shocking novel *Moll Flanders*. The pamphlets published at the time of her execution for returning from transportation are the first, and among the most vivid, convict narratives (Carleton, 1673a and 1673b). She was followed by the accounts of other forced exiles, such as those transported after Monmouth's Rebellion in 1685 (Morgan and Rushton, 2013: 75–80). More fictional still were the dramatic representations of Atlantic colonies on the stage, in the works of Aphra Behn. If Shakespeare's *The Tempest* was an oblique reference to the recent accounts of Barbados, Behn's plays such as *Oroonoko, or the Royal Slave* (1698) and, more explicitly, *The Widow Ranter, or the History of Bacon in Virginia* (1690) engaged with the colonial problems that were caused by political divisions at home. The latter was also responsible for the invention of one cliché – the low quality of the colonial gentry – and the myth that many of the gentry had been transported as criminals before rising to prosperity and power in the colonies. This was reinforced by satirical

14   *Exploration and settlement*

accounts of the American tobacco colonies, such as Ebenezer Cooke's *The Sotweed Factor* of 1708. His description of the tanned faces of respectable white Americans – 'tawny as a Moor' – established their status as a people who were not the same as European white gentry. Some of these images continued throughout the eighteenth century, until American independence.

Systematic information on British colonies, however, was not fully available until the late seventeenth and early eighteenth centuries: a key account was by John Oldmixon, who published in 1708 his survey of *The British Empire in America* in two volumes, based on secondhand sources, which brought the colonies closer to home. He reviewed the 'history of the discovery, settlement, progress and present state' of the major colonies from Newfoundland to Barbados, and so, 100 years after the settlement at Jamestown, the British could see the results of their efforts and, above all, the profits to be had from colonial enterprises. If de Rochefort had written to show the potential of transatlantic territories, Oldmixon wrote to show how profitable and advantageous they had already become in such a short time: his introduction is a long campaigning polemic justifying empire to those at home. Moreover, writing in the midst of what the northern colonists called 'Queen Anne's War' (the War of the Spanish Succession, 1701–1713), he was determined to show that, despite their sufferings through enemy actions, they had remained loyal to Britain. In 1708 the Massachusetts authorities petitioned Queen Anne for aid, proclaiming their losses in the war (see Chapter 5). These new colonies were, therefore, paradoxically both known and exotically strange for those left in Europe: by 1700 they had become familiar places on the maps of empires, yet with many alien features and types of peoples. In addition there were hints or indications in the texts that the 'European' society being created there was nothing of the kind, and that innovations in the forms of social relations, politics, and law were occurring. This became strikingly obvious to a wider public when, in both France and England, slaves arrived in Europe and Native American delegations travelled to negotiate with central governments (Bickham, 2007). Yet the 'English' empire of the late seventeenth century, as described in detail by Nathaniel Crouch (a pseudonym for Richard Burton) in 1685 in his *The English Empire in America; or a Prospect of His Majesties Dominions in the West Indies*, had become, with the uniting of England and Scotland in 1707 and a new war with the French, a *British* empire. In some ways it was this that provided the foundation of eighteenth-century British identity (Crouch, 1685; Armitage, 2000; Greene, 1998). Oldmixon's *The British Empire in America* set the seal on the culmination of 100 years of unification at home and expansion abroad (Macinnes, 2007: 82).

2.1 Exploration

Exploration was a continual feature of British and French colonialism throughout the period and was always incomplete: there was always a frontier that could be crossed and unknown territories mapped. The pattern of Caribbean islands was well understood, and exploration was confined to mapping the interiors of fairly small territories, with the exception of Jamaica, taken in 1655. Travel between Europe and the islands was almost a routine journey, and had long been so, mainly because of Spanish and Portuguese navigation. By contrast, the large interior of North America, away from the ports and coastal areas, remained mysterious for many years, and the mapping was only completed in the nineteenth century. Initial exploration had concentrated on inland bays or rivers, and then penetrated to the interior. Settlements by the British were essentially coastal to begin with, and the penetration of the back country was always difficult and gradual, seemingly up against an intractable landscape and native hostility. Thus, although building on the work of their predecessors, the British and French had difficulties understanding the land and peoples into which they intruded. As a result, exploration was a perpetually changing process throughout this period: with regard to native peoples, there were always new contacts to be made, new negotiations undertaken, and arrangements established that accommodated both natives and Europeans. This is still going on to some extent in the Amazon, but, in the seventeenth and eighteenth centuries, rivalry in North America between the European powers gave exploration a military edge and a more political purpose. Some of the expeditions were driven by geographic curiosity and were private ventures, but from the 1670s onwards, when the French strategy was to encircle the British colonies from the west, in a line from north to south from Quebec to New Orleans, there was always an undercurrent of imperial policy. For the British, exploration was rather more piecemeal, as dictated by the need for new land for settlement or trade routes westward. Agreements with native peoples, and the threat of war with them, induced some caution at times. Colonial governors might take the initiative in encouraging exploration and mapping, but the need for new settlements and trade routes, and war with the French, drove British curiosity. The French, with fewer settlers (see Chapter 3), were more likely to depend on either the initiative of Jesuit missions or the needs of the military for greater geographic knowledge. Even with territories where the essential map of the landscape was well known, the details of reliable transport or communication routes still needed to be investigated. Commercial and military communications and centres of interaction with natives had to be created, though many developed without official initiative. This was partly because Europeans were intruding into a well-established pattern of social and economic networks created over many years by native peoples. Although there are celebrated explorers whose names tend to be preserved in the names of rivers and features of the European's maps, the more detailed work was carried out by less well-known figures. Many, as might be expected, were army or naval officers of the European powers, and it is worth noting that soldiers' stories were often travel or exploration narratives. Many of the initial explorers of **New France** were clerical, many of them Jesuits, and their names and brave exploits are rightly famous (Jolliet, Marquette, Duluth, and Radisson among them) (Kellogg, 1917). The documents chosen (see Documents 2.1 and 2.2) to illustrate the process are, by contrast, from relatively low-ranking travellers, whose contemporary notebooks or retrospective memoirs documented what were often difficult and dangerous journeys.

Because the French controlled the St. Lawrence and routes to the Great Lakes, which in turn led to the west and then south to the Mississippi, they had a better picture of the interior and its peoples than the British were able to obtain. The English-speaking colonies came up against woodland and mountain on their western frontiers, which were difficult to traverse and map thoroughly. The rivers emptying eastwards into the Atlantic provided poor access to the west. The result was that traders, in particular, provided much of the detailed knowledge of tracks and people, though precise pictures of the west were, for a long time, hard to come by. The French, too, faced uncertainties, in part because they believed much earlier sixteenth-century accounts of the ways the rivers connected; perhaps, it was even hoped, offering a route to China. Both the geography and the attitudes of the native peoples to the French were uncertain, and several explorers became captives (as Hennepin, discussed below, did among the Sioux he encountered). The French explorers and their expeditions between the 1630s and the 1680s provided the basic understanding of the country in the north, west to Chicago via the Great Lakes, and south to the Mississippi (Kellogg, 1917).

Typical of the difficulties faced were the mixed achievements of René Robert Cavelier Sieur de La Salle, known as de La Salle, whose journeys provided both the link between French possessions in Canada and the Gulf of Mexico and the rationale for the establishment of Louisiana and New Orleans. He attempted to follow his brother into the Jesuit order as a missionary in Canada, but, impatient over their suggestion that he wait, crossed the Atlantic without their explicit acceptance. Although de La Salle traced the Mississippi to the Gulf of Mexico in 1682, he was unclear where this outlet was and on a subsequent expedition went too far west, ironically intruding into the Spanish territory of Texas. He proved unable to find the river mouth he had discovered by coming down from the north. The foundation of Louisiana, which de La Salle proposed, was the first serious challenge to Spanish claims to hegemony over the Gulf of Mexico and its coastal lands (de La Salle, 1677; Weddle, 1991). The British came to know about these ventures when accounts were published in London in translation. Detailed accounts of de La Salle's travels were published in 1699 by Louis Hennepin, a friar with experience of his expeditions, and in 1714 by Henri Joutel, de La Salle's companion on his last expedition to the mouth of the Mississippi: both provided invaluable information (Hennepin, 1699; Joutel, 1714). More detailed histories in the latter eighteenth century still depended on French sources in translation, such as Le Page du Pratz's *History of Louisiana,* published just as the French lost control of northern colonies in 1763. In establishing bases at Mobile and New Orleans, the French had by the early 1700s placed themselves firmly in the Gulf as a challenge to the Spanish, who, following the Seven Years' War 60 years later, successfully demanded it back and were granted Louisiana by the Treaty of Paris in 1763.

Thus trade and military rivalry drove much of the exploration, with the French seeking to connect their Canadian possessions to Louisiana and the south by river, while the British colonies often looked for trails and roadworthy routes westwards towards the Ohio for both trade and eventual settlement. European ideas of travel continually came up against the intractable forests where roads could not be made, or only made with great difficulty. This was always a problem for the British engagement with the western areas during war against the French in the eighteenth century. A parallel problem was their difficult relationship with native peoples with whom they needed to make an alliance against the French.

Expeditions were therefore rarely purely geographic or scientific in purpose: while maps and map-making were essential, the explorations that produced them were never entirely for purely academic purposes. The landscape, its peoples, and their potential were always of great official interest and the findings were reported to metropolitan governments in Europe, while heroic tales of the explorers were frequently best-sellers in print. This had the advantage, as noted above, for the British that many French explorers' narratives, printed in France, could be acquired and even translated for their own advantage. Scientific knowledge was exchanged, too, as well as samples of plants and trees. The New World was one of new drugs derived from strange plants offering new opportunities for medical treatment. There were other lucrative products from the local fauna. The tiny insects called cochineal, that produced a deep-red dye, were a highly profitable Spanish monopoly in Mexico and had to be stolen by an undercover botanist, Thiery de Menonville, and smuggled to St. Domingue for successful breeding. His raid was sponsored by the French Ministry of the Marine. Not all these investigations were for commercial profit: as Londa Schiebinger has shown, some work was done by women (sometimes disguised as men) on new medical abortifacients (Schiebinger, 2004: 39–44; Delbourgo and Dew, 2008). Explorations were not all for simple imperial purposes, therefore: the narratives of exotic fish, plants, and animals, and their environment, were attractive to an increasingly large reading public, and the specialists in botany and medicine were equally interested.

However, in every potential or actual conflict between Europeans and natives, or in a general war between European powers that also involved natives, the nature of the ground of the fighting became a matter of urgent investigation.

2.2 Maps and cultural misunderstandings

Maps are not innocent texts: they indicate levels of knowledge and ignorance and, above all, reflect the power of their authors' society. They frequently make claims, particularly where boundaries and frontiers are obscure or contested.

> Maps are now no longer seen as uncomplicated pictures of the geographic world: they are now understood to reflect power relations and embody the knowledge and ignorance, articulations and silences of the wider social world. Map accuracy and provenance are no longer the only considerations in this new history of cartography: it is now important to uncover maps' narrative context, their truths as well as their lies, and to see the act of mapping as a political act as much as a scientific practice.
>
> (Short, 2009: 12)

They also embody assumptions of importance and significance: the size of a town or city on the map may indicate their population size, prestige, or their political role. Maps also indicate claims and include territories which are regarded by their authors as 'owned', in much the same way that monarchs of England continued to claim rule over France long after the English were expelled. John Mitchell in 1755 included many villages populated by Indians, as Native Americans were called by settlers, within his depiction of a 'British America', and, by looking westward, created a fictive claim to all the land from the east coast to the Mississippi (Anderson, 2016).

The extent to which native inhabitants of territories participated in the creation of colonial maps has attracted a great deal of attention from historians. It has been suggested that, almost from the first, the maps of the New World drew extensively on native knowledge and even adopted some aspects of native cultural modes of representing space: for example, by measuring distances not in absolute numbers of miles between points, but in terms of the times needed to traverse between them. The results were not strictly geometric maps with a fixed unit of objective measurement such as mileage; rather, they showed topology from the point of view of practical usage, informing people on connections and linkages and distinguishing the easier from the more difficult ways of travel, represented in visual forms that could be understood by both native and European. Some Europeans, such as governor and colonial officer Thomas Pownall, were impressed by the accuracy of native maps (de Vorsey, 1992: 720–721). Far from having no idea of property (private property was a different matter), most natives had a clear idea of their people's territories and drew clear maps of their key features. Nancy Shoemaker (2004) makes the point that, while there were different viewpoints of emotional or religious significance – with memories differing, too, particularly of the dead and their burial places – there was general agreement between natives and Europeans about the essential geographies of 'white' and 'red' territories, even to the point of graphic portrayals in drawn maps being similar. In many different ways, therefore, native informants influenced the production of maps by Europeans, who often formed their opinions about feasible routes of exploration and trade from them (Short, 2009). The presence of native peoples on maps, acknowledging both their existence and their title to territories, was a feature of many earlier map-makers' drawings. Some peoples were deliberately excluded, but in the case of the British, according to one scholar, 'well into the eighteenth century, for much of the continent blank spaces signified geographic ignorance of North America rather than an effort to erase Indians' settlements from maps' (Anderson, 2016: 484). There was genuine, almost academic, interest from some colonial administrators: Francis Nicholson, governor of Maryland between 1721 and 1728, seemingly made a point of collecting native maps that showed the peoples neighbouring one another over a huge territory to the south and west of Virginia and the Carolinas. This clearly affected British understanding of the locations of natives on their western fringes and beyond, though placing them accurately on a more orthodox European geometric map always proved difficult. Reinterpretation of native representations required imagination as well as accuracy, and needed more additional information than the British, particularly, possessed up to the middle of the eighteenth century (Short, 2009: 28; de Vorsey, 1992: 721; Lewis, 1987, 2004). Their attitude to natives and native titles to land was always ambiguous, simultaneously seeking both land and allies on the western frontiers in what was a contradictory approach throughout the period (Anderson, 2016).

Explorers, particularly those sent to investigate specific routes, saw accurate map-making as one of their primary duties, along with the collection of information on the peoples and their attitudes to the British or French along the way. Examples of this are types of low-key, careful mapping undertaken largely by military men.

2.3 Documented examples

Although the main route between Louisiana and the northern French colonies was well understood by the end of the seventeenth century, there were many details that required further investigation. Louis XIV's minister Colbert had proposed an encirclement of the British by occupying the Mississippi route to the west. The abandonment of this policy left the problem of the isolation of the new colony of Louisiana from the Canadian possessions. Detailed memoirs of officers in the French service suggest that they were still attempting to fulfil Colbert's plan. For example, Lieutenant Dumont, who spent many years exploring the back country, leaves a vivid picture of his voyages, revealing the very diverse kind of society developing in Louisiana. There were many slaves, both native and African, and a situation fraught with danger as alliances between these could as the editor notes, develop into rebellion. His language is reflective of a very fluid situation:

> Terms and systems of racial identity were quite different from what they would become two centuries later, and the classifications of freedom

and unfreedom were more significant than those of race. The term *esclave*, or slave, could refer to one of the Africans brought by French slaveowners from West Africa, to an America Indian held by a French slaveowner, or to a native or European or African captive taken by the Indians in a raid such as the Natchez uprising of 1729.

(Dumont, 2012: 67)

His own travelling was in part an evaluation of the French settlements' vulnerability to this kind of attack, at which the Natchez in 1729 had been particularly adept. It was because of their devastating attack that Dumont devoted much space to the people and their culture.

The Natchez uprising took place on the night of November 28, 1729, thirty years after the French first settled in Louisiana and just over a decade after the founding of New Orleans about ninety miles away. It was a strategically planned and well-executed surprise attack that left more than 200 dead (mostly male) out of a Natchez population of 400 colonists and 280 enslaved Africans; a further 80 women and 150 enslaved Africans were taken captive while about 20 Frenchmen escaped.

(White, 2013: 502)

With a population at this time of just over 2,000 French and 1,500 Africans, this was a devastating loss. Moreover, Louisiana's most fertile agricultural settlement was shattered, as the Natchez (or the Théoloëls – People of the Sun) 're-exerted their authority over the land and their political and military dominance of the region' (White, 2013: 502).

Reviewing the state of the French settlements he encountered, Dumont compared them with the Tower of Babel, given 'the confusion of human languages'. There were fur traders from Canada, settlers from the Rhineland-Palatinate, 'exiled French convicts', African slaves, as well as soldiers and 500 prisoners, of whom 300 were deserters. He notes some official policies, as when 60 women were sent from France at one point, landing at Dauphin Island (near Mobile) to provide a more balanced gender distribution in the population (Dumont, 2012: 23–24, 125, 148).

More detailed, and with a far more precise effort at deliberate map-making, was the expedition of Régis du Roullet in 1732, from Mobile to the Choctaw nation (Document 2.1). He surveyed the length of the Pearl river, possibly with a view to establishing whether it would be a viable route of attack on the Natchez, who had taken refuge with the largely pro-British Chickasaws. In his precise notes and maps of this journey he noted the native names of important features, and of their villages, providing explanatory translations for most of them. He also commented on whether the way could be made more passable, or whether in certain seasons alternative ways around obstacles such as swamps would have to be taken. He also proposed ways of using levees to prevent flooding at certain points. Du

Roullet was apparently aided by a small accompanying party of natives, but nevertheless showed great practical initiative and skill. To finish his route by coming down the river towards New Orleans, he spent four days building a small 'fort' for security and then built a *pirogue*, a small rowing boat, to embark on the rest of the journey. His map-making skills are evident in the surviving chart of the river and its settlements, and his desire to be precise is revealed in the lists of villages and their populations of male warriors (Mississippi Provincial Archives, Vol.1: 148–149, 150–154).

A second example of this kind of expedition is represented by the efforts of the British to establish what they called the Venango (or Wenango) trail, from north-western Pennsylvania to Niagara, in 1760 (Document 2.2). The situation had been transformed by the victories against the French at Quebec and Montreal, and the north-western areas of Pennsylvania had been cleared of French forces. No attempt, though, was made to rebuild the forts and strongpoints, and it was part of that reclamation of the western areas that led to a number of careful expeditions to assess possible transport routes, among them the trail that led from Niagara to Pittsburgh. The aim was to facilitate the transmission of official messages and communications, as well as supplies and troops. As a result of the successful journey by Captain Charles Lee (later a general in George Washington's army), who travelled with messages from Niagara over a distance of more than 320 miles in 16 days, a more detailed survey of the territory was undertaken, with a view to securing the route (Stephens and Kent, 1941: 169–173). Colonel Henry Bouquet led troops from Fort Pitt to Presque Isle, where an earlier fort was designated for restoration. The journey was of about 140 miles and established the Venango trail as a viable route for the army. Careful attention was paid to the terrain, its roughness and adaptability for transport purposes, and to the availability of water supplies. Some of the route was through a swamp, which was 'laid with logs, but much out of repair'.

These examples could be duplicated at almost any time in the seventeenth and eighteenth centuries and were the model for subsequent transcontinental expeditions undertaken by the independent United States. Everywhere, at all times, geographic curiosity was mixed with strategic political and military interests. While the exploration narratives are eloquent testimony to the determination and enterprise of their participants, they also reflect the different national anxieties and interests of their sponsors.

3 New societies

3.1 Migration
   3.1a Varieties of migrant
   3.1b Numbers
3.2 Native encounters
3.3 New societies, new economies
   3.3a Slave societies
   3.3b Servants and convicts
3.4 Conclusion: New World, new societies

3.1 Migration

3.1a Varieties of migrant

There were many different types of migrants to the British and French Americas, not all of them French or British. There were many different reasons for moving. Some chose to move, while others, most notably African slaves and European criminals, were compelled to do so. The official processes for staffing the colonies with military forces and administrators also differed markedly. Enticements to emigrate, promises of work and land, were mixed with forms of more forceful inducement. A key group of migrants, **indentured servants** – *les engagés* for the French – remained an important element of migration to many British colonies, particularly for Maryland, Virginia, and Pennsylvania until the War for Independence, providing particular skills for the plantation and urban economies. This was the case despite the predominance of African slaves which had been established by 1700 in tobacco production. In the Caribbean, too, their early recruitment was vital, and they became indistinguishable from the forced migrants of military and criminal expulsion, from Ireland as well as Britain, up to the end of the civil wars. Their economic importance declined sharply by 1700, as their labour in sugar production was replaced by African slaves. French attempts at recruiting servants in this way were intermittent, faltering by the end of the seventeenth century and negligible in the eighteenth (Debien 1952; Gaucher et al., 1959, 1961). This group of migrants points to major interpretative difficulties, too, which will be addressed here: the thin distinction between 'free' and 'forced' migration, and the importance of economic changes in determining the demand for different types of labour. Even if indentured servants were not captives in war, as during the Jacobite rebellions, or convicted criminals sent in large numbers after the English 1718 Transportation Act, the idea that all chose freely to move to America needs careful sceptical scrutiny. There were too many allegations of young people being 'spirited away' by force in the late seventeenth century, and attested examples such as that of Peter Williamson from Aberdeen in the eighteenth, to be confident that free migration was universal. Yet some servants had skills to offer. Wareing (2017) has established these were at a premium, in the sense that the skills were needed in the colonies and allowed negotiation of better terms for both passage across and final employment in the colonies. Others, less skilled, poorer, or more desperate to leave, were likely to be at the mercy of the shippers and their captains, with less certainty of favourable conditions once their contracts had been sold to employers on arrival.

Slaves from Africa were the largest category of forced migrants, and were chosen by gender as well as for their particular skills. The development of the rice economy of South Carolina after 1700 led to attempts at deliberate recruitment of slaves from rice-growing areas of West Africa. By contrast, many 'free' settlers joined their co-religionists in the New England colonies in the seventeenth century, and there was some interchange of people during the English Revolution of the 1640s as Puritans on both sides of the Atlantic joined in a common cause. Opposition to the religious exclusivity of places such as Massachusetts also took on an Atlantic dimension, as networks of Quakers published accounts of their repression in America by way of protest in England in the 1660s, the outcome of a remarkable growing exchange of print culture (Morgan and Rushton, 2013: 44–48). Forcing migrants was also part of Oliver Cromwell's policies in Ireland in the 1650s, when people dreaded being 'Barbadosed' into servitude. These were not slaves, however badly they might have been treated, and remained with the same rights as other indentured servants (Newman, 2013; Handler and Reilly, 2017; see Section 3.3c below). For military migration there were also contrasts. Whereas the French Ministry of the Marine had its own armed forces and posted them throughout the French colonies, British colonies tended to rely on local militias for their defence, recruited from white settlers and their servants, with only the occasional injection of troops from Britain in times of war. Only colonial governors were sent out from Britain, with few troops or support staff, before the mid-eighteenth century wars.

The problem of gender imbalances remained in many French and British colonies: most migrants, unless they were travelling in family groups (as happened frequently among emigrants to New England), were single males. There were steps to counter this: Louis Dumont recorded the arrival of 60 'girls' on an East Indies ship, sent by the French government to Dauphin island off Mobile (now in Alabama, then part of French Louisiana) in the early 1720s to populate the colonies (Dumont, 2012: 125). By contrast, the British tended to leave things to the colonial market for labour to attract different kinds of workers: the result was that a sizeable minority of servants sent from Britain were female. This was true even of transported convicts. Though men could make up 90% of transported convicts from most rural areas, women at times comprised a third or even a half of the convicts from cities such as Bristol and Newcastle upon Tyne, particularly from the lower courts on conviction for petty larceny (Morgan and Rushton, 2004: 48–50). Among slaves, the concentration on the strength of men produced early gender imbalances, particularly in the Caribbean, and it seems that it took several generations for a more balanced distribution to develop. The role of women in the slave economy seems to have been slow to develop as a result, but in the eighteenth century they had specific roles in the plantation economies, particularly in weeding gangs. Here they replaced earlier gangs of servant women who had been used in places such as Barbados in growing indigo and cotton. The presence of many women slaves and the advantages of having a self-reproducing slave population, however, did not mitigate the levels of exploitation in places such as Jamaica, where labour discipline and punishments remained severe until the end of slavery in the nineteenth century (Beckles, 1985; Paton, 2017; see Section 3.3b below).

All these types of migrants – soldiers, slaves, free settlers, indentured servants, transported convicts, and state-sponsored women – took part in the collective enterprise of forming new societies in the Americas, alongside, and sometimes with, Native Americans. However forced their migration, their impact on native peoples and the local environment made them actors rather than just passive witnesses. The official intentions of both metropolitan administrators and local colonial officials came up against many difficulties and challenges that forced new solutions and institutions into being. The process was not one of wholesale transfer of European social relations and institutions to the other side of the Atlantic, but one of selective adoption or reproduction, innovative forms of law and legal processes, and new forms of political management.

3.1b Numbers

Historians have expended great efforts over the years calculating the numbers of migrants, their characters, and destinations. Karen Kupperman notes that:

> Huge numbers of people migrated westward across the Atlantic in the centuries after 1492. Millions were enslaved and had no choice about either embarkation or destination. The others were free, but a very high proportion of the free migrants felt some compulsion in the choices they

made. Many fled economic restrictions at home and signed up for a period of servitude to pay their way over. Others feared or experienced interference with their ability to practise their religion and chose emigration in hopes of being able to worship as they saw fit. The Americas offered opportunity to some, and the fortunate were able to make good on that promise.

(Kupperman, 2012: 44)

Christopher Tomlins – whose book is significantly called *Freedom Bound* – notes 'the simple ubiquity of movements of population – whether indigenous, European, or African, whether transoceanic or intraregional, vast or small, voluntary or coerced – and an accompanying consciousness of movement'. Secondly, imbalances arose rapidly through the swift growth of the 'introduced populations': during the two centuries up to 1800 the non-indigenous peoples of the mainland English colonies grew by more than 2.7 million. 'Though rates of population growth varied across regions and periods, natural increase quickly outpaced increase attributable to immigration' (Tomlins, 2010: 67). Settlers were simply more successful than natives, and free whites more than black slaves. By 1700 there had been more than 390,000 British migrants to the Americas (in addition to 200,000 to Ireland), compared with 45,000 French: this contrast remained throughout the eighteenth century, too, and the French colonies in North America were never as populous as the 13 British (Benjamin, 2009: Table 5.3, 259). Death rates varied, of course, depending on patterns of disease and near-starvation in the early years, but after 1650 natural increases accounted for the population growth in the British colonies almost more than immigration. In parallel with this European rise, Native American peoples experienced catastrophic declines in population, displacement from the territories, and loss of economic security. To the Shawnee of the Ohio valley, white people were like pigeons: invite in one couple and they would be followed by 'troops' who would take the land from the inhabitants (Tomlins, 2010: 67–68; Benjamin: Table 6.2, 321). As the weeks needed by ships to cross the Atlantic shrank, and the frequency of sailings increased, there were both more opportunities to migrate or to join an increasing number of seafarers and traders criss-crossing the ocean (Steele, 1986: 50–54). Though slow by modern standards, communication became easier and more routine after 1700, even safer for those on ordinary voyages. For slaves, there was a different, more dangerous, journey.

After initial difficulties, therefore, white settler societies flourished, yet were extraordinarily diverse in character, with people of many different origins. Religious diversity was one feature, particularly in the British colonies, as different incomers concentrated in different places. Puritans fled to New England to achieve religious freedom, while Sephardic Jews settled the English and Dutch Caribbean islands, escaping from under the shadow of persecution from the Spanish (Kupperman, 2012: 47–48; Zacek, 2009). British colonies also attracted French Huguenot and German settlers (mostly Protestants), as well as British and Irish. There were class differences, most notably in the slave colonies where gentry and business families invested in land while poorer whites were recruited to do the work, soon to be followed by African slaves. The result is that relatively few were free settlers, with precise numbers in each of the categories of free, indentured, or enslaved difficult to establish. Overall, Davies argues, 'it appears that by the end of the seventeenth century the king of England had perhaps 350,000 to 400,000 subjects, including slaves, in the New World; and that the king of France had about 70,000, also including slaves. What proportion had been born in the New World is anyone's guess' (Davies, 1974: 85) The British had also 'settled' about 200,000 in Ireland in the course of the seventeenth century (Benjamin, 2009: 259). Everywhere, opportunity was seized by some: as Steele comments, 'by 1675 those who had migrated to escape the Old World were succeeded or outnumbered by those who intended to reap the harvest of the New World' (Steele, 1980: 3). Servants may have been the largest category of white migrants, estimated at 350,000 in just under 200 years by Dunn (1984: 159). Philip Morgan suggests that white emigrant labourers may have totalled even more, perhaps as many as 500,000 out of a total European migration to the British colonies of 750,000 (Morgan, 1993: 18). It is generally agreed that about 50,000 of these were British criminals, largely English, who were sentenced to, or pardoned for, transportation in the eighteenth century. The use of pardons provided increasing numbers who had escaped hanging and been sent to the colonies (Morgan and Rushton, 2004). The crucial shift from the seventeenth to the eighteenth centuries was from the Caribbean to the North American colonies, Canny (1994: 64) suggests: whereas about 190,000 British migrants went to the West Indies before 1700, thereafter the huge majority of migrants aimed for further north.

The situation in the French colonies was very different. There were few instances of waves of migration and the populations of many North American colonies remained small until well into the eighteenth century. DuBois (2009) summarises the evidence:

> Though the French government focused much energy on the colonization of Canada, over the long term, especially when war with England forced it to make choices, it centered its military and political attention on the Caribbean. The French colonies in North America, in contrast to the British colonies, attracted comparatively small numbers of settlers. A maximum of 70,000 settlers departed for French Canada, and another 7,000 to French colonies in Acadia, Île Royale, and Terre Neuve. Louisiana, meanwhile, received no more than 7,000 settlers during its time as a French colony, with about 6,000 slaves arriving during the same period. Many more French settlers, meanwhile, went to the

French Caribbean, though no historian has established a precise figure for this migration. Some have estimated as many as 300,000 over the course of the seventeenth and eighteenth centuries, although that number is probably too high, and the total may have been as low as 100,000. By far the largest group of arrivals in the French Americas were African slaves.

(DuBois, 2009: 139)

By contrast with the Caribbean, the French North American territories were underpopulated compared with both their Caribbean and the northern British colonies. Settlement was intermittent and sparse, and the rate of natural increase in the settlements seems to have been low. The evidence for individual places confirms this overall picture: in Canada, **New France**'s population grew from about 4,000 in the 1660s to more than 16,000 by the early 1700s, and more than 37,000 in the 1730s (Pritchard, 2004: 423). 'The main point of contrast with New England is of course in immigration. Only in the late 1660s and early 1670s did New France receive relatively large numbers of recruits from the mother country. For the whole period of 150 years of French rule in Canada, the total of immigrants has been put at no more than 10,000, roughly what Virginia expected to receive in half a dozen good years' (Davies, 1974: 78). The whole of North America had fewer than 42,000 white French by the 1730s, with perhaps another 32,000 in the Caribbean, who controlled about 160,000 black slaves, though the total number of slaves transported remains obscure for the seventeenth century (Pritchard, 2004: 424). Pritchard argues that there were five types of migrants to Canada and the West: indentured servants (*les engagés*), soldiers, 'eligible' young women (500 poor white women were sent from the general 'hospitals' or prisons of Paris and Rouen, for example), convicts, and freemen. Of these the indentured servants were the most important settlers, with perhaps 39% settling in Canada, nearly all in the seventeenth century. The idea seems to have been abandoned by the 1670s. Significantly, more than 20% of the soldiers may have stayed, though up to a quarter died. Between 1683 and 1727 more than 4,500 soldiers were sent to 'New France' (Pritchard, 2004: 23–24).

The French, therefore, despite inducements and coercion, never created a steady stream of white emigrants to the colonies. Unlike the British, they forbade the settlement of both Protestants and Jews. By the last quarter of the seventeenth century little had been achieved – 'settlement had been left largely in the hands of devout lay Catholics who aimed to erect a colonial society of Christian perfection in order to aid the conversion of the natives' (Pritchard, 2004: 73, 78). Perhaps only in Acadia (Nova Scotia) did settlers create a well-founded agricultural society comparable to, say, that of New England. Gradually parts of New France followed that pattern in the eighteenth century as farming replaced trading with the natives. In Louisiana, developing slowly after the 1690s,

> fewer than 5 percent of the whites were free men. Given that 91.7 per cent were indentured servants, transported prisoners, women, soldiers, and children, the remainder are best viewed as some form of coerced labour. Despite the impressive numbers though, the entire scheme failed. An estimated 2,000 white immigrants deserted or died of ill treatment during the crossing or returned to France. At least half of all the white migrants either died or abandoned the colony before 1726.
> (Pritchard, 2004: 26)

Even without the fears of disease and death, the French empire remained only in part one of emigration and settlement, which left the North American colonies at a disadvantage compared with the growing prosperity and population of the British. Even when a sizeable population had developed, their opportunities in their own colonies were restricted. Most colonial officials were appointed from France and were not born in the colonies. These administrators, moreover, had a great degree of control over local economic life, licensing trades and occupations and regulating their collective associations (which the English called guilds). Only the church deliberately created patterns of local recruitment, and by the mid-eighteenth century more than three quarters of local clergy in French Canada, the curates, were Canadian-born. This reflected a policy that had also been applied earlier to native peoples, as the Catholic church to some extent tried to adapt to different communities through conversion and recruitment of local personnel (Moogk, 2000: 189, 213, 259).

3.2 Native encounters

In the Caribbean as much as in North America, European intruders came in contact with native peoples. The initial impact was often one of disastrous epidemics and population loss as natives succumbed to European diseases, but displacement and war added to the decline. Despite the polite words of Charles de Rochefort praising the French and British for being more civilised towards natives than the Spanish, populations declined steadily once land was needed for European settlement. This did not mean that they became a negligible force affecting the development of the colonies. On the contrary. As Pritchard remarks:

> The most extraordinary feature of this dismal account of death and social destruction is that, despite the devastation visited upon the native peoples of the Americas, the survivors continued to play important roles in the history of the French colonies: as warriors fiercely resisting

colonial incursions, as partners in trade, as agents of imperial conflict, and as independent actors pursuing their own tribal policies.
(Pritchard, 2004: 10)

Pritchard notes the collapse of the native population in St. Domingue and suggests that native communities declined to a few hundred in the Lesser Antilles by the last quarter of the seventeenth century. Some fled to St. Vincent, where there were about 6,000 in 1683, two thirds of whom were said to be **Black Caribs** (that is, a fusion of native and African). At the same time there were estimated to be 1,500 native 'bowmen' in St. Vincent, Dominica, and St. Lucia of whom 400 were black (Pritchard, 2004: 8–10, quotation on 10). The 'Black Caribs', in part at least native and African, were a force to be reckoned with after the British took over St. Vincent in 1763 and the object of two wars, resulting in their eventual expulsion and transportation in the 1790s (see Chapter 5.). The evidence from the British Caribbean in the seventeenth century is less specific: the small Indian population in Barbados was probably brought in as slaves from South America or from other islands, and Jamaica had been emptied of its native population by the Spanish long before the English took it in 1655 (Davies, 1974: 262). In the Lesser Antilles, however, fierce conflict was experienced. **Caribs**, in contrast to the Arawaks, offered fierce resistance to colonisation, mounting attacks on the English in Antigua as late as 1640 and forcing the French into a long war between 1636 and 1639 in Martinique and Guadaloupe. Their absence from Barbados might have been a key factor in the success of the initial English settlement. 'The Caribs are interesting and important for their relatively long resistance to Europeans and European influences. This resistance was not total even in the seventeenth century' (Davies, 1974: 265). Elsewhere the impact of the British paralleled that of other European nations. 'For Native Americans, the encounter with Europeans unfolded in a disastrous context. Beginning with sixteenth-century explorers and traders and intensifying as permanent European settlements developed in their midst, native peoples throughout coastal North America experienced devastating epidemics of Eurasian diseases' (Davies, 1974: 219).

Meinig emphasises the wide contrasts between the colonies of different nations in their strategies towards Native Americans. In many ways these reflected the different economic interests of the Europeans, particularly clearly in the case of British and French relationships with native peoples, both rather different to those of the Spanish and Portuguese predecessors. In part, relationships with natives varied according to the different patterns of dependency on each side. New Englanders famously needed native assistance in growing corn (maize – hence Thanksgiving in November), while natives developed an increasing demand for metal tools, woollen clothing, and guns. In exchange, beaver pelts and deerskins became a major items in European demands on Indian traders. The modes of exploration and settlement established priorities in ways that had profound consequences for the natives. In addition, colonial outposts varied as to whether the contacts with natives were for commercial reasons such as trade, by association with them, such as the fishing of the Newfoundland Banks, or were for deliberate settlement and farming, as in the New England colonies. The development of permanent settlements of large populations produced dynamic interactions with native societies very different from those of outposts, where trade and barter for rare goods were the key objectives. Despite the fact that 'a powerful sense of European superiority was latent in all such encounters', there were different relationships established with the natives (Meinig, 1986: 65–66, 70). Meinig therefore proposes contrasting models of relationships with natives, depending on imperial intentions and then the varied *systems* created by the different empires. To start with, he says, there were eight 'recurrent general patterns', with exploration and 'gathering' resources such as fish part of those early expeditions. Once contact with natives was made there could be barter, on relatively equal terms, or plunder through 'military opportunism, seizing whatever might be of value in European markets'. This would naturally lead to a fifth stage of development, the creation of outposts for the purposes of control and exchange, leading to a sixth stage of 'imperial imposition', the appointment of governors and formal structures of command. Finally, there was permanent settlement by outsiders and the creation of 'imperial' colonies, with a 'transfer of full complex of institutions' (Meinig, 1986: 65–66).

These suggest different structures of power between incoming Europeans and natives: plunder, implantation, and imperial imposition and inclusion of territory into an official colony all reflect dominance over native peoples and denial of their claims to place or economic rights. This might arise with an accompanying ideology of **terra nullius** – holding that the land was empty of any population with a claim to it, and therefore belonged to no one except the Europeans who seized it. The others indicate concessions to the natives, of equality in exchange or barter, or rights to land if not offshore resources. Perhaps the dominance of economic interests is over-emphasised here. There was also the more cultural and racial aspect of identity, as Sandberg remarks: 'from the earliest contacts between Native Americans and Europeans, ethnic identities shaped violence in the Atlantic'. Moreover:

> Within the borderlands, individuals' identities seem to have been incredibly flexible and changeable. Studies of ethnicity and violence in the Atlantic world often oppose 'colonizers' to 'indigenous peoples', envisioning a statist imperial programme suppressing resistance by the colonized. Yet, the importance of nonstate actors in early modern Atlantic world ethnic violence makes such a focus on states extremely problematic.
>
> (Sandberg, 2006)

Above all, 'where Native American and European colonial communities lived in close proximity in borderlands, blurred cross-cultural identities and mixed-ethnic populations emerged' (Sandberg, 2006: 6, 7, 8). Therefore relationships were not quite so hostile, involving absolute differences and uncompromised opposition, as some contemporary narratives imply. Nevertheless, Meinig's model of native-European relationships has some value. He suggests that three largely distinct types of social relationship developed. First, the earliest of all in date, there was *stratification*, as in Mexico, where the subordination of suppressed natives in a racial hierarchy of exploitation through the forced labour of natives (the ***encomienda*** system) was the foundation of the new economy. Second, there was *articulation*, as in French Canada, where European and native economies coexisted and interacted, exchanging goods while remaining to some extent distinct from one another. The relationship was one of practical equality. Finally, there was *expulsion* – as in Virginia and Massachusetts, where there was literally no place for natives in the economy or society (Meinig, 1986: 71–72; G. Morgan, 1984). Therefore, while the Spanish developed forms of stratified exploitation of peoples subjected to compulsory labour, at least while the native population was sufficiently numerous, the French in Canada attempted to develop relatively equal links of exchange between their economy and those of the natives, with a growing interchange or even merger of personnel in order to secure mutual trade benefits. The French fur trade in Canada depended on native suppliers and Europeans needed native skills to participate in the supply. By contrast, in colonies such as Virginia and Massachusetts there was a consistent policy of expulsion of native peoples after the initial careful negotiation: once sufficient numbers of settlers had been imported, land hunger dictated aggressive policies towards native territories and peoples. As noted below, natives had a residual role as forced labour in Massachusetts, a role allocated to African slaves in Virginia. Despite the different racial attitudes among the whites, it seems that economic circumstances were more critical in deciding which strategy was adopted.

Within both the British and French colonies, therefore, there were great variations in the developing relations with Native Americans. By 1700 Virginia had become set in its policies of ethnic cleansing, yet further south, in newer colonies, relations with Indians were very different. Rather like the French in Canada, English settlers in Carolina had extensive trade relations with Native Americans, depending on the Indian trade for deerskins and, at the beginning, slaves. 'In fact, Carolinians founded their colony on Indian trade for deerskins and Indian slaves. They found no difficulty in finding allies who provided deerskins and slaves in exchange for metal goods, clothing and guns' (Benjamin, 2009: 313). At the same time, unlike in the French Canadian colonies, many whites, and rising numbers of Africans, arrived there after 1700. Increasing hostility among natives resulted as white farmers and planters sought land up-country, but there were still extensive trade relations with them during the first half of the eighteenth century. In many colonies, therefore, self-interest forced colonists into relationships with Indians. The result, suggests Thomas Benjamin, was that 'the most complex political and commercial relationships between Europeans and Indian peoples anywhere in the Americas existed in North America in the seventeenth and eighteenth centuries' (Benjamin, 2009: 298–299). In every zone of fluid border and frequent contact, a 'frontier exchange economy' developed and mutual demands for goods led to substantial and profitable trading (see Grant-Costa and Mancke, 2012, and Usner, 1987).

Trade relations of relative equality and mutual need, however, did not mean that natives could not be enslaved, nor that they could not in their turn create slaves from the European intruders. One of the key forms of interaction between native and European societies was the exploitation of enslaved captives on both sides. Warfare produced captives who, in places such as Massachusetts, were treated by Europeans as servants or slaves. Native warfare, whether against fellow natives or Europeans and their native allies, also involved attempts to replace their own losses by capture – an essential process for powers such as the Iroquois, who experienced serious losses of fighting men in their wars of expansion. One of the people they preyed on, the Huron, suffered continual losses, despite French attempts to redeem Christian Huron from the Iroquois through a kind of ransom market. In a similar fashion, many British colonists found themselves either becoming, or dealing in, native slaves. This complex pattern of practices has only recently been re-emphasised in the histories of British colonies, though it had been noted and studied in the early twentieth century (Lauber, 1913). In these relationships some captives could therefore become part of the society of their captors. Others could be profitably enslaved and traded, or exploited locally. Following this pattern, Europeans often had native Indian slaves, and natives often held European captives.

This pattern of native enslavement has been underestimated, according to Newell (2015), with regard to New England in particular, where the *unfree* labour of native servants was common: 'slavery flourished . . . and Native Americans formed a significant part of New England's slave population'. Yet more attention has been paid to the situation of white servants, and, particularly, white captives among the Indians, than Indians among white settlers. 'Somehow Indian slavery virtually disappeared from post-World War I scholarship on New England.' There were similar patterns of native slaves being actively sought and exploited by the French in Louisiana, though there the slaves were in larger groups on small plantations rather than in the households of family farmers (Newell, 2015: 2–4; Usner, 1992). Yet, as Newell has established, 'throughout New England before 1700, Native Americans represented the dominant form of non-white labour' (2015: 5). The brutal wars against natives, such as the Pequot War in 1636 which led to the enslavement and expulsion of many Indians, and King Philip's War of 1675–1676, both close to being 'total wars', were key events in this process. After the Pequot War, 15 boys and two women were sent to Providence

Island, off the Nicaraguan coast, where they were described as 'Cannibal Negroes'. These wars could be described as the first 'total' wars, yet this was not the aim of either side involved. In terms of strategy, Starkey concludes, the New Englanders followed a piecemeal approach and accepted the limited aims of Indian warfare. In effect, though, for some of their enemies in particular, the wars were total, as Indian communities were destroyed or driven out (Starkey, 1998: 80; Kupperman, 2012: 178). This reflects longstanding practices of extreme violence in these northern colonies, and generated a level of hatred among the whites of their native enemies not found elsewhere (Perrault, 2006). After King Philip's War, enslavement and indentured servitude were integrated into penalties in the judicial system: 'colonial courts increased the sentencing of Indians to terms of servitude and even slavery as punishment for crime and debt. This new technique of judicial enslavement added many hundreds of additional Indians to an already sizeable – and reproducing – population of additional Indian slaves and servants in New England cities, towns and households' (Newell, 2015: 11). Masters could also impose conditions where their slaves married free Indian women. Patience Boston, a Maine Indian woman, recalling the circumstances which led to her killing her master's grandson, recorded in 1738 that in one indentured contract 'I was Married to a Negro Servant; and because his Master would have it so, I bound my self a Servant with him during his Life Time, or as long as we both should live' (Boston, 1738a, unpaginated). This pattern of native enslavement had equivalents in other British colonies where Europeans either tapped into established native networks of slave trading or practised the enslavement of captives in war. In South Carolina there were 1,400 Indian slaves in 1708 (500 men, 600 women, the rest children), taken in the recent wars against the French and the Spanish as well as against Indians themselves, the governor reported, making up a quarter of the total slave population. Yet this declined soon after as African slaves were imported in large numbers and came to be the dominant element of the workforce by the 1720s (Lauber, 1913: 106; Gallay, 2002). After 1700 the presence of Indian slaves declined, partly because of metropolitan interference. Whereas during the Pequot War 'English colonists asserted their right to Indian slaves under the doctrine of the "just war", which permitted enslavement of enemies captured in a defensive conflict', 100 years later the Duke of Bedford told Governor Shirley of Massachusetts that he regarded Indian captives as prisoners of war, not slaves or captives. With legislation against trading in native slaves in Massachusetts and Pennsylvania, at least in the northern colonies, Indian slavery had all but disappeared by the mid-eighteenth century (Newell, 2015: 10, 202; Lauber, 1913: 188–195). Levels of violence remained high, but the gradual reduction in the native presence in Massachusetts reflects inconsistent policies in the eighteenth century. Contrary to images of simple removal, expulsion, or extinction, however, a complex and lengthy process is documented by Jean O'Brien in one part of Massachusetts. The native population suffered continual restrictions, harassment, and exclusion as a result of the deep mistrust towards them held by the white settlers. In the end they were squeezed out entirely (O'Brien, 1997).

French practices differed little from those of the British. As Rushforth comments, 'between 1660 and 1760, French colonists and their Native allies enslaved thousands of Indians, keeping them in the towns and villages of New France or shipping them to the French Caribbean'. A continent-wide network of slave raiders and traders developed, he suggests, and both colonists and Indians alike engaged in the violence that generated slaves and kept them under French control. In the North, in New France, native slaves were the major source of unfree labour in the seventeenth century and beyond, while in Louisiana and the Caribbean there were increasing numbers of African slaves. This goes against our conventional image of the French 'cultural adaptations and creative innovations' that accompanied coexistence in New France (discussed above), as proposed by Meinig. For example, in Louisiana in the first quarter of the eighteenth century it was not unusual to come across small plantations with only Indian slaves, though Africans were steadily increasing (Rushforth, 2012: 10–11; Dumont, 2012: 148). Despite sharing many of the same social structures of unfreedom and exploitation with other European cultures in the Americas, it seems that racist attitudes of absolute differences of superior and inferior races were lacking in much of French America (Aubert, 2004).

Our knowledge of the other 'side' of this seizure and enslavement process, namely European captivity among the Indians, is detailed and highly personal. This is partly the product of the explorers' narratives discussed in Chapter 2, some of whom endured lengthy periods of confinement, partly also from the regular reports of the French Jesuits, and also from the burgeoning pamphlet literature pouring from the printing presses of British America. Concepts of natives' 'savagery', supported by the evidence of those who had endured captivity among them, for the British settlers and the French Jesuits alike, provided a consistent worldview of the cultural gulf between the civilised and the savage. This dichotomy survived to the end of the nineteenth century. The texts also give us some of the most moving narratives of suffering and survival. In the north-east, one fear was of cannibalism, a genuine threat to some prisoners among the Iroquois, though the general impression from the first encounters in the Caribbean was that natives everywhere were cannibals (Boucher, 1992). This was a danger to French Jesuits, who celebrated several 'martyrs' to this practice while also living in dread of it. The Jesuits, adopting the Huron as their main allies, were willing to understand their practice of cannibalism during times of starvation, according to Kelly Watson, but regarded the practices of their enemies, the Iroquois, as gratuitous barbarism, a judgement reinforced by allegations of sadism and sodomy. In part, because Iroquois women were closely involved in deciding which prisoners to keep and which to kill, the fear of cannibalism and torture reflected deep anxieties among European men about their own masculinity. Both Jesuits and Puritan captives, in their writings, regarded their ability to endure suffering as a reflection of their strong faith, and in some individual instances they were able to survive astonishing levels of pain. Nevertheless, these seventeenth-century experiences of native warfare and capture set a pattern for the future, and fear of torture and painful death haunted white men's minds in North America for another two centuries. (Watson, 2015: 129–133, 140–142).

Captivity narratives became something of a genre in the English-speaking colonies of North America, in parallel with the stories of torture and martyrdom produced by the Jesuits in New France. Because the New England colonies had their own printing presses by the late 1680s, stories of all kinds were published for an eager public. A culture of story-telling, memoirs, pamphleteering, and preaching allowed for colonial experiences to be made public. Many of the features of later captivity narratives were already established by the early 1700s. One common theme was the fear of capture and enslavement of white women, which held a fascination for British colonists and for white Americans in general, until the end of the 1800s. The John Ford 1956 film *The Searchers,* starring John Wayne and set in the late nineteenth century, encapsulates some of the oldest legends, racist fears, and ambiguities. Absorbed into Indian society, women might be forcibly married and the mothers of native children, and therefore unable or unwilling to return to be objects of pity or contempt in white society. Those seized as young children might be so assimilated as to be indistinguishable from Indians themselves, and incapable of being reintegrated into white society. Captivity narratives printed in English began in New England as a result of captures in King Philip's War (1675–1676), when the fears of captivity were accentuated by the severe loss of lives on both sides. The very religious tone of Mary White Rowlandson's account of her 11 weeks' captivity, the death of one child, and the loss of others set the framework for many of the other early narratives from New England, which emphasised divine providence and personal faith as the key forces ensuring endurance (Vaughan and Clark, 1981: 29–76). The survival of the story-teller is related to the goodness of God and their own personal faith in Him and his goodness. These New England stories are therefore, in a sense, *redemption* narratives. Later accounts of their experiences by former captives were more factual and perhaps less striking, often concentrating on the details of Native American society and culture, and their personal treatment. This seems to mark a shift to a more secular worldview, or at least one that placed less stress on personal salvation and destiny, by the middle of the eighteenth century. Certainly, the captives' stories seem to have become factual, and are almost ethnographic in their detail about native societies, practices, and attitudes. Pauline Turner Strong notes the shift between the late seventeenth and the middle of the eighteenth century as one from 'providential hermeneutics' – that is proof of God's judgement and forgiveness, as preached by people such as Cotton Mather in Massachusetts, mixed with some secular elements – to a more matter-of-fact style of 'proto-ethnographic' narrative which offered authentic experiences and details (Strong, 1999: 152).

Many stories published in the eighteenth century, both factual and fictional, made promises of being based on 'authentic' experiences, from Daniel Defoe's novels such as *Moll Flanders* to the biographies of criminals – and their confessions on the way to the gallows – published as pamphlets or by the chaplain of Newgate Gaol in London (now known as *The Newgate Calendar*). Many stories included details of events and experiences in the American colonies, such as the biographies of English criminals sentenced to transportation there, which described the sufferings of servitude, their escape, and return to Britain. It was these that influenced Defoe. Thus the language of 'authenticity' was a particularly strong feature of the mass of personal publications produced in the eighteenth century. For British readers, the account by Peter Williamson, reprinted many times in Britain in the mid-eighteenth century but only much later in America, was reinforced by his publicity tours of Britain performing Indian dances and songs. In several versions of his life he alleged that he had been sold to 'spiriters', and ended up in the colonies as a young indentured servant, where he was apparently captured by Indians as well as being involved in fighting them. His story fuelled fears of a different kind of captivity – that of being being kidnapped and taken to the colonies (Colley, 2002: 188–192).

If there was a degree of predictability in the literary form of these captivity narratives, suggesting that the printers probably had a controlling part in their production and acted as authors and editors to influence the narrators' styles of expression, the range of people at their centre became more varied in the later eighteenth century. Clearly some stories were told by those who never thought they would be caught in Indian country. This is most obvious among the small group of captives taken from ships that were wrecked on the Florida coast. One was unusual in being the memoirs of an African-American servant: as Strong remarks, 'Black captives are relegated to the background in these narratives, often remaining unnamed. The publication of *A Narrative of the Uncommon Sufferings and Surprizing Deliverance of Briton Hammon, A Negro Man—Servant to General Winslow* in 1760 broke this silence and anonymity, at least to a degree' (Strong, 1999: 184). Certainly, when African slaves were killed or captured, or even liberated by European forces, they were rarely named. Another of what might be called these *accidental* captivity narratives was the story of New Englander Jonathan Dickenson, who at the beginning of the eighteenth century published his account of being wrecked in Florida, threatened by Indians, and rescued by Spanish soldiers. His narrative, deeply religious, was titled *God's Protecting Providence, Man's Surest Help and Defence* (1700). There were other Florida episodes and shipwrecks: an English sailor from Workington in north-west England had a similar experience to that of Briton Hammon after a shipwreck in Florida. *The Surprising Adventures and Sufferings of John Rhodes, seaman of Workington* (New York, 1798) is a very long and detailed account of capture by Indians and imprisonment by the Spanish. What makes both of these men remarkable, it should be noted, is that they belonged to the poorest class of servants and hired men, in effect the proletariat of the Atlantic World who have left few personal records or memoirs.

More large-scale captures, however, occurred in war as part of Native American strategy. This disproportionately affected some border communities, though, as Calloway points out in his overview of 'north-country' captives from New Hampshire and Vermont, the idea of a clear and well-defined border is scarcely applicable in this period (Calloway, 1992). Border territories were porous areas of cautious co-existence of Europeans and natives, where peaceful relationships of trade and exchange may have been countered by the exploitation of forest and hunting, or the straying of cattle into native fields of corn (a particular issue behind King Philip's protestations). In these circumstances capture might have been intermittent, almost personal, or systematically directed at whole populations of intrusive Europeans. There were also, particularly as sporadic raiding moved to large-scale conflict, *systematic* captures – in 1704 in Deerfield, for example, when a large raid took dozens. This was the worst of a series of raids over many years. Deerfield lost at least 125 captives between 1677 and 1712. Two accounts concerning Deerfield men survive, most famously in a personal account by John Williams, *The Redeemed Captive Returning to Zion,* and in Quentin Stockwell's story 'of his captivity and redemption' as reported by him to Increase Mather: they were taken from Deerfield in 1677 and 1704. As Colley points out, many of these captives were sold or transferred to the French and had to be recovered in either prisoner exchanges during war or in the post-war bargaining over prisoners (Vaughan and Clark, 1981:79; Colley, 2002: 153). Smaller-scale captures in marginal places were equally deliberate but could be even more devastating for a small community. Well into the eighteenth century there were repeated patterns of threat of capture as raids and seizures destabilised communities which had thought themselves relatively safe.

Land and captives were, therefore, the key areas of dispute between Europeans and Native Americans throughout the period. Yet there were also strategies of trade and alliance on both sides that produced collaboration and shared experiences of war in the conflicts firstly between France and Britain and, later, between Britain and its colonies. Diplomacy was an essential part of the formal relations between settlers and natives, though the British were more inconsistent and piecemeal in their strategies. In the mid-eighteenth century they acquired key mediators with the Indians and perhaps came to trust them as allies. Yet, even when agreements were achieved, there is much to be said for Calloway's denunciation of the long history of white deception and treaty-breaking: very few treaties were observed by the Europeans, and the British settlers in particular repeatedly broke agreements about territorial limitations to their own settlements. Land hunger was a recurrent feature as populations grew (Calloway, 2013).

3.3 New societies, new economies

Colonial societies in the Caribbean and North America were highly diverse, depending on the character of their settlers, the social relations they created among themselves, and the forms of economic production and trade that developed. Neither Britain nor France could control the social and economic development of their colonies, and the different economies developed without any central direction. A comparison of the diversity of colonial societies in British and French North America reveals some similarities in the kinds of social relations developed, particularly where slavery prevailed, but also some remarkable contrasts. In no sense did either imperial power create a single type of colonial society in the Americas. John M. Murrin, quoted by Philip Morgan, pointed out that 'the seventeenth century created, within English America alone, not one new civilization on this side of the Atlantic, but many distinct colonies that differed as dramatically from one another as any of them from England . . . not one, but many Americas, and the passage of time threatened to drive them farther apart, not closer together' (Morgan, 1993: 2). Another way of characterising this variety is summed up in the historical survey by Eric Nellis (2010), who calls the British colonies 'an empire of regions'. A broad view incorporating British and French colonies reinforces this perception and requires exploration of the reasons for the colonies' varied development. As we have seen, the history of white expansion in North America could be divided into distinct phases, each exercising greater pressure than before on the native peoples: encounters were followed by colonies, and colonies became empires. The common process did not produce a convergence of the colonies, whether British or French, into a North American 'society'. On the contrary, their origins lay with a diverse collection of promoters, some of whom retained influence over the colony for a long time: many concerned with Virginia had been involved in Ireland, and others were impressed by the trading companies which had been set up to make profits in Russia and India. Settlers in general had little involvement in the first steps and thus little influence on the initial direction of the colony, although Puritan interests in Massachusetts bought up the initial stock company in order to establish their own controlling, and intensely religious, interest. Even in religion, English colonies were divided, with Virginia implementing Church of England structures while Maryland was a Catholic colony and New England was divided into rival forms of Calvinist Protestantism. Each had its own supporting proprietors and stockholders, who had different levels of control over the direction of their development.

The hopes of the promoters were reflected in some of the unrealistic advice they gave to the early settlers. Richard Hakluyt thought that, in conquering lands which were very hot, the English might replace the Italian and Spanish suppliers of wine and olive oil: he optimistically regarded the natives as likely labourers in these vineyards. There were repeated exhortations to

Virginia's settlers to dig for gold or silver or, as second-best, copper. Within a couple of years of the 1607 settlement the fertility of the land was noted, but it was still unclear what should be grown. One early governor and planter, Sir George Yeardley, wrote to London:

> For the present state and condicon of this Countrie, it wants only Supportes, round and free supplies, both of men and moneyes, to make good the mayne and profitable endes of a moste happy plantation. Concerning the Countrie and the soile thereof, wee finde it fertile and full of encrease, bringing forth goodly Corne, many kinde of Fruites, naturall Vines and quickly rendring us our owne Countrie seedes, and Rootes which wee bury therein, as prosperous and unchangeable for tast and quantitie as England it selfe. For these Comodities of pitch and tarr Soape ashases. Wood Iron etc. most true it is Noble Sir, that there they bee most plentifully to bee returned home, if soe bee it the meanes and skifull workemen together which fit provisions for those Labourers (untill the Colour may quitt some of theis Charges, by planting their owne Vines, sowing their owne Corne, and broodinge their owne Cattaile, Kine, Swine, Goates etc. which would shortly be, and had bin ere this, had the Government bin carefully and honestly established and carried here theis 3 yeres passed) may be provided and sent over to worke in those businesses.
>
> (*Records of the Virginia Company* Vol. 3, 1933: 30)

Under John Smith, food supply and proper planting in Virginia, following the Indian style of mixing rows of maize between ones of vegetables and fruit, was regularised, but the adoption of the sweet form of tobacco from the West Indies provided the key step to a profitable economy. Tobacco, and the money to be made from its large-scale production, continued to shape Virginia's history until the nineteenth century. No such choice was available to those further north, where both religious inclination and the environment dictated an economy of mixed farming. Elsewhere in the South, in South Carolina in particular, the best crop proved to be rice, given the low-lying and humid land close to the coast. Further inland, conditions were more difficult, but the colony began by supplying timber and tar for the ships of the Royal Navy; the switch to large-scale plantation production between 1700 and 1730 was driven by the profitability of rice. This shaped the rise of slavery and was the basis of the recruitment of slaves from rice-growing areas of West Africa. The use of Native American slaves was rapidly surpassed by the increasing numbers of Africans, who provided the labour force for the export economy. As Ira Berlin noted, in South Carolina, 'throughout the low-country, rice was king' (Berlin in Morgan, 1993: 88, 89, 90).

At the base of the new societies were new forms of economic production drawing on a variety of crops and animals from Europe, Africa, and the Americas themselves. In the early modern Atlantic there were many forms of biological exchanges and transfers, not least the movement of deadly diseases such as smallpox from Europe and yellow fever and malaria from Africa. Diseases invisibly accompanied the people on the move and had a devastating impact on native peoples in the Caribbean and North America. More deliberate and experimental were the movements of commodities for production by Europeans, who also adopted local products of value such as indigo, tobacco and, above all, maize and potatoes as additions to some of the standard crops of European agriculture. Products were exchanged and production on both sides of the ocean was transformed: by the eighteenth century, crops such as potatoes had become part of the means of survival for the poor in Europe. There were parallel experiments in transferring the production of European and African crops across the Atlantic – cereals such as wheat, barley, and oats, and, for the Europeans, relatively new crops such as cotton, sugar, and rice, along with animals such as cattle, horses, pigs, chickens, and sheep. Finding which environments suited which commodities took time and sometimes near-disastrous experimentation. Initially Europeans depended on local knowledge and native advice, as suggested above, before developing economies that could be profitable in the growing transatlantic markets. They were often bewildered by native farming techniques and it often took at least two generations for these to be copied successfully. If the sponsors and financiers of colonies thought in terms of profitable exports to Europe, most settlers were more concerned with land and economic survival on what land they could acquire. With many commodities undergoing uncertain conditions and fluctuating prices, particularly for crops such as indigo, there were recurrent problems even for the best-organised producers. Even if the colonial relations of production seemed pre-capitalist, as the reinvention of slavery was – it had died out in the Middle Ages in countries such as England – the value of many of the products depended on the burgeoning systems of capitalist trading and marketing. In many ways this was the first stage in economic globalisation, albeit under conditions of imperial rivalry and colonial control. Fortunes could be made and the customers in Europe became accustomed to the new consumer goods, even if they understood little of the conditions under which they were produced.

After initial struggles with food, disease, and the natives, the colonies established a reasonable standard of living; yet, in Virginia in particular, people would remember the 'starving time'. By the 1650s the English-speaking colonies had attracted large numbers of settlers and were in many ways economically stable, with Virginia exporting large quantities of tobacco while the New England colonies became deeply involved in supplying foodstuffs and timber to the Caribbean. Within this complex of possibilities it is not surprising that colonies could develop in contrasting ways, depending on the commodities which they found viable and profitable, the kinds of migrants they attracted or imported, and the social relations of their production. Though both France and Britain had slave and non-slave economies, and concentrated on sugar and tobacco in the former, there were great differences between the plantation economies and the rest. This variation was greatest among the British economies of North America, with its differences between northern and southern colonies. Contrasts between the image and reality of the British colonies are pervasive: the image of New England is one of free settlers seeking freedom of worship, compared with the repressive character of early Virginia, peopled by fortune hunters, the sweepings of jails and **bridewells**, and forced migrants from Britain and, after a short time, Africa. They were united in a need for land, and expansion into native territories began from the beginning; but in terms of social and class relations the resulting societies, with one a society aiming at being one of 'saints', were a contrast between what Daniel Boorstin has called the New Englanders' 'city upon a hill' and Virginia's rule by 'English gentlemen, American style' (Boorstin, 1958). The key institution in New England was the town, a legal and constitutional entity rather than a large urban settlement. It was through towns that land was allocated, law administered, and taxes raised. Later the welfare system that in some ways reproduced the English **Poor Law** of 1601 was managed through towns and townships. There was little like this in the southern colonies, Virginia and the Carolinas, where urban centres were a coastal feature while the key units in rural areas were the county and the parish. The novelty of the New England town has been stressed by historians: Powell (1963: xviii) pointed to the way that, from the first (to quote Edward Winslow of the Plymouth colony), New Englanders claimed that 'we came here to avoid the hierarchy, the holy days, the Book of Common Prayer, etc.', meaning the structures of deference and rituals of the Church of England. Yet they also claimed a level of equality before their God and in their dealings with one another that British colonial governors, for one, found at times impossible to tolerate. Given the many hierarchies of England – economic, legal, civic, and in terms of religious exclusion – the nature of the Puritan society in America was bound to be different in significant ways. Some political developments occurred outside the formal character of the charters, such as the town meetings of Massachusetts and New England, an extension of Congregationalist principles of self-government to the secular sphere. 'The distinguishing characteristic of the first New England towns was the primary assembly of adult males as the ruling body. The assembly in the beginning in several towns was held weekly but soon gave way to a monthly meeting.' While all adult males were allowed to attend and speak, only freemen could vote and being admitted to the freemanship was a slow and grudging affair – most were shareholders in the Massachusetts Bay Company (Zimmerman, 1999: 19, 20–22). New England created new inequalities between servants and employers, freemen and others, but the population had a sense of being a breakaway society.

The gradual disintegration of the original egalitarian Puritan communities in New England can be seen in the classic study of Dedham, Massachusetts, by Kenneth Lockridge (1970), which was in his view unmistakably an 'American society' in its original Puritan ideals. Yet as time went on it also suffered growing internal inequalities accompanied by differences between political factions that undermined that original sense of equality. It was characterised by unusually favourably economic conditions, longevity, and good health, as well as organisation. He notes, though, that the era of 'communal utopianism' came to an end as social diversity, growing inequalities, the changing character of New England, and the general broadening of horizons altered the community. This process was also partly because of the internal problems of maintaining communal coherence which had already developed by the middle of the seventeenth century, reinforced by legal disputes with local Christian Indians over land. Equality at the practical level of the economy simply proved impossible. This study was an idealistic view of an early Puritan community and regarded as over-simplistic at the time of its publication. Massachusetts was wracked by many problems, some of them fiercely religious and of its own making. There were always inequalities of wealth and power, partly in terms of education and religious training, which meant that Puritan ideals of equality could be sustained theologically – all were equal before the throne of God – but were unworkable as the economy developed. The levels of inequality in the growing towns such as Boston, and between the coastal settlements and those further inland, were a feature of New England society by 1700.

British colonies in the South might over-simply be described as plantation or slave societies (see below). There were great differences between large and small farmers, and the numbers of acres and slaves they owned, and it is clear that politics in colonies such as Virginia was mostly dominated by a few very rich families. The differences between the British northern and southern colonies, however, can be exaggerated. Both had slaves, for example, and employed and dealt in slaves. As Adams and Pleck put it (2010: 5), 'most New England masters owned only one or two slaves who lived in spaces such as the attics of their master's home. In 1700 the black population of New England numbered about a thousand, roughly half of whom lived in Massachusetts'. Most lived in towns, working alongside white servants (p. 5). There were few plantations in the rural areas of the North, unlike in the South where large numbers of slaves were employed in producing cash crops for export. The absence of towns (except for the ports on the coast) in the South marked a very different form of society. Respectable white people gathered for crucial rituals in the management of the colony, such as the monthly meetings of the county courts, which met at courthouses as often there were few other buildings (apart from taverns) nearby. Some communal entertainments such as race days or the theatre in Williamsburg (Virginia) – which George Washington personally appreciated – also provided a forum for meeting and socialising. This was more of a gentry society than that found in New England, and the elite made use of any opportunity for gathering and socialising. Yet society in the slave colonies was also distinctive in that the subordinated groups, servants and slaves, made many efforts to escape and the result was a surveillance society that was constantly alert to the threat of wandering escapees and accustomed to stopping and interrogating suspect parties of travellers. A key mechanism for masters of slaves and servants was advertising runaways in the colonial newspapers, whose role in policing the society became increasingly important after their establishment in the 1720s and 1730s. These advertisements have provided historians with many accounts of the character and appearances of the 'silenced' groups in southern society; the individuality, defiant attitudes, and forms of personal resistance of the runaways emerge in some of the details. Their styles, adopting distinctive forms of dress or personal decoration despite their poverty, suggest that in the face of oppressive economic circumstances there was an underlying need to express their own identities. The challenge represented by runaway servants and slaves was different: slaves were taking their masters' property, literally 'stealing themselves', when they ran away ('Steal away, steal away to Jesus,' the nineteenth-century spiritual went), while servants were in breach of contracts and were often punished with extensions to the length of their service to compensate their masters for the financial losses incurred. Both could be whipped – servants by order of the courts as well as by their masters – but the punitive mutilation or even killing of slaves by their owners were not crimes. For both, running away was a form of resistance. Servants had a measure of protection from abuse through their resort to the courts, which had the duty to enforce and supervise their contracts, but slaves had no such support. Though there were some parallels with the kinds of anxiety that mobility and running away provoked in Britain, this society was far more like an open prison for many of its inhabitants compared with the mother country (see Chapter 5 for running away as resistance).

Few of these characteristics were shared by the French colonies. The authorities had a clear idea of urban life and tried to export their model when towns were founded. New Orleans, among others, was laid out on a distinctively French urban design when founded in 1718, complete with a grid layout of streets and, where diagonals met, a circular roundabout. This, ironically, influenced the layout of crossroads and intersections in the first planned city following US independence – Washington, D.C. Njoh (2016: 25) remarks that 'efforts to export French urban culture to North America were deliberate and elaborate'. French rural outposts followed more military designs with defensive bulwarks, though these were also found around towns such as New Orleans and Quebec. French colonial societies were, though, like those of the British, varied, and this reflected their economic bases. Settler farmers were found in the North, particularly in the Acadian area of Nova Scotia, where artful management of irrigation and drainage produced prosperous family farms. Quebec, by contrast, was a place of small towns which had built up close relationships with the natives to exploit the fur trade, and, increasingly, small scattered farms. Only towards the mid-eighteenth century did farming develop. Further south, in Louisiana, a plantation economy was established despite great difficulties in relations with local native groups. As for its major town, New Orleans, its latest historian, Dawdy (2008: 234) remarks that 'the "founders" of Louisiana came from a culture of military privateers and *coureurs de bois* [literally 'hunters in the woods'; i.e., vagabonds] whose livelihoods depended on the violation of imperial law': they skimmed profits from the Indian trade, used royal ships for their own purposes, and, unsurprisingly, she calls it 'rogue colonialism'. Unlike British colonies, French settlers do not seem to have developed a print culture of their own, so the kinds of locally produced memoirs, pamphlets and, above all, newspapers, so common for Anglo-America, are missing, along with the insights they might have given to ordinary social relations.

The degree of variety of these colonial societies was to some extent limited by the central controls exercised in the two empires. It would be only a slight exaggeration to say that the French empire tended to impose legal uniformity on its colonies: the laws of slavery, for example, the *Code Noire*, were the same everywhere. Ironically, in the early 1700s Louis XIV declared slavery to be illegal in France itself, 70 years before the same decision was made in England. By contrast, the laws governing servants and slaves in the British colonies had to be invented in each one because there were no clear laws of slavery in England (see below). There was considerable mutual influence, and creative copying, but the laws had to be passed in each place. With regard to more general laws, of crime for example, it was usually assumed the common laws of England prevailed in the colonies. This was sometimes stated explicitly in the founding charter of a colony, and the involvement of governments in their charters made a difference as to whether there was a transfer of the 'full complex of institutions' complete with a governor and other formal structures (Meinig, 1986: 66). Throughout the British colonies some form of legislature, assembly, or council, usually highly unrepresentative initially, was formed to enact new laws and regulations for the new society. Unlike in the French colonies, therefore, the governors of British colonies always had to deal with local law-making and the need to persuade local representatives of different kinds to implement both British trade regulations and policies. The potential for conflict was there from the beginning. Debates were often genuine: for example, to what extent did English laws passed after the foundation of a colony apply there? Were they automatically extended to the colonies? This was occasionally a highly important political matter, as in the case of the 1679 *habeas corpus* law giving guarantees against arbitrary imprisonment. Many assumed that the law enshrined much more ancient common-law liberties and therefore did not need to be copied or inserted into colonial statutes, while others took steps to do just that explicitly. The 'rights of Englishmen' were assumed and continually evoked in the colonies, even if the legislation underpinning them was vague and uncertain.

There were policy continuities in the British colonies, all of which had some semblance of a Poor Law to deal with the problems of poverty and other forms of distress. Yet even here there were differences in both the methods of financing and the units of administration of the system, which varied from one colony to another. The basic principle of local responsibility was retained, so the legal framework was exported almost intact to the colonies which adopted a 'close copy' of the English system: for example, 'individual relief, local control and a "parish of settlement" requirement' were all put into force in Virginia by the late seventeenth century (Hitchcock, 2016: 10–11). This was not universal, as the role of the Church of England parish was unusually prominent in Virginia and South Carolina. Elsewhere,

> Colonial administration of the poor laws was left to the smallest unit of government. In New England, the town was responsible for executing the statute. The Town Meeting made the decisions, which were carried out by the selectmen, tithingmen, or overseers of the poor, civil officials. In the southern colonies where, as in England, the Anglican church was established, the parish was the administrative unit. There, the board of vestry, a group of men, usually twelve in number, chosen by the freeholders to oversee the religious affairs of the parish, was also charged with the responsibility of caring for the poor.
> (Trattner, 1999: 18)

As in England, aid for local people, particularly to neighbours known to the authorities, was often generous, but there was a great reluctance to help strangers. It did not take long to become 'local' (usually three or six months' residence, far shorter than in England), but seaport towns and other communities were grudging towards those who arrived poor and who seemed to expect instant assistance. Through these provisions in the British colonies, communities accepted their responsibilities for, and obligations to, their unfortunate members. In the late eighteenth century several even experimented with urban institutions such as a poorhouse (Philadelphia and Charleston) or a mental hospital (Williamsburg). In effect they were also accepting the inevitability of poverty and other misfortunes striking their fellow Americans (Lockley, 2005; Mackey, 1965). This is only one example of the apparent similarity between the home country and the colonies, but it demonstrates the way that different conditions in North America affected the implementation of what may seem a standard English institution. There were many other areas of difference and innovation, not least the law of land and property, which was much simpler and more easily administered than in England. The convergence or divergence of the colonies from the home country's legal and political culture became more than just a theoretical issue in the eighteenth century, and some historians such as Jack P. Greene have suggested that after 1700 there was a process of *convergence* among the colonies in British North America, with the formation of a distinctively American collective culture and political setting. This common ground overrode any social and religious differences between the colonies.

A key factor may have been the social character that marked the free white settlers:

> Certainly in the 1760s and 1770s, as earlier, the most impressive aspect of the free population of Britain's American colonies was the extraordinarily large number of families of independent middling status, which was proportionately substantially more numerous than in any other contemporary Western society.
>
> (Greene, 1993: 37)

This group was far more independent-minded and, in economic and political terms, more active in its own interests. And those in it knew their own minds.

3.3a Slave societies

The idea of a slave society is not as simple as it might appear. Even if the economic base of exploitation is understood, it is still difficult to grasp how such a system survived the potential for violent conflict. Yet slave societies had persisted for centuries and, while the European colonial form of slavery differed significantly from both classical European and traditional African models, it was in essence the same structure of oppression as its predecessors. 'Slavery took many forms in the early modern Americas, and this variety persisted in both indigenous and colonial settings long after the African slave trade overshadowed other slaving cultures' (Rushforth, 2012: 8). The scale of forcible migration and the intensity of the work regime in producing some of the cash crops were unprecedented. For both Britain and France, therefore, slave relations were new and required considerable innovation, both legally and economically. One area that needed foundation was law – as noted above, the slave laws in the colonies had to be created and enforced, and for the British colonies the crimes and punishments created by slave laws drew on some ancient British traditions and some Europe-wide styles of punishment. The principle of destroying the bodies of rebels and those who committed treason, wives who killed their husbands (by burning), and servants who killed their masters (hanging, frequently followed by the corpse being hung in chains or 'gibbeted') was part of English law at the time, but some of the punishments inflicted on rebellious slaves were even more savage. This became widely publicised in the rebellions in Antigua in 1736 and the New York 'conspiracy' of 1741 (though a particular focus of alarm in the latter was the participation of disaffected poor whites (see Chapter 5). Whites were hanged but slaves could be burnt alive; in Antigua, slaves endured the continental European punishment of breaking on the wheel. Even lesser punishments were distinctive: slaves convicted of serious crimes against their masters could be transported out of the colony, as some of the New York rebels were. This became more common in slave laws after the American Revolution. For no other category of offender was transportation inflicted in the British colonies.

The colonial laws validating and enforcing slavery often contradicted the freedom offered in the imperial centres of Europe. In the eighteenth century both France and Britain declared that, legally, there could be no slaves in those countries. Brett Rushforth notes that in 1704, when the slave 'Louis' demanded his freedom on setting foot in France despite the opposition of Michel Bégon, the author of the *Code Noire*, Louis XIV declared that slavery had been abolished years previously. So, while 'Louis' was free in France, the slave traders were free to go on buying African slaves, and the slave holders in the Americas were free to go on exploiting them. 'Legal pluralism, rather than legal uniformity, defined slavery in the French Atlantic world' (Rushforth, 2012: 77, 133). Seventy years later, in 1772, the case of James Somerset came before Lord Chief Justice Mansfield in London, the question being not whether slavery was legal in England but whether someone could be *taken out* of England into slavery. Somerset had been brought to London by his master, and when plans were made to leave for the colonies he sought legal help from the abolitionist movement to challenge his master's right to take him back. There were ancient laws from the eleventh century forbidding the export and selling of people into slavery, and this was one factor that led to the plaintiff winning his freedom. From then on it was said that once slaves set foot in England they were, in practice, free. This did not, however, alter their status in the colonies, where they could still be subject to extreme repression and violence (Ogborn, 2008: 265, 279; Gould, 2003). The growing idea that slaves should have rights in law affected practices towards the end of the eighteenth century.

The British Parliament was forced by political opposition to both the slave trade and slavery itself to introduce some safeguards for slaves: they could no longer be regarded as property and killed by their masters. This was partially established in a crucial case in Grenada in the 1770s, which came to the notice of the London authorities when they sent a questionnaire in 1788 to all their slave colonies requesting information on the economic and legal standing of slaves. In a prosecution of a white man for murdering a slave, the prosecutor quoted Edward Coke on the definition of murder as the slaying of a sentient being, and, moreover, used him to argue that since the thirteenth century (in **Magna Carta**, no less) a feudal subordinate – a 'villein' – had legal rights of address against crimes such as assault and murder committed by his feudal lord. If slaves were like feudal serfs, went the argument, they shared these rights. In at least one case in Grenada in 1775 these arguments were decisive in securing the conviction and execution of a man who killed a female slave (see Document 3.3). It was the rights of 'villeins' that had run through the discussions in Somerset's case. In the British colonies of the Leeward Isles in 1798 there were major reforms, known as the 'Amelioration Acts', encouraging marriage among slaves, protecting female slaves from violence during pregnancy, and even making killing a slave murder, though prosecutions of masters were hesitant and at times unsuccessful. In this way the slave-owning class attempted to forestall the criticism of the anti-slave-trade campaigners and the abolitionists who were successfully portraying an image of cruelty as being the central characteristic of slavery. In many ways the legal confusions of the new French Republic, which officially abolished slavery in 1794 and then allowed its return, was matched by the profusion of laws in the British colonies. In this period, at the end of the eighteenth century, both empires found themselves confronting challenges to the established inequalities of rights between classes, races, and even genders.

Slavery depended on the reduction of individuals to mere property, and it has been one of historians' aims to try to reconstruct the lives and experiences of individuals within the mass of the exploited. This is not easy for the earliest period, the seventeenth century, in particular. Whereas there are some memoirs of indentured servants, the printed lives of slaves only emerge (in English, notably) at the end of the eighteenth century. Most of what we know about slaves' appearance, attitudes, and actions is given to us by their owners, when they ran away or are recorded as otherwise troublesome in diaries and journals. Slaves rarely speak to us directly. Resistance is visible in many small personal actions of disobedience, non-compliance, and escape. Yet it is also true that full-scale slave revolts were rare, with the exception of Haiti in the 1790s (see Chapter 5). Most slave societies worked within a structure fraught with conflict and a potential for extreme violence – but they worked, for the most part. In some circumstances, remarkably few white people dominated a large African population. At Golden Grove plantation in Jamaica, in 1765, there were only five white men – a senior overseer and four assistants who also acted as accountants – in charge of more than 371 slaves, of whom 190 were male. 'More than 80 per cent were adult men and women, suggesting that a large proportion had been brought to Jamaica in the Atlantic slave trade.' That year there was a near-revolt by the slaves, with one overseer from the estate attacked, shot dead, and then beheaded by what were described as 'new negroes', that is, new arrivals from Africa. While there were numbers of children on this plantation, they were not at this time sufficient to replace the older workers as they became 'wore out', and newly shipped slaves were continually needed to replenish the workforce. In this, Golden Grove was typical of a great many Jamaican plantations (Higman, 2005: 172, 197, 201).

Comparison with plantations in British North America offers a glimpse into two very different economic and demographic regimes. Both were settler societies in terms of the white experience, and yet also slave societies. Dunn (2014) took a plantation in western Jamaica, Mesopotamia, and one from the Virginian tidewater, Mount Airy, and undertook a careful analysis of the slaves, their forms of work and treatment, and their opportunities for family life in the two places. The most striking difference lay in the life expectancies of the two slave groups: in Jamaica the plantation was frequently having to import new slaves to replace those who had died, while in Virginia the estate in the latter half of the eighteenth century exported a surplus to be marketed to other plantations. The regime of discipline seems to have been different, too, with greater severity – perhaps reflecting fear of revolt – in Jamaica compared with Virginia. Another crucial difference seems to have been that the Jamaican owners were rarely present at this plantation after 1750, many living in England, while the Virginian planters treated their estates as their homes. This was the key distinction – the Virginian landowners were Virginian, in ways that, for most of the period before 1800, the Jamaican planters were not Jamaican. Yet both elite racial groups wanted to be seen as essentially embodying British values, to be judged accordingly, and, in the American case, demanded what were regarded as the traditional legal and political liberties of British subjects. Zacek (2010) confirms that this was already the ideal of the Leeward Islands' planters by 1700, and their political system, of assemblies and legislation, resembled that of Britain's two houses of Parliament. In the face of conflict with their colonial governors sent from London, both they and their North American equivalents became more strident in demanding their rights.

The lives of ordinary slaves are only recorded in fragments, usually when they caused trouble for their owners by running away or being intransigent in other ways. The physical realities of slavery emerge from an increasing combination of archaeology and history. The small buildings that comprised slave houses, grouped near the big house of the owner, are often found in both contemporary paintings and in the archaeological record. This can be seen in those few plantations open to the public today. Carter Grove in Virginia is one example (with the tourists in mind as well as educational purposes). The sizes of the slave houses seem to have been variable, with the smallest little more than three metres by two and the largest three or four times that size. It is likely that dimensions varied according to the family size in Virginia and other northern colonies, and, as Philip Morgan points out, some were for families and others for single people rooming together. Whatever the variety of inhabitants, these were not barracks: the planters accepted that the accommodation should afford slaves a degree of privacy (Morgan, 1999: 111–112). A number of excavations have reflected on the stories indicated by both the built and working environment and the burial practices of slave societies. Slave graveyards have been a particular focus of archaeological ambition, though very few have been identified and excavated. The largest number of slave interments so far identified was excavated on Barbados by Jerome Handler and his colleagues at the Newtown plantation. The excellent state of the plantation's written records provided an unusually detailed framework for the excavation. Most of the evidence consisted of the way bodies had been interred, the range of people buried, and the evidence displayed on the bones and teeth. Cultural information can be inferred from the forms of the burials and the condition of the bodies. A few of the Barbados skulls displayed teeth which had been filed in what seemed to the excavators to be a West African style, and a prone burial (face down) was also considered to be a possible survival of African practices. Most characteristics of the layout of the body, an east-west orientation for example, were typical of all eighteenth- and nineteenth-century interments. Thus, of the 104 remains discovered by Handler and his colleagues, there was evidence of what might loosely be described as 'survivals' of African practice and of the adoption of new practices influenced by both European and New World experiences (Handler and Corricini, 1983; Handler, 1995, 1996).

Some caution should be taken when seeing these practices as simply African or European: as Jamieson has commented (1995: 40, col. 2), 'neither a search for "survivals" nor an anthropological emphasis on "phenomenology" seems suited to the study of African-American mortuary practices'. In other words, we cannot simply assume that features found in the ground can be interpreted as transfers from Africa, nor can we make simple guesses concerning their meaning for those who took part in the burial rituals. With that in mind, the use of mounds to mark burials, and practices such as leaving gifts and objects on the grave subsequently, do suggest a determination by slaves to mark someone's passing and their continuing value to their community in ways that seem similar to African practices (Jamieson 1995: 48). The scattering of shells on Gullah graves (on the islands off South Carolina, largely from the nineteenth century) also suggests some continuity. Moreover, slave narratives indicate, as Jamieson suggests, that 'funerals may have been one of the few times that antebellum communities could assume control of the symbolism around them, and thus create the dignity at death that negates the "social death" of their slave status' (1995: 55, col. 1). The concept of 'social death', by which slaves were non-persons in law and society, was introduced most powerfully by Orlando Patterson (1982): though almost a non-person in life, it is a paradox of slavery that through death and burial the individual may finally have achieved the standing of personhood. Farnsworth (2000) argues that archaeologists have failed to explore evidence of brutality and violence towards slaves: in a small number of instances, Jamaican graves contained heavy weights attached to slave bodies, suggesting they were buried with the instruments of punishment (being chained to a weight was one of a range of penalties for trying to run away). Other bodies suggest that hunger and near starvation were common experiences, as teeth in particular show evidence of 'growth arrest lines' where normal growth had been halted temporarily by poor diet (Watters, 1994; Corrucini et al., 1982; Handler and Corrucini, 1983). In some islands, such as Montserrat, widespread deaths of slaves from starvation were reported in the late eighteenth century as the food supply was reduced by exceptional climatic conditions (Watters, 1994).

The health of slaves, as Dunn's work indicates, differed in the Caribbean and North America, with the latter showing increasing self-sufficiency of supply as plantations encouraged and maintained large numbers of slave children. The West Indian regimes were more deadly, not just because of the prevalence of diseases but because of the forms of work and exploitation. The health of women was the key to the difference in African population growth, and there is evidence that Caribbean women were worked harder during pregnancy, and their children less valued, than in the North. Paton (2017) suggests that, even though from the 1780s the Jamaican authorities became keener to encourage slave fertility, providing a bounty for babies born and in a number of colonies passing laws forbidding the flogging of pregnant women, the measures had little effect on the poor rate of reproduction of the slave population. The owners still depended on the slave trade. Work remained hard and the pressure to undertake heavy labour whatever the slave's condition undermined all official efforts to encourage a rising population of slaves through natural reproduction rather than importation of new individuals. Interestingly, one white indentured servant, William Moraley, commented on the Virginian planters' practice of encouraging marriage and family life among their slaves, regarding it as being to their financial advantage (see Document 3.1). This is to some extent confirmed by historians, though, as Kenneth Morgan points out, there were some differences between Virginia and the other slave colonies in the Carolinas and Georgia (Morgan, 2007: 84–95). Certainly, family life among slaves in the Caribbean was more difficult to achieve as so many factors undermined its stability (Moore et al., 2001). In other respects, things were improving for slaves in the British Caribbean at the end of the eighteenth century, as several colonies passed laws for the 'amelioration' of slave conditions, clearly with an eye to the mounting criticism and widespread campaigning for the abolition of both the slave trade and slavery itself. Masters' powers were gradually restricted as laws against cruelty – and, above all, the right to kill your own slaves – were passed. It was a small beginning on the way to abolition of the slave trade (1807) and slavery (1833).

3.3b Servants and convicts

As mentioned earlier, the deployment of servant labour was one of the characteristics of British colonies. Yet the use of indentured servants – that is, workers bound for a set number of years to work for an employer, often by way of compensation for the cost of their travel to the New World – was one of the features of both the British and French colonies. They should properly be distinguished from their fellow unfree workers, African slaves, despite the recent use by some historians of 'white slavery' to describe their condition. In many ways this idea follows the popular eighteenth-century usage of 'slavery' to describe servants' conditions (see Document 3.2, Father Mosley's account). This modern adoption of the term, though, is criticised from both the historical and political viewpoint by Handler and Reilly (2017). They argue that 'white slavery' is a misreading of the history of the main features of servitude in the colonies, however convenient it may be for those trying to establish that Europeans suffered comparable abuse to that directed at slaves. Nevertheless, the mixture of voluntary and forced migrants who made up the population of indentured servants endured a structure of exploitation and, at times, brutal discipline, but it was not lifelong or hereditary. The colonial system of servanthood bore superficial resemblance to that set up in England in 1563 by the Statute of **Artificers**. The indenture signed at the start specified a term of service, the mutual obligations of master and servant, and the rights of the servant on completion of the term of service. In England and Wales the usual term of service in agriculture was a year (or a day less, to prevent the servants establishing rights of settlement and poor relief in the parish). Customary rules specified the maintenance, wages, and clothing to be given to the servant, according to age, gender, and level of skill. Above all, the conduct of both parties was subject to legal scrutiny through local magistrates. Studies suggest that servants in a largely rural economy, serving in a framework of annual contracts, could generally rely on magistrates to safeguard their interests. Examples of abuse were usually penalised and the servant released from the contract. With the exception of the young, physical punishment by masters and employers became increasingly illegitimate. This was not a perfect or tension-free system, but large parts of the agricultural economy depended on it until the nineteenth century. The annual contracts of English servants, supervised very carefully by local magistrates and without the employers' rights of corporal punishment, abandonment, or neglect, were very different from the forms of indentured service in the colonies, even if they contained some of the same elements, such as redress through the law.

Adaptation of English structural relationships therefore involved their transformation. British colonies departed substantially from the 1563 model, varying both the legal length and the practical realities of this form of labour. From the beginning, in the first half of the seventeenth century, colonial conditions were much harsher. The laws were very different: all colonies, beginning in the first half of the seventeenth century, passed laws regulating servants which specified severe penalties for disobedient behaviour or trying to escape. By 1700 all had followed the examples of the pioneers such as Barbados and Virginia, with the latter in 1661 developing complex rules and regulations as well as severe punishments. The penalties involved both corporal punishment and extension of the length of service (Hay and Craven, 2004, have the most comprehensive survey of the statute laws). Female servants who became pregnant might have their service extended and their child also bound to labour. There was no standard practice with regard to the length of service, which varied in time and place, for nearly 300 years: reasons for this diversity were partly due to the quality of the worker, their age, gender, and level of skill. Whereas the English law carefully distinguished apprentices from servants, day labourers from annual contracts in agriculture, and domestic from other types of servant, the colonial legislation tended to lump them together under a single law.

The kinds of work and the local economy varied between colonies. Another reason for diversity was political, as the rebels of Ireland and Britain in the Civil War, and those from Monmouth's rebellion in 1685, were sentenced to ten years' servitude. There were waves of political exiles after every defeated rebellion: it solved the problem of what to do with those who surrendered. As Davies comments:

> the list is a long one; scarcely a civil commotion took place in the British Isles between 1650 and 1700 that did not deposit some human sediment on the other side of the Atlantic. It is not a record to be proud of. But there is no reason to think that these reluctant emigrants necessarily made bad colonists; on the contrary, those who survived and stayed in America were probably as good as orthodox indentured servants, if not better.
>
> (Davies, 1974: 92)

British criminals, increasingly sent in the seventeenth century to the **Chesapeake** colonies of Maryland and Virginia as an alternative to the death penalty, and in the eighteenth as a routine punishment for petty thefts, mostly served seven years. The usual *sentences* in British courts were seven years for minor theft and, for those reprieved from the death sentence, 14 years or life, but in the northern colonies there are no records of any indenture for more than seven years for convicts. This was the case even if the sentence of reprieve had specified 14 years or life (Morgan and Rushton, 2004). Elsewhere, Handler and Reilly (2017) argue the norm was three to five years in places such as pre-1660 Barbados. For voluntary servants, Virginia had four years as standard, in contrast to the seven for **convict servants**.

The treatment of servants was much harsher than in England, where (with the exception of adolescents) servants could not be flogged by their employers. Yet such punishments, often, but not necessarily, with the approval of magistrates, were common in the colonies. Working there was more like being on a naval ship than an English farm. Edmund Morgan argues that:

> in Virginia a master had little reason to treat his servant well in order to obtain a renewal of his services at the expiration of his term; and a servant had little reason to work hard in order to assure being rehired, because men would not bind themselves out for a second long term when they could make more by working for themselves.
>
> (Morgan, 1975: 92)

This may not be the whole picture: in many parts of the mid-Atlantic colonies there were few opportunities for independent landowning, or working as free labourers, so many servants fled to cities such as Philadelphia. The status of servant was different from that of slave, as William Moraley acknowledged from his own experience (see Document 3.1), but they could be sold – or, rather, their contract could – to another employer without their permission and even left as a legacy on the employer's death. They were to some extent a commodity with a price. Though some servants were able to complain to magistrates about abuse, and obtain some degree of redress, the odds were stacked against them. Their work was on isolated plantations and farms in colonies such as Virginia, and there was no freedom of movement for them to go to court. Moraley was sure that few of them won their cases. Servants were kept under strict control and, despite their various forms of defiance and resistance (see Chapter 5), they could not threaten the system. Importantly, 'no servant rebellion in Virginia ever got off the ground' (Morgan, 1975: 217) – not even in Barbados. Newman regards the servant system as ensuring 'total control' over all the servants' time: this, he argues, was – particularly in the seventeenth century – a loss of freedom worse than that suffered by African slaves.

> It was white men and women from the British Isles who first experienced such a dramatic reduction of personal freedom, not African slaves. Labourers were the most expensive commodities purchased by planters, and local laws and the "customs of the country" allowed planters to fully exploit their investments. Consequently, and because of the lengthy terms that many served, these servants more fully resembled pauper or vagrant apprentices, bound to serve a master for as long as a decade.
>
> (Newman, 2013: 95)

Controversially, he portrays the situation, whereby 'the heavy deployment of vagrants, convicts and prisoners – people judged to have forfeited many of their rights, including the right to life in the British Isles – meant that in seventeenth-century Barbados white labourers could be, and were, worked as virtual "white slaves"' (Newman, 2013: 246). Though this was often an image used in British printed accounts of colonies throughout the period, this is very much an extreme view of the situation of workers who, though clearly exploited and severely regulated, had a different *future* from that of slaves once their period of servitude was over.

In the first half of the seventeenth century Barbados and Virginia were the main destinations of servants. In Barbados by the 1650s Richard Ligon observed:

> The Island is divided into three sorts of men, Masters, Servants, and slaves. The slaves and their posterity, being subject to their Masters for ever, are kept and preserved with greater care than the servants, who are theirs but for five yeers, according to the law of the Island. So that for the time, the servants have the worser lives, for they are put to very hard labour, ill lodging, and their dyet very sleight.
>
> (Ligon, 1657: 43)

At the same time, Royalist soldier Heinrich von Uchteritz was one of 1,300 prisoners taken after the Battle of Worcester (1651) and transported to Barbados a few months later in 1652 to indentured servitude. He was the only one to have escaped and returned home, he claimed. He described the workforce of great plantation owners: his own had 100 'Christians' (white servants), 100 Africans and 100 'wilde' (i.e., 'savages') or Amerindians. He was fed largely on potatoes and cassava, both strange to him, and forced to do the work usually performed by slaves who, he thought, lived in cabins resembling dog kennels (Handler, 1970). Ligon noted the wretchedness of the servants and attributed to it their rebellion in combination with the African slaves.

> Mischiefe has been done, by the negligence and wilfulnesse of servants. And yet some cruel Masters will provoke their Servants so by extream ill usage, and often and cruell beating them, as they grow desperate, and so joyne together to revenge themselves upon them. A little before I came from thence, there was such a combination amongst them, as the like was never seen there before. Their sufferings being grown to a great height, and their daily complainings to one another (of the intolerable burdens they labour'd under) being spread throughout the Island; at the last, some amongst them, whose spirits were not able to endure such slavery, resolved to break through it, or die in the act and so conspired with some others of their acquaintance, whose sufferings were equall.
> (Ligon, 1657: 45)

The rising was given away by an informant, and the leaders executed. It seems that African slaves did not join in, but this was the nightmare of a society where both servants and slaves were employed together – particularly if the servants were Irish (because their loyalty was always doubted by the authorities, given that their transportation had often arisen from conditions of resistance to the British in the first place). The levels of cruelty directed at white servants are not easy to establish, though printed accounts by those who returned later in the century suggest the discipline remained severe. By the late seventeenth century, as the black to white ratio grew to one of overwhelming African dominance, there seems to have been a kind of grudging acceptance and integration of the poor whites among the planters in places such as Barbados.

The major destinations of British servants after 1700 were the mid-Atlantic colonies of Pennsylvania, Virginia, and Maryland, with the smallest, Maryland, taking remarkably high numbers of servants, including transported convicts. Overall, according to a 1764 survey, Maryland had more than 23,000 adult white freemen and 5,000 adult male servants – 1,507 of them transported convicts. In addition, the numbers of free women matched those of men, but there were fewer servants, only 2,200 with 386 convicts among them. There were more than 20,000 adult slaves and slightly more than 21,000 slaves under the age of 16. The servants were heavily concentrated in just four of the 14 counties, making up 20% of the labourers there, the rest being black slaves (see Document 3.4). In other, poorer, counties, both free servants and convicts were fewer in number, indicating that it was the richer, more productive areas with larger farms and plantations that drew in the white servants. There was also active recruitment of convict servants in particular to the ironworks of Maryland, which were being developed by investors such as the Baltimore Company to produce a major export from the colony. In the tobacco plantations, servants generally seem to have worked in digging ditches and hoeing the rows of tobacco plants. Details of how their work differed from that of slaves are hard to find, but clearly some artisans such as carpenters and blacksmiths were in great demand as servants. This kind of data are missing from elsewhere in British America, but estimates of 50,000 convict servants, and many more through free migration, suggest that, until the American War for Independence, this form of labour was vital for large sectors of the colonial economy. The prospects for these servants were not good, as it seems that few achieved success. In a western county of Virginia, according to one historian:

> slaves and white servants ranked lowest in both status and opportunity, and their record as freeholders reflects this state of affairs. Only one free black owned real estate in Augusta County, and former indentured and convict servants hardly fared better. Out of the 216 bound adult males known to have served before 1770, only sixteen (7.4 percent) eventually acquired land in the county. Of those sixteen successes, nine immigrated as members of freeholding households before the establishment of Augusta County's independence in November 1745. These retainers apparently used their masters' successes to enhance their own prospects for attaining a freehold.
> (McCleskey, 1990: 452)

This was from a county still expanding westwards, with some opportunities for striking out into new lands. But success was rare for the poorest whites. Moreover, contemporary accounts from the coastal areas further east confirm this: Father Joseph Mosley, a Jesuit on the eastern shore of Maryland, wrote to his sister in England about the fate of servants who, he thought, had been deceived by wild promises of a prosperous future.

> It has been a fine poor man's country; but now it is well peopled; the lands are all secured and the harvest for such is now all over. The lands are mostly worked by the landlords' negroes; and, of consequence, white servants, after their term of bondage is out, are stroling about the country without bread.
> (Hughes, 1908: 342; see Document 3.2)

Nowhere in the British colonies were there real opportunities for advancement, and this perhaps explains the continual pressure for new lands in the west to be taken and exploited.

Neither servants nor, particularly, convict servants were as common in the French colonies. Though some Indians, such as Caribs in the West Indies, were indentured as an alternative to enslavement in the seventeenth century, servants from France were in short supply. Political repression produced some candidates: at least 2,000 Huguenots in 12 ships were sent to the Caribbean colonies as indentured servants in the 1680s. Assisted migration was tried in the 1660s and early 1670s but the French government received complaints that the resultant servants were of poor quality and were requested to send no more 'idiots and cripples'. Nevertheless, the *engagés* made up about 39% of seventeenth-century migrants to French Canada (Pritchard, 2004: 8; 19, 23). Without volunteers, the French authorities turned to compulsion. As Davies observes, 'transportation in seventeenth-century France was seldom inflicted as a punishment by the courts; it would have reduced the number of convicts needed for the Mediterranean galleys. On the other hand, more as an administrative than as a judicial act, intendants from time to time rounded up rogues and vagabonds and sent them to the colonies' (Davies, 1974: 92). The result was that, in the early eighteenth century at least, small numbers of indentured servants and convicts (from the jails) were found in Canada. In Louisiana, where half of the 9,000 migrants and African slaves imported between 1718 and 1721 died or fled, there were only 233 indentured servants. Slaves had quickly come to dominate the labour force. Nevertheless, census data suggest that servants were still useful. In the 1720s, Louisiana census records indicate that 'the largest plantations in Natchez were the Sainte Catherine and White Earth concessions, worked by 38 French indentured servants, 50 African slaves and 4 Indian slaves' (Caillot, 2016: 90 fn. 185).

The official policy of criminal transportation was therefore intermittent and almost randomly applied. There was nothing in France to match the comprehensive legislation of the English 1718 Transportation Act (which excluded Scotland). The lingering commitment to the use of Mediterranean galleys provided an incentive to continue galley slavery as a major criminal punishment. This was managed in Marseilles, where there were jails to hold and then distribute the prisoners. An Atlantic policy developed in the mid-eighteenth century, when Brest in Brittany was chosen for a site of penal hard labour in reconstructing the port. Out of this, convicts became available for shipping across the ocean. Yet this was not deliberate policy, and few were sent (Pierre, 2017: 27–29). Servants in general proved problematic in several of the French colonies, particularly where the fur trade was the dominant form of the economy: there were simply not enough basic labouring jobs for servants to do. In other places the hard labour was better performed by slaves. Women were even more difficult to accommodate. As Kupperman has observed:

> Young women did go as servants, and colonial promoters always urged the colonies to make sending women a priority, but they faced life in largely male establishments with few of the protections they would have

had at home. In the middle of the seventeenth century, the French government sent a large number of women under the age of twenty-five as potential wives for settlers.

(Kupperman, 2012: 60)

These young women – *les filles de roi* (literally the 'king's daughters') – were sent out with the added attraction that they brought a dowry and were under the tutelage of nuns until they married. Only slowly, however, did the French Canadian colonies develop a settled population on this basis and, while their local militia were a formidable addition to the French army in times of war, there were never enough people to provide a rival to the more heavily populated British colonies.

3.4 Conclusion: New World, new societies

The kinds of societies produced in the British and French colonies were not foreseen by their founders and were in many ways always changing in certain respects throughout the period from 1650 to 1800. Little that was taken across the Atlantic remained the same as it had been in Europe. Laws, political institutions, forms of economic and social relations, and cultures all had to adapt and change. Much had to be invented since there were no templates for a slave society in western Europe at the time, and new forms of economy grew up around those oppressive relationships. The cash-crop monocultures producing sugar, rice, tobacco, and cotton that were created in the slave colonies were the first imperial outsourcing in European history and set a pattern that was later followed in the production of tea or rubber in the Indian subcontinent, south-east Asia, and Africa in the nineteenth century. The plantation 'complex' became a global phenomenon throughout the British empire long after the death of slavery itself. Other social relations in the colonies that shaped their development were with native peoples and, as we have seen, these extended from relatively equal patterns of trade to ethnic cleansing and enslavement. The biggest losers in conflicts, first between Britain and France and then between Britain and its 13 colonies, were the natives. Among white settlers, social differences between the economically secure and the poor were characteristically one-sided, particularly where indentured servitude prevailed, and the poor in general found themselves under greater regulation and control as such class differences grew. The poorest were often found in the growing cities such as Philadelphia (Pennsylvania) where welfare programmes were often made up of a doubled-edged strategy of aid and institutionalisation, where economic help was accompanied by enhanced forms of incarceration in workhouses governed by a regime of hard work. The French colonies in North America did not experience this level of poverty, though the people in New Orleans came closest in the variety of their origins and their economic problems. In the Caribbean the French colonies seem to have had a wider range of plantations in terms of size and numbers of slaves, and this formed a middling group of whites who were absent in British colonies such as Jamaica. This had profound implications for the ability of the white population to suppress slave uprisings, since poorer whites were essential to the formation of armed militias (see Chapter 5).

The nature of the social identities of these colonies posed a fascinating but difficult problem. In fighting each other, the British and French colonies grew to some degree closer to their metropolitan authorities, partly because of the necessity of asking them for help and support during the wars. This does not lead to the conclusion that they thought of themselves in any simple way as 'British' or 'French'. Though the leaders of the British colonies maintained strong relationships with Britain, often sending their sons to be educated there, and had widespread trade links with British ports and businesses, they increasingly felt distinctively different. In the end the North American colonies became alienated and fought a long and bitter war for independence. Historians debate whether this was in part due to ideological and cultural differences with Britain that had grown up since the seventeenth-century processes of colonisation. The British conquest of French North America cut off the French settlers from France – yet these settlers had already become the first population to be designated as 'Canadians'. By 1800 this identity was shared by the settlers of British origin, too, still loyal to Britain (to the puzzlement of the newly independent Americans) but distinctively different. Colonial identities were therefore more fluid and uncertain during this period, perhaps because it was also a process through which the British and French in Europe were also going at the same time. National identities were to some extent still under formation in this period, a work in progress. Only gradually were patriotic certainties developed – 'We shall never, never, be slaves', sang the British in the cheap patriotic song *Rule Britannia* – but the slavery they referred to was rule by an absolute Catholic monarchy, such as those in France or Spain. In 150 years of continual warfare, the two 'nations' came into much clearer focus, both in Europe and in the colonies.

4 Wars across the Atlantic

4.1 The Second Anglo-Dutch War (1665–1667)
4.2 King William's War (1688–1697) or the Nine Years' War
4.3 Queen Anne's War/the War of the Spanish Succession (1702–1713)
4.4 The War of Jenkins' Ear/War of the Austrian Succession (King George's War) (1739–1748)
4.5 The Seven Years' War/French and Indian War (1754–1763)

From the 1660s to the early nineteenth century the sequence of wars between the French and the British, ending in the defeat of Napoleon at Waterloo in 1815, shaped the history of the two nations and the fates of their American colonies. In addition they affected the way the identities of the two nations and their offshoots developed. Both French Canada under British rule and the independent United States of America were born of war, of victories and defeats. Some historians have argued that a developing patriotism – the sense of being British or French – was both the cause and the consequence of more than a century of wars between Britain and France. The two national identities were forged in opposition to one another (Colley, 1992). The encounter with the Americas, though, left both nations transformed. In one way, the more that European forces were sent to the Atlantic colonies the more it became clear that warfare on the two continents could be utterly different. Moreover, the scope of the Franco-British wars extended almost globally after 1700, and, indeed, the Duke of Newcastle in the late 1750s in the middle of the Seven Years' War argued that 'Ministers in this country where every part of the world affects us in some way or other, should consider the *whole Globe*'. This was following a comment directed against William Pitt (the Elder, secretary of state in charge of foreign affairs and military strategy) that he had concentrated on the needs of his own department – he 'looks too much to his own part of the world *only*'. But the different perspectives reflected a situating of competing demands from what were now increasingly global empires. In this diversity, both empires were forced to adapt to local conditions and forms of conflict. At home, ordinary people with their increasing literacy eagerly lapped up accounts of triumphs and defeats, as war could range from the Caribbean to the

Philippines, or from Canada to India (Watts, 2007: 2). Yet a common narrative was hard to achieve, particularly for the settler societies of the British North American colonies. Experiences and memories differed between the colonies and Britain, as each called the wars by different names. The designation developed in North America at the time, and followed by historians, became King William's War 1688–1697, Queen Anne's War, King George's War, the French and Indian War, while the British remember them by their original cause of conflict; the War of the Spanish Succession (Queen Anne's) 1702–1713, the War of Jenkins' Ear and the War of the Austrian Succession 1739–1748 (King George's), and the Seven Years' War 1754–1763 (the French and Indian War – which, for the Americans, lasted more than eight years). For many, the experience of war was a continual experience, and each generation had its own forms of participation, their own experiences of defeat and victory, and their own losses, both in terms of human life and economic devastation. That there were different memories and contrasting narratives of the wars as between the mother country and her colonies, at least on the British side, only became significant at the point of imperial breakdown in the American Revolution.

In retrospect it seems inevitable that the two empires would contest control of the territories from the Caribbean to the Arctic. Imperial envy and rivalry had shaped the formation of colonial ventures since the early part of the seventeenth century. The anti-Spanish faction in Jacobean politics in Britain naturally looked to colonial expansion as a means of curbing the power of Spain on the western side of the Atlantic. France, too, had seen its western venture as a means of establishing herself as a truly Atlantic power, perhaps in control of the north-west passage to China. Ambitions were greater than either country's capacity to deliver them: secure and growing settlements proved hard to establish and many colonies suffered from native hostility and economic vulnerability. Many endured a 'starving time', as Virginia did at the start, and slow growth. By 1650, though, the British and French had a firm toehold in North America and the Caribbean, and populations of most colonies were rising (Roper, 2009). Equally important, doubts about the expense and difficulties of colonisation had been replaced by enthusiastic big-power competition, uninhibited by any scepticism about the importance of colonies in the grander scheme of national power.

James Axtell, who calls the situation in North America between the early seventeenth century and the middle of the eighteenth a 'skewed triangle' of three cultures, French, British and Native American, summarises the structure of the conflict as follows:

> France and England glowered at each other across the narrow channel that kept them at arm's length. In the great arena of European power politics they were inveterate enemies, forever concocting alliances with competitors and launching military and economic adventures in hopes of gaining at least temporary advantage. When these behemoths tangled,

not only the European continent but half the world was their battleground. Many of their sharpest contests were joined in the wooded fastness of eastern North America, where the allegiance of strategically placed native groups was often a crucial ingredient of success as well as a principal prize. In America, the Indian allies of the two powers, like their counterparts in Europe, fought for their own interests, jumping from one side to the other, standing neutral, or occasionally daring to take on all comers in order to preserve their independence as long as possible. For the Indians the stakes were particularly high. English farmers and speculators coveted their land while French traders and military officers sought to reorient their material life and labor.

(Axtell, 1985: 4)

Some historians such as Grenier have claimed that the primary conflicts of this triangular warfare, in alliance with and against Native Americans, shaped colonial ideas of warfare in ways that European commanders could not comprehend: he calls this 'the first way of war' in America, an unlimited warfare directed at the removal or even extirpation of the enemy from threatening areas. This form of war was not easily understood by British commanders but became a natural response of settlers and natives to conditions on the porous frontiers of northern America (Grenier, 2005; Calloway, 1992). There was always a contradiction between settlers' genocidal tendencies and the need for peace: Daniel Boorstin characterises the British settlements as engaged in 'defensive war and naïve diplomacy', because they never formed significant alliances with native peoples from the outset and, moreover, found it difficult to defend their settlements successfully (Borstin, 1958: 345). The French embraced the form of native warfare first in their championing of the Huron against the Iroquois, and later in their use of native fighters against the British. By contrast, this type of total warfare initially had little place in the military visions of British officials sent out from England. Yet those who had suffered Indian raids in the seventeenth century, the white settlers, endorsed it, even if they were not particularly adept at it. There is a tendency to trace a tradition of heroic, armed self-defence among the British settlers in America, a precursor to their success in the War for Independence: 'in America war had become an institution for the citizenry as well as the warriors. The colonials were in the habit of defending themselves on neighbouring ground instead of employing professionals on a distant battlefield' (Boorstin, 1958: 351). The 'myth of preparedness', says Boorstin, of an armed citizenry always ready to fight in defence of their society, has entered American consciousness. Connected with the need for a volunteer militia, it has also entered the US Constitution as the second amendment. Yet historical evidence does not confirm the myth in any simple way. Though part-time soldiers, the white North Americans could be formidable fighters in both British and French colonies, but their civilian settlements were always vulnerable to attack. In the frontier areas, warfare was mostly unorthodox, and it was only in the Seven Years' War that European armies faced each other in their traditional manner on the battlefield on the Heights of Abraham at Quebec: elsewhere, ambush and raids on civilian settlements dominated. There were, therefore, contradictory cultures of war-making at work in North America and very contrasting ideas of the laws of war. Prisoners, paroles, and exchanges of captives were normal between white men, but no such rules applied to the Native Americans who were regarded as an example of de Vattel's *nation féroce* (or savage people) to whom such niceties could not be applied as they themselves did not observe them. Towards such people there were no laws of war, no legal limitations to the level of violence. By contrast, among the white adversaries all the formal rules of European warfare were observed in matters such as capitulation and parole, with rights of associated white civilians included in the surrender terms of the military personnel (see Document 4.1, the surrender terms of Port Royal, Nova Scotia, in 1710).

4.1 The Second Anglo-Dutch War (1665–1667)

There was conflict between the French and British from the 1660s onwards, beginning, ironically, as part of the second conflict between Britain and the Netherlands. At the outset Louis XIV declared war on Britain. While the British authorities for six months previously had been trying to mobilise against the Dutch, the news came in April 1666 of the French entry to the war (Marley, 2008: 250–251). The forces at the disposal of the British were largely buccaneers and settlers, and the former were remarkably reluctant to waste their time attacking the Dutch when there were lucrative targets still to be found among Spanish possessions. The British were nominally at peace with the Spanish, and it took months of negotiations with the buccaneers for the governors to mount any serious attacks on the Dutch. The war was a desultory to-and-fro affair in the Caribbean, with the British navy having some success after reinforcement from Britain. On land, British attempts to extend their share of St. Kitts to the French part of the island were disastrously unsuccessful and the French seized Antigua and Montserrat. In their attack on the latter, the French were counting on both superior numbers of troops, more than 1,000, many of them from professional regiments sent out from France, and the fickle loyalties of the Irish on the island. The French forced a surrender by the British governor after capturing many non-combatant civilians and families, and 2,000 Irish inhabitants agreed to swear loyalty to Louis XIV. Meanwhile, in Europe, peace negotiations were taking place, and the eventual peace agreement, the Treat of Breda of July 1667, established a pattern that would go on for another century. Possessions seized in the war were returned, so the British retrieved Antigua, Montserrat, and their half of St. Kitts. Fighting still went on, however, as the news took months to reach the West Indies fleet, and both French Cayenne and Dutch Surinam were severely damaged by British forces in the autumn.

Subsequent conflicts in the seventeenth century were largely the Franco-Spanish War (1673–1679) in which individual British buccaneers participated as French privateers, pursuing their traditional Spanish targets. In the eighteenth century the scale of warfare, particularly between navies, increased and the British came to rely less on the use of these irregular forces. In the seventeenth century the British Royal Navy suffered from the general weakness of naval facilities available in the Caribbean, and it was only in the 1740s that appropriate docks and places of repair were created for the navy, which thereby established a permanent presence in the West Indies (Ward, 2011). As the scope and intensity of fighting grew with each conflict, the wars on the western side of the Atlantic increasingly drew on military as well as naval resources from Europe. The British in particular seem to have been reluctant to send out large numbers of troops. In the second Anglo-Dutch war some troops were sent out from England, namely 800 to Barbados, accompanying William Willoughby in March 1667 (he was the younger brother of Francis, deceased, who he was in effect replacing) (Marley, 2008: 257). In the next decade the 'rebellion' of Nicholas Bacon provoked the London authorities to send 1,000 men of the 1st Foot Guards to Virginia in early 1677, though they arrived just after Bacon's Rebellion had ended with his death the previous October. The French Ministry of the Marine, by contrast, had its own corps of troops and deployed them in both Canada and the Caribbean. As we shall see, these were often supported by units of regular regiments sent out in each of the major conflicts with the British.

4.2 King William's War (1688–1697) or the Nine Years' War

The Glorious Revolution in 1688, in which William of Orange was invited to replace the Catholic James II, provoked war within Britain and Ireland, and between the Netherlands (and Britain) and France. Like the restoration of the monarchy in 1660, this political transformation required some astute and swift changes of loyalties among the leadership of the British colonies (Lovejoy, 1972; Stanwood, 2011). Events such as Leisler's Rebellion in New York anticipated the new Protestant regime of William III, against a rearguard defence by the governor of James's rule, but Leisler's *coup d'etat*, driven by anti-Catholic rhetoric, was ended with his execution (though he was granted a posthumous pardon). Protestant ideologies thereafter underpinned loyalties to Britain, in what has been called a 'protestant empire', in the colonies as strongly as in Britain itself (Pestana, 2009). Finding a way through these treacherous times in the mid-1680s to the Glorious Revolution often involved mutual accusations of treason, and divided loyalties remained for another half-century in Britain. The existence of rival claimants to the British throne produced unique consequences for the warfare of the 1690s, however, with the highly unusual feature of Jacobites (supporters of exiled

James II) acting as privateers against British shipping under licences issued by their rival monarch: according to the rules of war, these were treated as legitimate actors by both the British and, more importantly, the French (Le Pelley, 1944; Bromley, 1987: 139–166). When James died in 1701 there was no rival crowned 'king' of Britain to issue the privateer patents in France, even though Louis XIV acknowledged his son James (the 'Old Pretender') as the rightful monarch. Jacobites at sea could thereafter be denounced by the British as pirates, perhaps, in some cases, with good reason: certainly, some pirates adopted some of the images of Jacobite resistance to the German (Hanoverian) George I, perhaps as a means of showing defiance rather than as a reflection of devoted political opposition (Bialuschewski, 2011).

More seriously, the upheaval of 1688 and a convergence of conflicts in Europe produced a prolonged war, known variously as the War of the League of Augsburg, the War of the Grand Alliance, King William's War or, more accurately in terms of the grim experiences on both sides of the Atlantic, the Nine Years' War. As James Pritchard has emphasised (2002), this war involved many participants, including natives in the Americas as well as unprecedented numbers of European countries. The range of countries arraigned against the French in Europe was extraordinary, and in North America in particular the pattern of warfare of orthodox and unorthodox styles of fighting set a pattern that continued for another century. For some this war also marked the 'rise' of Russia and Great Britain, the former as a European, the latter as an increasingly global, power (Clark, 1970; Pritchard, 2002)

In the Americas, the North endured continual raiding across the frontiers from both sides, with the European powers making use of Indian allies, a pattern of deployment that continued to the American War for Independence. This resulted in many deaths in the attacked settlements. The British allied themselves with the Iroquois, but, because of their more numerous settlements, were in fact more vulnerable to raids, massacres, and the loss of captives. Redeeming captives therefore became part of the negotiations with the French as much as with Native American opponents (see Chapter 3). For example, in August 1689 the town of Lachine near Montreal was attacked by more than 1,000 Iroquois, allies of the British, who killed more than 20 residents and carried off a further 200. This proved an immediate setback for the French, as some of their allies promptly defected to the British. The result was a war of 'stinging raids' (Haffenden, 1970: 486). The following year, 200 French Canadians and Indians attacked Corlaer, now known as Schenectady, and killed 60 inhabitants, seizing 25 and leaving the rest. They retreated with 50 horses laden with booty. A counter-attack by pro-British Mohawks killed 18 of them during their retreat (Marley, 2008: 31, 315). This kind of raiding and killing produced many prisoners for both sides, largely in the hands of the native allies, which made their ransoming or exchange a process both more drawn out and more difficult. Not all attacks were carried out by Native Americans. The assault on the British

Newfoundland settlements by the French was led by the governor of the French part of the island in 1697. The campaign destroyed more than 30 fishing villages, killed 200 men, and captured a further 700 (Marley, 2008: 328).

In terms of orthodox military strategies in the North, the French under Count Frontenac, their ageing but effective commander, aimed to seize New York by land attack and deployed forces which, though they contained French officers, were largely made up of Native Americans. With their alliances of greater longstanding and more secure, the French adopted the raid with their native allies as their primary tactic. The Native Americans, 'masters of frontier warfare', could strike at settlements 'almost at will' (Starkey, 1998: 85). By contrast, through the combined use of naval and army resources in waterborn assaults, the British struck by sea and river at both Nova Scotia and Quebec. Both sides were ultimately unsuccessful, but the different modes of attack and defence set a pattern for subsequent wars.

In the West Indies the war of the islands was resumed. The British were again expelled from St. Kitts at the start of the war, when the French ordered all British inhabitants except the Irish Catholics evacuated to Nevis. A year later a large-scale campaign brought it back under British control. Elsewhere the British attacked both Guadaloupe and Martinique, while the French in 1694 attacked Jamaica, devastating some areas and leaving with shiploads of plunder. None of this was very decisive, though losses in ships and men, and to civilian communities, were substantial in some incidents. The French commanders sent out from France concentrated their forces in particular against the Spanish and their lucrative cargoes of gold and silver, leaving the fighting in the islands to local forces. This was despite the growing counter-attacks by the British and the Dutch. The French did manage to restore their finances by some seizures of Spanish treasure. With this kind of strategy in place, the established buccaneers of St. Domingue played a negligible part in the war. In fact, pirates in general stood aside from this official conflict (Pritchard, 2002).

From the far North to the Caribbean, King William's War 'did not prove very instructive for all parties involved. The British and the French learned that colonial warfare in America was both expensive and indecisive. Most of the gains the two nations had made against each other were eliminated' by the conditions of the peace (Kessel and Wooster, 2005: 181).

4.3 Queen Anne's War/the War of the Spanish Succession (1702–1713)

War was resumed soon after William III's death in 1702. Little had changed except that the Iroquois had signed a 'Grand Settlement' with the French in 1701 and therefore were of little help to the British in this war (Kessel and Wooster, 2005: 19).

James Moore, governor of South Carolina, in 1704 led a raid towards St. Augustine in Spanish-held Florida; 1,000 Creek allies and 50 South Carolinian volunteers attacked and sacked Apalachee villages. In one raid, 400 were killed. Moore returned with 1,000 captives who were sold into slavery. His assaults 'demonstrated the profitability of slave raids into Indian lands' (Kessel and Wooster, 2005: 218), although there had been a less effective raid at the start of the war in 1702 (p. 261). The Yamasee were also armed in support of the British. In the North, one of the worst incidents in the war, and the worst since King Philip's War in the 1670s, was the Deerfield (Massachusetts) raid in 1704: 48 people were killed and 112 captured by pro-French Indians. Not surprisingly, in 1708 Massachusetts petitioned Queen Anne in emotive terms, outlining their sufferings at the hands of Native American raiders; 'Bloody Villanies and Outrages' and 'divers barbarous Murders' had been inflicted on them by people assisted and protected by the French (see extract in Document 4.2). They were determined to show that they had participated fully in the war:

> We have been sharers in Common with other our fellow Subjects to a great Degree in Losses, both of men and Estate, at home and at Sea, both in the former and the present War, our Trade is greatly diminished, and we are very much Exhausted; our yearly Expence for our necessary defence, and to prevent the Incursions of the Enemy is vastly great.

They went on to argue that the best tactics would be imitation of those of their enemies: 'the most probable Method of doing Execution upon them and Reduceing them, is by men of their own Colour, way and manner of living'.

This kind of raiding, with killing and capturing of civilians, dominated the northern war, with a few exceptions of more orthodox moves, such as by the British against Port Royal in Nova Scotia and an equally unsuccessful Franco-Spanish expedition against Charleston, South Carolina. The French did seize St. John's in Newfoundland. In 1710 British troops finally captured Port Royal and, the next year, French Acadia, securing control of Nova Scotia. These gains were kept under the 1713 Treaty of Utrecht.

Accounts of the fighting were printed, as was noted in Chapter 3, where the captives among the Indians left strikingly explicit and very religious tracts. Unprinted sources can also reveal some of the problems of the British settlers pursuing an unorthodox foe, and of the military making war in the European way.

4.4 The War of Jenkins' Ear/War of the Austrian Succession (King George's War) (1739–1748)

There were two causes of what became a continuous war, in which the pace and scope of the fighting extended from the Americas to India. The assault on Captain Jenkins, whose severed ear, reported if not actually displayed to Parliament, caused the British government to declare war on the Spanish, seems disconnected to the problems of the Austrian succession, which provoked a general European mobilisation in 1742. Captain Robert Jenkins' problems with the Spanish coastguards off Cuba in 1731, when his ship, the Glasgow brig *Rebecca,* was intercepted and searched and he was assaulted, were, however, typical of the anti-smuggling measures taken by the Spanish authorities in the Americas. The British Parliament heard from Jenkins seven years later, and it authorised privateering against Spanish vessels by way of reprisal and as a means of persuading the Spanish to negotiate. When this failed, war was declared in 1739. The problems of succession to the Austrian throne (the question of a woman, Maria Theresa, occupying the throne) led to France and Prussia's opposition, and Britain, the Netherlands, and Saxony's support for her. In 1744 France therefore joined Spain in war against Britain.

The fighting, however, was on an unprecedented scale, eventually embracing the Caribbean and North America, Europe, and India (where it is known as the First Carnatic War, in which the dominance of the British on the east coast of India was exceeded by that of the French in the south). It was the first time that the fleets of Britain and France engaged on three continents. Things began in the Caribbean between the British and the Spanish. In November 1739 Admiral Vernon captured Porto Bello – 'the success was seen in Britain as the first of many to come, as Vernon, an able but impossibly quarrelsome commander, enjoyed extraordinary popularity' (Anderson, 2014: 18). But the three admirals, Ogle, Vernon, and Wentworth, could not work together, and attacks on Cartagena (Colombia, March-April 1741) and Santiago de Cuba in July-August 'were humiliating failures'. The Cartagena assault included 4,000 Virginians led by the lieutenant-governor of the colony, William Gooch (in office 1727–1749), and George Washington's half-brother Lawrence. This was the first time that North Americans had been recruited for Caribbean operations. Recruits were certainly needed as disease killed many of the British forces: almost three quarters of the 10,000 men sent out in October 1740 were not alive two years later, as prevalent diseases such as yellow fever took their toll. With the French also sending naval forces, there was by early 1741 'in the West Indies a concentration of the European naval power far greater than any ever seen before' (70 ships of the line between them, with more than 50 guns each) (Anderson, 2014: 19–20). After the disastrous efforts of 1740–1741, 'the West Indies saw relatively little large-scale fighting': one British minister commented in 1741 that 'now America must be fought for in Europe' (Anderson, 2014: 180). This was not quite true, as in 1744 the British successfully attacked and seized St. Martin's and the French made an effort by way of reprisal to take Anguilla in 1745; they were repulsed by local forces, with some loss of life.

In the southern colonies of British North America, Georgia's founder and first governor James Oglethorpe deployed the white and native forces of the newly established colony (the charter had only been granted in 1732) to probe the Spanish defences in Florida, making several attempts in 1739 and 1740 to capture strongpoints such as St. Augustine. Even with naval backing these efforts proved unsuccessful, as most Spanish outposts were too heavily fortified. In this sector, Native Americans fought on both sides, with the Yamassee attacking Georgia's settlements by way of reprisal, including Oglethorpe's own property. In 1742 the Spanish attempted a large-scale invasion of Georgia, producing a fierce response from forces under Oglethorpe's command which required substantial reinforcement, and they were eventually repulsed. In defence as in attack, Oglethorpe relied on naval supplies and transport, a strategy that was mirrored by his Spanish opponents. This conflict set a pattern for the following 40 years in terms of British ambitions to take control of Florida and expel or restrict the Spanish forces that were seen as a threat to the southern colonies (Marley, 2008: 395ff). In the Caribbean the presence of more French reinforcements, particularly naval vessels including ships of the line, led to some initial clashes before the French had officially entered the war. In the North, fighting between British and French forces began in 1744. The French persuaded the Micmac Indians to declare war on the English and attack them in their base in Annapolis Royal, Nova Scotia. The Massachusetts governor, William Shirley, declared war on them and began to plan a strike-back. The successful New England attack on Louisbourg in 1745 was led by Shirley and his commander of the militia, William Pepperell, and involved more than 2,000 colonial troops. The surrender was a major reverse for the French and was received as a great shock in France: Louisbourg was regarded as their strongest outpost on the east coast. The success was widely praised in England and Pepperell was knighted. The return of the fortress to France under the Peace of Aix-La-Chapelle in 1748 was criticised in England by the newspapers and the political opposition in Parliament (Anderson, 2014: 182–183). Fighting continued along the northern frontier, with the French making a major effort in 1746 to retake Nova Scotia and liberate the French settlers there, the Acadians, but failed to bring the forces together: ships were scattered and disease undermined the strength of the troops (Marley, 2008: 406–407). Towards the end of the war, Charles Knowles, risen from captain to admiral, achieved a major defeat in 1748 of a Spanish warfleet off Havana. He was unable to follow this up, as peace agreements had been signed with Spain. The Treaty of Aix-la-Chapelle followed soon after.

4.5 The Seven Years' War/French and Indian War (1754–1763)

Axtell (1985) makes the point that the eventual success of the British in the Seven Years'/French and Indian War was by no means inevitable. In the previous 100 years they had frequently been outmanoeuvred and confounded by French successes in previous wars, and the French exploration of the back country from Canada to Louisiana gave them a greater strategic sense of the North American context. Conflicts along the frontier began in the early 1750s and significant French successes had been achieved before war was officially declared. In 1753 a young George Washington was ordered by Lieutenant-Governor Dinwiddie of Virginia to go to the back country of Pennsylvania and demand that the French remove a fort (Fort Le Boeuf). They refused, so the British attempted to construct one of their own. But the place was seized by the French, fortified, and renamed Fort Duquesne. The next year Washington re-entered the territory to build a fort near Duquesne, Fort Necessity. After advancing towards Duquesne he achieved an initial successful ambush of a small French force. As large French forces gathered in retaliation, Washington fell back to a poor position at Fort Necessity, which he had not had time to strengthen. With about 400 men he should have been able to put up a strong defence, but the French were almost twice as numerous, the weather was atrociously wet – which dampened the gunpowder – and, after almost a day's fighting, Washington was forced to surrender. The condition of surrender, signed on 3 July 1754, allowed him and his men to retreat but undertake not to build another fort in that area. Aged 22, and a colonel, Washington had suffered his most humiliating defeat, followed the following year by the slaughter of General Braddock's professional forces, where Washington acquitted himself bravely in covering the retreat of the survivors.

By contrast, the by-now almost traditional New England assault on Nova Scotia in 1755 was a great success, with the French forced to abandon two forts, including Fort Beauséjour, and concede the Bay of Fundy to the British. For the local French settlers, the Acadians, this proved disastrous, as the British lieutenant-governor of Nova Scotia, Charles Lawrence, drove them into exile and, with the help of many New England ships, transported thousands of them – at least 7,000 – to the other colonies. He did not have official endorsement of this policy, and, indeed, seems not to have consulted any of his superiors in London. The pretence was that they had refused to take the oath of loyalty (as specified in the 1710 articles of surrender, see Document 4.1, and subsequent treaties), but this had not been seen as a problem before. The Acadians were consequently scattered as far south as South Carolina and, because Virginia's governor refused to accept his allocation, some shiploads were even sent to England. The Acadians' arrival was unannounced in some places, Virginia among them, and colonial governors were uncertain what to do: South Carolina tried to distribute them between the parishes of the colony. At the end of the war the Acadians who had arrived in England, concentrated in Bristol and Southampton, were sent to France, which they did not much like since there was no land for them to settle on (at one point some families were relocated to a Breton island, Belle Île-en-Mer, in 1765). Many managed to return to Canada, and others were returned to the Americas. It is from this population, eventually reassembled in Louisiana after enduring many sufferings, that the term 'cajun' derives, applied to the French-speaking people there and their culture as a distorted pronunciation of 'Acadian'.

> By the close of the campaign, the combination of deportations and flight had effectively depopulated Acadian Nova Scotia. The entire scheme, so chillingly reminiscent of modern 'ethnic cleansing' operations, was executed with a coldness and calculation, and indeed an efficiency, rarely seen in other wartime operations.
>
> (Anderson, 2000: 114)

It was the largest forced removal of a civilian population undertaken by the British since Oliver Cromwell's brutal displacement of Catholics in Ireland in the 1650s (Plank, 2001; Morgan and Rushton, 2013: 127–152; Hodson, 2012).

On land, to the west, military efforts by the British proved no more successful than before, with General Edward Braddock's army pressing into French territory in July 1755 and stumbling into ambush and defeat near the Monongahela river, on his way to attack Fort Duquesne. Though the conventional volley tactics of the British redcoats drove the Canadians (white troops) into retreat, the Native Americans on the French side destroyed the British force. Of perhaps no more than 1,300 men, more than 900 became casualties, with 63 of Braddock's 86 officers reported killed or wounded. He was badly wounded and died on the retreat from the battlefield. George Washington had volunteered to serve with Braddock and managed to escape injury: he organised the final retreat. More than a year later, in 1756, the British government finally declared war against the French, who had seized a British base at Minorca: the fighting in North America had not been sufficient for London to be provoked into open warfare. Even with reinforcements and a more coherent sense of purpose, though, the British did not fare well against the new French commander, the Marquis de Montcalm. At Fort William Henry in August 1757 Colonel George Monro's 2,500 men were besieged and forced to surrender. As they marched through the countryside they were attacked by Montcalm's Indian allies and up to 500 were captured, though Montcalm managed to ensure the release of them over subsequent weeks by paying his allies for their freedom. Once again the war of the border outposts was going the French commander's way. The natives, though, had caught smallpox from their prisoners and suffered serious losses. These early battles showed the contrast in strengths between the two sides: while the British dominated on water, the French and, more importantly, their native allies, were supreme on land in the forests of the north and west.

The appointment of William Pitt as secretary of state produced a decisive change in British policy and in relationships with the colonial societies in the Americas. Money was the key: he was willing to fund his European allies' armies in the war against France on the continent and, moreover, to underwrite the colonial authorities' war efforts aimed at an invasion of French Canada. Above all he treated the colonies more as allies than subordinates and made sure that colonial officers held the same status as those in the British army sent out to America. The Americans, with a growing sense of difference from (and resentment of) the British officers, were reassured. Visible signs of Pitt's commitment took the form of many thousands of troops sent to North America for the campaigns in 1758 to take the major French forts, Louisbourg, Ticonderoga (Fort Carillion), and Fort Duquesne. With those in British hands, the way to invading Canada would be open. New commanders came with the troops, and the tide was turned in 1758. In June and July the British forces attacked under James Wolfe and Lord Amherst, laying siege to Louisbourg and forcing a French surrender. They thus gained control of the mouth of the St. Lawrence river, and the waterway to Quebec from the east. Then Fort Carillion (Ticonderoga) was attacked, in the hope of opening up a way to Canada from the south, but Montcalm had time to reinforce his defences and the Anglo-American army was repulsed with severe losses. There was more success at Fort Duquesne, promptly renamed Fort Pitt, now Pittsburgh, five years after Washington had stumbled (Marley, 2008: 423–424). The final step in Pitt's plan was achieved a year later when Fort Carillion fell to Lord Amherst with negligible casualties. At this point, it seemed, a proper assault on French forces in Canada could begin.

So began the year of miracles – an *annus mirabilis* – on all fronts, from Canada to India. In the Caribbean in January 1759 British forces captured French Guadaloupe after massive naval bombardment and some spirited infantry attacks (Marley, 2008: 426). The most significant naval defeat for the French was the destruction in November 1759 of a large proportion of their fleet in Quiberon Bay (off Brittany, north-west France), which in effect led to their abandonment of the seas to the British, who were from then onwards unchallenged. This meant that reinforcing their armies in India and North America became almost impossible. By then the British victory at Quebec in June had been reported, and the situation of French forces in North America was becoming desperate. The British had advanced up the St. Lawrence river, and in this move 'the navy was essential and a partner in the military success' that followed: 'the assault on Canada proceeded entirely on water: up the St Lawrence River and also upon the rivers and lakes of northern New York' (Baugh, 2011: 8, 11). The tactics adopted by Wolfe in the face of a well-defended Quebec city were at first unsuccessful, but his landing of more than 4,500 men upriver, and getting them on to the Heights of Abraham, became part of his legend. The subsequent battle, with Montcalm emerging from the defences unaware of how many enemy troops faced him, was in many ways an orthodox European conflict, as lines of infantry exchanged volleys from muskets. The British had eluded the rifles of the Canadian militia men and native troops by simply lying down in the grass. Their sudden rise to fire on the advancing French infantry proved decisive. Both commanders died of their wounds, and the death of Wolfe was immortalised by American painter

Benjamin West, working in London. In this painting West invented the modern hero portrait, almost by accident. Though the French returned to besiege the British forces in Quebec the next year, the arrival of Royal Navy ships with reinforcements led them to retreat to Montreal. In further fighting, more of French Canada was brought under British control and by September 1760, when Montreal was surrendered to Jeffery Amherst's army, French Canada passed to complete control by the British.

The conflict was not entirely over at that point, as, with old scores to settle, the British launched in 1762 the campaign to regain control of Newfoundland. Against some 600 French troops on the island, Lord Amherst eventually mustered 1,200 New York troops, landing and forcing a surrender. By that time the French expeditionary force had seized or destroyed more than 400 fishing vessels. In the same year, Grenada and St. Vincent in the Caribbean were occupied by the British. In the latter there was a large population of free '**Black Caribs**' who the British came to suspect remained loyal to the French (see Chapter 5 under 'Maroons' for the subsequent conflicts). They also gained Tobago and Dominica, all of which they retain after the 1763 Treaty of Paris; the Spanish gained Louisiana, a serious reverse for more than 70 years of French development there.

Summing up the Seven Years'/French and Indian War, Anderson remarks:

> Warfare on the fantastic geographical scale of the Seven Years' War in America had been conceivable because Parliament was willing to grant the sums necessary to fund far-flung campaigns; because the British people were able to shoulder the taxes required by a war vaster than any their nation had ever fought; because the colonists cooperated in the imperial enterprise with an enthusiasm and a vigour unprecedented in their history.
>
> (Anderson, 2000: 412)

Though the British government was in debt and short of money (and raising money through taxation to pay off the debt was the crux of the post-war dispute with the American colonies), the French government was in far worse condition and was in effect close to bankruptcy. The ability to finance global war marked the distinctive character of British politics and institutions compared with the French. In one crucial respect – the ability to tax, borrow, and spend – the British state was supreme (Eloranta and Land, 2011). In the phrase of Daniel Baugh, the Seven Years' War was the greatest 'great-power contest' in history so far, and the French lost the fight in both America and India. Though they had kept a toehold in the Caribbean islands, the French had lost their North American and Indian empires (Baugh, 2011). When a French army next landed in North America it was to achieve the secure independence of the United States.

The American Revolution (see Chapter 5) was in some ways a conflict by proxy, with the French supplying weapons and supplies to the American patriots and the British using all means at their disposal to prevent this. There were two crucial naval engagements, and a French army took full part in the siege of Yorktown in 1781, which forced British commander Lord Cornwallis to surrender. The first clash between the British and French navies of any significance was in the summer of 1781 off the **Chesapeake**. The Royal Navy fleet, based in New York, fought an indecisive engagement with the French fleet under de Grasse and returned with its damaged ships to effect repairs. This left the French a clear opportunity, for the first time, to disembark substantial land forces to assist George Washington in his move against Cornwallis, who had landed in southern Virginia. Bottled up at Yorktown, under artillery fire and infantry assault, Cornwallis was forced to surrender. This did not end the war. De Grasse redirected his fleet to the Caribbean, hoping to break the British stranglehold on the region which they had preserved – along with its valuable sugar plantations – throughout the failures in the American Revolution. Admiral George Rodney, who had spent most of 1781 trashing the Dutch colony of St. Eustatius, confronted him off Jamaica and achieved a remarkable victory at the Battle of the Saintes in 1782. This was partly because technical innovation had been forced on the British authorities. The Royal Navy, in desperation at the poor state of their ships when the war began, had resorted to copper-bottoming them as a means of preventing further decay and fouling, and almost by accident had enabled their ships to be more manoeuvrable. This proved decisive in Rodney's victory. The American war ended with the British giving up the 13 colonies and acknowledging the independence of the United States, but their valuable slave colonies in the West Indies, and the Anglo-French territory of Canada, remained safely in their hands.

There were less than 10 years of peace. The French Revolution, and particularly the execution of the French royal family in 1793, led to the declaration of war by Britain. Moreover, the slave revolt in Haiti, mingled with the threat of a general revolution, gave the fighting in the Caribbean during the 1790s a particular resonance. The British feared contagion by the revolutionary fervour spread by the French, and mistrusted all populations in their Caribbean colonies who could not be totally subordinated. They intervened by sending an army into Haiti, with disastrous results, and turned on a number of minorities, such as the **maroons** of Jamaica and the 'Black Caribs' of St. Vincent. A revolt by slaves and free people threatened British control of Grenada, to which the British responded with traditional prosecutions for rebellion and treason (see Chapter 5). Fighting began in 1794 with the British seizing Martinique, St. Lucia, and Guadaloupe, and, though the French retook the last, British forces continued to expand their activities and took Trinidad from the Spanish, thereby establishing a foothold in South America for the first time. As in earlier conflicts, the Royal Navy provided the British with the key form of security as well as the vital means of attack. The French navy in Europe was blockaded in port for long periods, in Brest and Toulon, and this remained a core British strategy until the decisive victory over the combined fleets of France and Spain at Trafalgar in 1805 gave Britain control of the seas. In the meantime, as the United States came to more open trade arrangements with Britain, there was a great danger of war between France and the USA. Over two years, 1798 to 1800, there were a few naval engagements in the Caribbean and some seizures of French traders by American privateers, but negotiations led to the end of what has been described as a 'quasi-war'.

By 1800 the French were still active in Haiti, and held on to islands such as Guadaloupe, but conflicts with the British were largely a minor sideshow to the large-scale warfare in Europe that characterised the Napoleonic era until 1815. The British kept – and even extended – their Caribbean holdings and maintained Canada's borders against the USA. The profitable sugar plantations were preserved as an integral part of Britain's imperial wealth, even as the movements critical of both the slave trade and slavery itself grew at home. Both powers had to reflect on failures; the French in the Seven Years' War and the British in the American Revolution. Though the British kept many of their colonies, Brendan Simms' summary of the period – 'three victories and a defeat' – neatly defines their eventual failure to manage their own colonies and in fighting against people very much like themselves (Simms, 2007).

5 Resistance, rebellions, and revolutions

5.1 Resistance
5.2 Runaways: servants and slaves 'stealing themselves'
5.3 Rebellions
5.4 Slave conspiracies, real or imagined?
5.5 White rebellions/rebellious whites
5.6 Revolutions

The title of this chapter requires some discussion, as the differences between these categories may seem either too obvious or too arbitrary to be useful. The debate nevertheless goes to the heart of the problem of how to interpret the nature of popular opposition to the unjust and oppressive social relations created in the early modern colonies of the British and French empires. The three terms may be usefully applied to different situations; to distinguish the numbers involved, the level of threat to the established social systems, and whether those opposing the status quo had in mind a complete restructuring of society. One difficulty for historians is that a word like 'rebellion' may have been used casually by those in control at the time to characterise everything from personal protests to incidents of collective rioting and large-scale violence, whether aimed at political change or reclamation of conquered territory. Moreover, the level of rhetoric is at times extreme, as it serves the purpose of those favouring brutal reprisals to exaggerate the level of threat. The same might be said of the word 'conspiracy', whose use in a given situation may reflect the level of fear pervading the ruling authorities rather than the actual organisation of those opposing them. Paranoia may be a feature of all controllers of unequal societies – the fear of conspiracy between, for example, black slaves and poor whites. The result is that historical documents often throw around words such as 'rebellion' or 'revolution' in casual ways that can be deceptive. For historians, though, it might be a valid approach to distinguish:

- Resistance – refusal to conform or obey: this could be collective, but is most likely to be small-scale and personal

- Rebellion – a threat to the established order, attack on the ruling class or controlling authorities of an unequal society
- Revolution – following much the same violent process as a rebellion, but with an alternative social or political order in mind to be created at the end of the process

These distinctions are probably over-neat, because one may turn into another and all may occur simultaneously. Perhaps all revolutions begin with one person refusing an order, resisting arrest, or fighting back, but revolutions in the end depend on creating an organisation and undertaking deliberate, sustained conflict rather than random individual acts. Certainly there is some evidence that North American slave revolts often began with a spontaneous, almost accidental, act – of arson or theft – which turned into more seriously organised opposition. Above all, full-blown revolutions, in contrast with mere rebellions, depend on a plan to replace current social or political structures, and this was always the crucial weakness of many insurgencies in colonial societies.

5.1 Resistance

The colonial structures set up by Europeans in the colonies were deeply unequal and exploitative, and inevitably generated resistance and conflict at both personal and collective levels. The native defence of land and rights was just one aspect, providing a permanent external threat for settlers and colonial authorities. Internally, servants, slaves, small landowners, women, and the young asserted themselves against social forces of exclusion and exploitation. This does not mean that these actions should all be seen as part of a common struggle or that they should be perceived as a collective movement, though clearly some actions took the form of common revolt. Asserting their own identity and wishes against the controlling forces alone constituted a challenge, and could be subjected to suppression. For servants and slaves, maintaining memories and traditions from their country of origin, whether it was Catholic Irish servants or African slaves, was a means of asserting their cultural identities against a society that denigrated or feared them. If African slaves buried one of their own with rites and symbols derived from African religious customs, then they were in effect defying their reduction to mere chattels. When servants and slaves ran away they challenged both their subordinate status and the working of the economic system that relied on it. Everywhere in the Anglophone Atlantic, vocal women were in court because their words had assaulted others in the community and their insults provoked legal responses from their victims or from the alarmed authorities. Patriarchy had its limits, communities were finding. Whether there were similar limits to other systems of inequality is a key question for this chapter.

These individual actions constituted one common form of resistance to oppressive structures, in a social world where individualism was in some ways – economic, political, and cultural – becoming widespread (Wahrman, 2004). At the same time, early modern societies depended on economic exploitation for their success in developing both increasingly prosperous and productive European economies and also their colonial offshoots. Under these conditions, subduing the largely young workforce and suppressing their resistance was vital. This contradiction is also reflected in the unequal representation of women or African slaves in print before 1800, and the absence of consistent independent expressions by natives in the European empires. These groups, particularly slaves and natives, are in effect *silenced*, what Edwin Ardener called 'muted', by powerful forces, and in print and other written records are often more reported about, rather publicly, than reporting their experiences in their own words (Ardener, 1968). The historian therefore has to read sources with a view to detecting the 'hidden' transcripts or meanings, as Scott (1990) has suggested. In societies where every move may be observed, there may be subcultures of meaning created which the controllers may not understand; what Scott calls 'the often fugitive political conduct of subordinate groups' – 'the powerless are often obliged to adopt a strategic pose in the presence of the powerful' and we risk underestimating the extent of their resistance (Scott, 1990: xii). Behind the surface of an ordered society, in other words, there lie disorder, conflict, and potential violence.

5.2 Runaways: servants and slaves 'stealing themselves'

Everywhere in the British colonies, but particularly in North America, white servants ran from their service. It is striking that we know little about any parallel actions in French colonies, partly because servants, *les engagés*, were far fewer in number and there were fewer safe places to run to; though, in the South, New Orleans may have been an exception. Since one of our main sources of information is newspaper advertisements, our information is largely about British servants as the French colonies did not publish newspapers in such numbers as their Anglophone counterparts. Many descriptions of personal dress styles and ways of self-presentation derive from these newspaper advertisements for runaway servants and slaves. As has been noted earlier, the presence of many English-language newspapers, at least one per colony in British North America (often more in major centres such as New York and Philadelphia), allowed far more individual detail to emerge in print. In these brief but often striking descriptions the usually silent subordinated classes are shown very graphically in words if not pictures. Not surprisingly these adverts have attracted a great deal of attention from historians looking for new sources away from plantation and legal records (Waldstreicher, 1999; Prude, 1991; Smith and Wojtowicz, 1989; Morgan and Rushton, 2004) (See Document 5.1).

Servants and slaves often emerge as individuals in these newspapers. As Waldstreicher comments, 'recent work reveals a mid-Atlantic situation in which slaves' individual acts of running away proved to be profoundly destabilising, even comparable over the long term to the slave rebellions and other collective acts of resistance in the South and the Caribbean. Such seemingly individualistic acts, in turn, reshaped black life in the North and put enormous pressure on the slave system elsewhere'. More importantly, he notes that runaway advertisements were, in effect, 'the first slave narratives – the first published stories about slaves and their seizure of freedom . . .' (Waldstreicher, 1999: 245, 247). As Smith and Waldstreicher have discovered, there is a concentration of runaways in the mid-Atlantic colonies of Maryland, Virginia, and Pennsylvania, and the mixture of people and styles reflects a growing culture of 'disguise and self-transformation' which they adopted as they tried to survive unnoticed within the more cosmopolitan settings of towns such as Philadelphia and New York. Some British servants showed their political leanings in their appearances, as for example:

> John Jones, bricklayer and plasterer, aged 28 who ran away wearing English shoes and large brass buckles, on which is "May Trade revive, Wilkes and Liberty Number 45".
> (*Maryland Gazette*, 27 March 1766 and 20 September 1770)

Whether Jones belonged to the larger world of radical politics in London is unknown, but he wore his politics on his feet as a supporter of the government critic John Wilkes.

The way these men and women combined was also a matter of concern, particularly when white and black worked together. For many servants an experienced slave or someone who had spent more time in the colony could act as a companion and a guide to escape routes (see Document 5.1). Moreover, *how* they looked – or if they looked up at all – was also taken as an indication of their rebellious spirit. To have a 'down' or 'hanging' look was in some ways to be seen as the ideal, but to have an 'impudent look', meeting and perhaps challenging the master's eye, was an indication of a recalcitrant spirit. In less dramatic, but interesting, ways these adverts also show how styles of dress reflected a desire to maintain some kind of individuality, even if clothes were the uniform dull kind that employers bought for their subordinates. With both servants and slaves, White has indicated, descriptions of dress suggest that people were striving for something different from the mass: at least in the South, slaves were involved in making decisions about their appearance, suggesting they were choosing the clothes themselves (White, 2011). Another aspect that masters noted was accent and dialect – Irish, Scottish, northern English, or country-born (i.e., American), along with the source of their clothes, from Europe or America. Newly arrived servants still possessed their original clothes and perhaps a wig provided by the ships' captains on landing (Morgan and Rushton, 2004;

Waldstreicher, 1999: 259). Disguise was also important: some servants particularly were described as able to 'pass' as a free person, or with a particular skill. Few were quite so inventive as the convict women who passed as a man – and a doctor – or a fugitive princess handing out official jobs to the grateful colonials. Morgan and Rushton (2011) stress the way that women in particular could exploit opportunities for deception. Waldstreicher (199: 261–262) notes the continued skill of slaves up to emancipation in 'passing' for something they chose to be rather than just accepting the labels forced on them. Paradoxically we know about their personal appearance because they were so closely watched – as Scott suggests, 'the dialectic of disguise and surveillance that pervades relations between the weak and the strong will help us, I think, to understand the cultural patterns of domination and subordination' (Scott, 1990: 4).

For slaves who did not own their own bodies, dressing distinctively and showing their individuality were almost revolutionary personal actions. Yet the circulation of newspapers, and the repetition of runaway advertisements in so many of them, meant that a society highly tuned to policing illicit mobility could be very successful in tracking down and recapturing runaways. This is partly because of the paradoxical process of individual expression through dress, meaning that not all slaves or servants looked the same despite the uniformity of clothing issued to them by their masters. As Sophie White emphasises:

> Clothing is never simply the blandly functional or frivolously fashionable covering of the body. Rather, the act of dressing—of clothing, undressing, re-clothing—itself served another purpose, that of creating, affirming, and upholding identity on a daily basis . . . Those transplanted to the colonies and those born there had a stake in demonstrating that their seasoning and acclimatization to the new environment could be temporary and reversible.
>
> (White, 2013: 499)

This was true of both slaves and servants: maintaining or recreating some aspects of their original cultures were a means of defiance. These patterns run counter to DuPlessis' (2016) assumption that slaves were largely catered for, provided with standard uniforms in all but name, rather than making their own consumer decisions: minute differences which they could create in their appearances established a sense of individual identity for many people, and these small 'markers', chosen by their wearers, gave the masters and advertisers the means of identification. Times of dressing up also allowed some room for free expression. Formal community occasions often open up opportunities for subversion within the traditional ritual – exploiting the moment, so to speak, and turning it to other critical and oppositional ends, such as White noted in New Orleans' **Mardi Gras** celebrations. Such periods of defiance and challenge rarely have long-term effects, and only in exceptional circumstances provide a chance of changing social relations and systems permanently. White's study of the Mardi Gras, and the clash over appearances of slaves and the free, suggests uneasy relationships between the way people were *supposed* to dress and behave and the way they actually did present themselves when they could.

The most fortunate aspect of runaway servants' experiences in British North America was that there were several places to run *to*: Philadelphia, New York, and other port cities offered work on ships and, perhaps, a way home for the few. More importantly, there were also opportunities for work. Despite the widespread advertising of Maryland and Virginia runaways in the Pennsylvania newspapers, there was little systematic tracing and retrieving of them. Unlike slaves, their mobility was often a welfare problem in the cities they ran to, but this was not viewed as a challenge to the society as a whole.

5.3 Rebellions

Paranoia and suspicion pervaded all slave societies, or those where hostile natives came too close for comfort. Fear of Indian attack from nearby, supposedly 'safe', Indians was pervasive in both British and French colonies. Close proximity did not necessarily breed trust and peace. If the British in New England learned to hate natives in the terrible fighting and losses of King Philip's War of 1675–1676, then the French also learned some hard lessons, first in Canada and then in the South. Such raids were followed by reprisals, as shown in Chapter 4. The question raised above about the exact difference between resistance and rebellion is relevant here: natives did not acknowledge the authority of white colonialism and were always reasserting claims, often guaranteed by a recently broken treaty, to their land and rights. It tended to be white settlers who broke such agreements and natives who resorted to force to restore them. For that reason, 'resistance' and 'rebellion', as conceived here, are essentially forces *internal* to the societies set up by white settlers: collective resistance to that settlement falls into the category of fighting back against the warfare of conquest and invasion.

More reminiscent of rebellion were the consequences of running away. Wherever there were slaves there were repeated attempts not just at running away but to establish places of safety, in effect spaces of freedom. This has become known as *marronage*. **Maroons** – derived from the Spanish *cimarrón* for wild or untamed animal – were encountered by Francis Drake during his attack on Panama and gave him help. From then to the end of slavery, both maroons and their territories were a challenge to the control of slave societies over their subordinate races. Running away and creating spaces of freedom, nearly all defensible spaces, seem to indicate a force that could have undermined slavery as a system. Unlike servants, therefore, slaves in many colonies, notably in the Caribbean, had to create their own places of safety – there were no destinations to run to that could offer freedom (the nineteenth-century 'underground railroad' to the northern states of the US and thence to Canada had no eighteenth-century precursor). The opportunities depended partly on geography: even islands as small as St. Lucia offered an almost impenetrable interior. In Jamaica far more space was available, and runaway slaves were able to form whole communities and maroon 'towns' were established, to become the focus of colonial assault. These zones of freedom potentially threatened the existence of slavery if runaways were guaranteed freedom there. Certainly, some of the authorities, inspired by slaveowners, thought so from time to time, and there were military assaults against these territories and their populations. For long periods, however, some maroon communities coexisted amicably with slave societies, as long as they did not invite runaways but, on the contrary, promised to return them. What began in resistance in places such as Jamaica, for example, ended in peaceful coexistence.

Peace by treaty was not, however, the first intention of the British authorities in Jamaica. The maroons were alleged by planters to be dangerous predators, and the first military efforts against them were aimed at conquest and extermination of their independent zones. The Jamaica maroons were highly organised in several 'towns' and, remarkably, were ably led by three people, one of them a woman, 'Nanny', who has become an iconic figure in Jamaican history. The fighting in the 1730s was far from being the first conflict on the island, as Patterson (1970) suggests: there had been a long history of flight and resistance, internal rebellion, and the formation of safe refuges against white control since the British seized control in 1655. The slave society subsequently created was distinctively different from that previously developed on Barbados: there were few white smallholders, and the overwhelming pattern of landholding was in large estates controlled by a few families. As a result, white people made up only about 10% of the population and white control had to rely on military forces from outside rather than any local militia available for mobilisation in an emergency. The African slaves were also distinctive, for in the early eighteenth century, at least, a large proportion came from a single area – modern-day Ghana and, to a lesser extent, Dahomey. The 'Coromantee', or Akan-speaking peoples, therefore formed a large group – and it was as a Coromantee that the female leader 'Nanny' identified herself, along with the religious or magical practices that gave her much of her reputation among the Africans. In the late seventeenth century there were repeated revolts by slaves, many from this background, and attempts to pursue them into the more remote areas were unsuccessful. By the end of the century the escapees had set up 'a cluster of villages in the more remote areas of the eastern hinterlands'. By the 1720s two distinct bands of 'rebels' had taken territories for themselves – one, the Leeward band, in the centre of the island, and another, the Windward, in the Blue Mountains to the north-east. It was the conflict between the latter and the penetration of white estates into their territory – which incidentally impeded communication between the two bands – that provoked the violent conflict of the 1730s (Patterson, 1970: 299–301; Kopytoff, 1978: 288–290).

Though there had been intermittent conflict since 1731, the key period of fighting was 1735–1736 in what has come to be called the First Maroon War. Initially the British were optimistic that there could be a quick victory: in the northern papers, it was confidently reported, 1,700 soldiers had taken 'Nanny Town', the 'chief settlement' of the rebellious negroes, at the end of 1734 and were 'now in pursuit of those Notorious Black Rebels' (*Boston Gazette*, 24 February 1735). Things proved more difficult, however, and more troops were needed over the next year. The two main leaders, Cudjo (or Cudjoe) of the Leeward maroons and Cuffee of the Windwards, proved adept commanders. The latter was notoriously disciplinarian, ruling a group of about 300 fighters with some brutality. Cudjo, too, kept control over his subordinates and was reported to have opposed the casual killing of whites in their raids on plantations (Kopytoff, 1978: 295). Nanny – an *obeah*-woman, or healer-sorcerer – was killed in 1733 by a slave who was generously rewarded by the grateful white authorities (Patterson, 1970: 302). There were other leaders who were in charge of smaller settlements (often named after them), and the impression is that the white forces were invading a society of well-organised peasant farmers.

In the end the numbers of British troops told, and there were decisive moves in 1735 and 1736 that nearly destroyed the maroon territories. Early in 1735, the press recorded, 500–600 of the 'rebellious negroes' had been 'destroyed', and 'two of the greatest negro towns taken'. The remainder were surrounded by 1,600 men who were hoping to destroy them (*Boston Gazette*, 24 February 1735, dateline 7 January). This was over-optimistic, but the strategy of attacking the towns proved initially successful: even in the mountains the British managed to sack them and drive their inhabitants into the countryside where, it was said, they were liable to starve. The *New England Weekly Journal* (21 April 1735, dateline 10 April) reported that 'we hear from Jamaica, that the Rebel Slaves are all driven from their Towns in the Mountains, way to Leeward, and we hope will soon be reduced, many of them coming in half-starved'. By the middle of 1735, therefore, the British were hopeful of further success, but the maroons reorganised around other settlements and, despite the periods of relatively peaceful activity, remained a menacing force. By 1738 the white planters had concluded that the only solution was to come to terms with the maroons and, in 1739, treaties were signed with both maroon groups. The agreement guaranteed the independence and security of the maroon territories on condition that runaway slaves were not given safe refuge but, on the contrary, were returned to their plantations. Whether they realised it or not, this signalled an inevitable process of decline for the maroon societies, as, with a severe gender imbalance among the slave population which was overwhelmingly male and no means to replenish the supply of men through runaways, the population among the maroons fell over subsequent decades. Nevertheless, the maroons, who regarded these treaties as sacred, were astonishingly successful. They had fought the British almost to a standstill and forced a white ruling class to accept – in writing – a black society as their neighbours. This was unique in the British colonies.

Maroons turned up in small islands such as Barbados and in the mainland colonies. Other groups under this heading were a mixture of natives and slaves – the British on St. Vincent (after they had taken over the island in 1763) were keen to distinguish 'real' **Caribs**, the 'yellow Caribs', from the **'Black Caribs'** who they regarded as slave runaways. The eastern part of the island was still dominated by these groups, beyond British control, and provided an intermittent affront to British ambitions for complete control of the island. In the 1790s, in the revolutionary panic following the Haiti rising, both the Jamaica maroons, in the Second Maroon War, and the St. Vincent Black Caribs suffered a final attack and deportation from their homelands (see below).

5.4 Slave conspiracies, real or imagined?

Outright rebellions which threatened the systems of exploitation were few but were taken seriously by colonial authorities, who suppressed them with great savagery. In the seventeenth century, at least until the last quarter, one of the greatest fears among the British Caribbean governors and plantation owners was a combined revolt of Irish and African, as Beckles (1990) has documented. Wherever whites and blacks were in alliance, the authorities were always alarmed – and determined to respond with severity. From the middle of the 1730s for almost ten years there were reports of slave revolts and rebellions in many British colonies. Jamaica, South Carolina, Antigua, and New York were involved in panics concerning slave insurgencies. Most of these were short-run, but the First Maroon War in Jamaica, as discussed earlier, was a full-blown military affair which ended in a formal treaty between the parties. In the minds of the many readers of local newspapers, which by the 1730s were being published in all the major North American British colonies as well as in the Caribbean, these events were not isolated incidents. The result was what in the twentieth century would be recognised as a media-induced panic, as reports and letters came in from elsewhere, to be copied and repeatedly published throughout the colonies to a horrified public. In Britain the newspapers were equally sensationalist, craving reports of the latest horrors. In addition to rebellions, there were reported individual crimes by African slaves – rape, attempted and successful murders, usually committed within the households of their service. In addition, There were also many poorly recorded rebellions on board the ships on the way to America, though these were not reported as so much of a problem for whites afraid of violence in their own homes (Bly, 1998; Richardson, 2001).

Rebellion was, if the accounts are to be believed, accompanied by conspiracy and plots for the destruction of white power and population. Everywhere the reports were of slaves banding together to destroy. One of the rebellions that induced the most savage response from the British authorities was that in Antigua in 1736. The foremost historian of the island, Gaspar (1978), places the incidents of 1736–1737 firmly within the process of slave resistance. Contemporary accounts attributed the plot to the Coromantee (thought to be particularly good warriors) and created a horror story to justify the brutal response of the authorities. Yet here, as in New York five years later, the story told by the authorities was a cliché: the rebels were going to annihilate the whites and then elect their leader as king of the island. This was a standard official story of rebel intentions, as Lepore (2005) points out with regard to New York in 1741. The reports from Antigua certainly created a shock wave through the British colonies.

> This Island is in a very Confusion at present about the Negroes rising in Battle against us (the Plot happened to be found out just before it came to a head) and therefore we hope we shall find means to prevent it; it was so far gone that they had all their Posts, and was to attack us the 30th of this Instant, by blowing up the Ball House, and then a great Army to come into the Town to fight and devour Men, Women and Children. But as God would have it, we have all the Heads in Custody, and are every Day, as we find them guilty, putting them to miserable Deaths – Mr Kerby's Negro named Court, Mr Thomas Hansons' Tomboy, and Mr John Christopher's Hercules, were racked to Death in the Market Place. Mrs Lodge's Negro named Fortune (a Fidler), Mr Philip Darby's Jack, Mr Thomas Stephens's Frank, and Mr Anthony Garret's Venture (Carpenter) were burnt alive in the Pasture of Major Otta's.
> (*Boston Weekly Newsletter*, 25 November 1736. Extract from a letter from Antigua, dated 18 October)

The reprisals taken after their defeat were savage and widely reported (See Document 5.3). In summary, it seems that:

> In all, eighty-eight slaves were executed: five were broken on the wheel, six gibbeted, and seventy-seven burned. By a special act, forty-seven other slaves were banished, but the legislature postponed the transportation of eight major witnesses whose testimony was needed for the trial of some free coloured suspects.
> (Gaspar, 1978: 309)

Unlike the English custom, when being hung on a gibbet was inflicted as an additional punishment to the corpse of the executed criminal, these victims in Antigua were hung up alive and it reportedly took several days for some to die. The Antigua executions were a mixture of English and

European customs. They shared a number of features with English practice, not least the public brutality of the executions, whose effect it was hoped would be a deterrent to any prospective offenders. The formality and theatricality of the occasions were striking features of the process of cruelty. The punishments also contained elements of English law, under which those who, like servants killing their employers or wives killing their husbands, were seen as challenging the natural order of society, were found guilty of 'petty treason', and were sentenced to be burnt to death (though, in practice, they were often garrotted first). The burning of wives guilty of husband-murder was only abandoned in the last quarter of the eighteenth century. Slaves rising against, or killing, their masters fit this pattern of 'unnatural' crimes. The transportation of insurgent slaves out of the colony to be sold elsewhere, which was implemented in both Jamaica and New York, was also an adapted version of the transportation of British and Irish convicts to the colonies, a punishment which was not inflicted on white criminals in the colonial courts (there being nowhere further to send them). Such slaves were sold on an open market, which could mean removal to French or Spanish plantations. Yet the additional factors in Antigua – the 'racking' was in fact breaking the victim on the wheel, derived from practices found in Germany and elsewhere on the continent of Europe – were not English traditions, and show how slave laws in British colonies were in many ways local inventions rather than mere reproductions of English law (which had no legislation about slaves) that drew on many other influences. These events in the Caribbean were reported in detail in the North American as well as the London newspapers, with perhaps even greater levels of gruesome detail (See Document 5.3).

South Carolina in the 1730s was also disturbed by slave actions. Some attempts were unsuccessful, as reported in the northern papers:

> South Carolina, in December last a great number of negroes had run away into the woods with arms and ammunition, and planned something but were surprised and taken with all their arms, 2 barrels of powder, two of shot and 1 of flint.
>
> (*Boston Evening Post*, 15 March 1736)

In 1739, however, the threat seemed to the authorities much greater. In the Stono Rebellion, which started about 20 miles from the colonial capital of Charleston, South Carolina, more than 60 slaves attacked a storehouse for weapons and gunpowder, which they seized after killing the two guards (Doake, 2006: 35–36). As the fighting grew, at least 21 whites were killed and about twice that number of African slaves – making it probably the bloodiest rebellion in North America. Most of the rebels headed off towards St. Augustine in Florida, almost 200 miles away, perhaps trying to make contact with the Spanish since war had just broken out (The War of Jenkins' Ear) and they might have expected a welcome. The Spanish governor had promised freedom to all slaves who escaped from the British. It was believed at the time that they were mostly Catholics, which historians of Africa have suggested indicates an origin in the central African kingdom of Kongo, which had been converted a century before (Thornton, 1991). The effective deployment of guns was seen as a particular threat to white control. The revolt had started on a Sunday, when most of the white population would have been at church – and, even though they were legally obliged to carry arms to church, were in the position of leaving their properties vulnerable to attack (Berson, 2009). Although the white reaction was successful in suppressing the revolt, the slaves had almost succeeded, and it provided a well-remembered scare among the authorities for years afterwards. The revolt provoked a legal clampdown through several pieces of legislation, including the 1740 Negro Act, restricting the movements and activities of slaves, who were not allowed to gather in groups. Killing a slave became a minor offence for white owners, punishable by a small fine. This law set an example for several other colonies.

New York suffered two outbreaks of violence, much of it from the local authorities in response to perceived threats of a slave rebellion, in 1712 and 1741. In 1712 a plan by fewer than 30 slaves had a shocking effect on the city, partly because of their possession of guns and partly because of the number of white people killed at the start. We know most about it from the reports to London from Governor Robert Hunter:

> I must now give your Lordships an account of a bloody conspiracy of some of the slaves of this place, to destroy as many of the inhabitants as they could. It was put in execution in this manner, when they had resolved to revenge themselves, for some hard usage they apprehended to have received from their masters (for I can find no other cause) they agreed to meet in the orchard of Mr. Crook in the middle of the town, some provided with fire arms, some with swords and others with knives and hatchets. This was the sixth day of April, the time of meeting was about twelve or one clock in the night, when about three and twenty of them were got together. One slave to one Vantilburgh set fire to [a shed] of his masters, and then repairing to his place where the rest were, they all sallied out together with their arms and marched to the fire. By this time, the noise of the fire spreading through the town, the people began to flock to it. Upon the approach of several, the slaves fired and killed them. The noise of the guns gave the alarm, and some escaping, their shot soon published the cause of the fire, which was the reason that not above nine Christians were killed, and about five or six wounded.

He concludes, summing up the judicial response that there were:

> twenty seven condemned, whereof twenty one were executed, one being a woman with child, her execution by that means suspended. Some

were burnt, others hanged, one broke on the wheel, and one hung alive in chains in the town, so that there has been the most exemplary punishment inflicted that could be possibly thought of.

(Callaghan, 1885: 341–342)

He notes that there were also 'six having done that Justice on themselves' (that is, committed suicide).

Thirty years later, Daniel Horsmanden (1744: 55 footnote) compared the 1741 outbreak with this, recording that:

> Governor Hunter, ordered a cannon to be fired from the ramparts, to alarm the town, and detached a party of soldiers to the fire; at whose appearance those villains immediately fled, and made their way out of town as fast as they could, to hide themselves in the woods and swamps. In their flight they also killed and wounded several white people; but being closely pursued, some concealed themselves in barns, and others sheltered in the swamps or woods; which being surrounded and strictly guarded till the morning, many of them were then taken. Some finding no way for their escape, shot themselves. The end of it was, that after these foolish wretches had murdered eight or ten white people, and some of the confederates had been their own executioners, nineteen more of them were apprehended, brought upon their trials for a conspiracy to murder the people, etc. and were convicted and executed; and several more that turned evidences were transported.

The next year, 1713, the legislature passed a law with severe penalties to regulate 'Negroes and Indian slaves in the Night-Time'.

New York's second outbreak of violence, in 1741, was contentious from the start because, though the incidents of arson were real, contemporaries and historians have since responded to the testimonies of the arrested slaves and free, both African and white, with great scepticism. Comparisons with the witchcraft in Salem, Massachusetts, in 1692 were made at the time. Szasz (1967) takes the sceptical view that robbery was the aim of the several mixed groups, and that it was much later that ideas of conspiracy and popish plots were added ('perhaps by the interrogators, as in many European witchcraft trials'). Certainly, the first crime to be investigated was a burglary where valuable household goods were stolen and then searched for by the authorities. This produced the first executions and, in their aftermath, arrested servants and slaves began to spin stories of a large-scale plot to attack the white population. More than a dozen fires, including one in St. George's Fort defending the south of the island, added to the fear of the authorities. An anonymous letter to Lieutenant-Governor Cadwallader Colden at the time noted the comparison with the Salem witch trials and regarded the huge number of confessions and accusations (most slaves went from one to the other in their testimonies) as worthless. However, the most recent historian of the episode, Lepore (2005), in her book *New York Burning*, takes the evidence more seriously while being suitably sceptical of the self-justificatory and dramatic, almost hysterical, account produced by Daniel Horsmanden, recorder (the chief city magistrate) and member of the supreme court. Whatever the original threat to New York, the response of the authorities was a savage over-reaction. These were fevered times, however, and white people's paranoia was reinforced by the sensational claims that several of the 'conspiracies' of this period were linked, even co-ordinated:

> Besides the 15 Negroes in our former Papers mentioned to be executed for the late Conspiracy to destroy this City, and murder the Inhabitants, on Friday the 11th Instant, there was another Negro called *Willmos*, burnt here for being one of the Conspirators in the said Plot. At the Stake he confessed, as we hear, that he was concerned in the Rising of the Negroes at *St. John's*. Where he killed several White People with his own Hands; that he was likewise in the Plot at *Antigua*, where he turned King's Evidence, and he was guilty of that formed here. He impeached two White Persons who have been apprehended, one of which has since confessed himself guilty, and impeached several others.
> (*Boston Evening Post*, 20 July 1741, datelined 13 July)

Like revolutionary and terrorist scares in later centuries, this picture of the slave risings suggests an international conspiracy that is driven by almost professional agitators: it represented a slave society's worst nightmare. In the evidence it was said that the plotters wanted to fulfil the failed plan of the 1712 rebels (Horsmanden, 1744: 55). As in Antigua, the executions were conducted with deliberate brutality, creating a theatre of cruelty that was designed to deter any further dissent from the slave population or their white friends (Fearnow, 1996). More uncertain is whether there were slaves mustered or allowed to watch the ceremonial killings, though it is likely that many were.

Certainly, the level of arrest and prosecution was extraordinary. Lepore (2005: 246) reports that, among the slaves alone, 14 were burned alive and 16 hanged; a further 84 were transported out of the colony to any belonging to a foreign power (not to a British possession). They were distributed to Portugal, Madeira, Hispaniola, Cap Français, St. Eustatius, Curaçao, and other places. At least 208 had come under suspicion (that is 10% of the enslaved population in the city, though more as a proportion of males): all but a few were arrested and judicially processed in some way. A handful were identified as 'Spanish Negroes', at a time of the war against Spain. More than half of the named slaves were therefore executed or expelled. The four whites executed were condemned mostly for burglary or, in the case of John Ury, whose trial seemed almost an accidental afterthought, for being a Catholic priest (pp.192–197). Only tavern-keeper John Hughson was alleged to be a key player in the conspiracy: he was said to have been the leader and would have become 'king' of the city had the revolt succeeded. Star witness in the trials, servant girl Mary Burton, whose master John Hughson was hanged, was widely disbelieved by the end of the process but nevertheless was rewarded with £100 by the city, which she used to buy freedom from her indenture.

Of all the slave rebellions, the rising in Jamaica known as Tacky's Rebellion (1760–1761) was perhaps the one that came nearest to challenging the slave system and the control of a British colony. Hundreds of slaves died in the fighting and more were transported to be sold to Meso-American slaveholders, mostly in British Honduras (now Belize). The rising began in St. Mary's parish among largely Akan slaves (from modern-day Ghana), known to the British as 'Coromantee' or 'Coromantin', and quickly spread throughout the island. There were elements of magical belief among the rebels, who wanted to expel the whites and set up their own country: at least one traditional '*obeah*-man', or religious leader, was involved, giving Tacky magical protection against white men's bullets. As a result of this practice, subsequent Jamaican laws made *obeah*, known in Haiti as *voodoo*, illegal and there were attempts to suppress it. As the fighting spread, more were killed on both sides. With the help, significantly, of the maroons, who stuck to the letter of their 1739 agreement with the authorities to aid them against runaways, Tacky himself was killed and his severed head exhibited in Spanish Town, where it was promptly stolen, allegedly by fellow countrymen who resented this ignominious exhibition. After more fighting, the rebels were eventually defeated. By that time at least 60 white people had been killed, and 300–400 rebels. Even more were transported, after about 100 executions. The most severe exhibition was made of two men, leaders from St. Mary's parish, who were hung, alive, in cages and left to die: reports suggest that one lasted seven days, the other nine. Other punishments were less severe, but even the slaves who gave warning of the rebels' plans and evidence against them were punished – several were transported off the island.

There were further disturbances in 1765, again starting in St. Mary's among slaves of the same ethnic origin, having some time before taken an oath to stay secret and await their opportunity. The leader was alleged to be a slave who had been tried but acquitted of rebellion in 1760. After a couple of white men, one a slaveowner, were killed, they were suppressed by a quick military response. On investigation it was alleged that the slaves on at least 17 plantations had been involved. Vivid accounts of these rebellions were provided in Edward Long's *History of Jamaica*: he took the view that the Akan were naturally warlike and this, accompanied by religious fervour, made them prone to rebellion. The key factor, more likely, as discussed in Chapter 3, was that, because of the high death rate, Jamaica was continually having to import new populations of slaves and these retained an unusual degree of solidarity among themselves as well as a strong common culture. In other slave regimes, newcomers were always in a minority and they were socialised into obedience by their more experienced fellow-workers (Long, 1774: 455, 457, 458, 461–462).

5.5 White rebellions/rebellious whites

On occasions subordinated whites acted collectively to express their discontents. Conflicts between colonial central authorities and the leading figures of their colonies were not uncommon, but rarely involved large-scale violence. In both empires the new 'possessions' proved troublesome. Pritchard (2004) notes repeated refusals by French colonies in the seventeenth century to comply with instructions, usually quarrelling over a number of problems stemming from the situation in France. Shortage of supplies to the colonies produced rebellion in Martinique in 1666 and St. Domingue four years later. No repressive reaction came from France. The collapse of the market for tobacco – and the monopoly of the Senegal Company in buying and marketing it – caused great difficulty in 1680 in Cap Français, which was calmed only with a bland reassurance from the governor. In many of these islands, divisions between rich and poor generated reluctance among the latter to serve in the militia, and in the 1690s St. Domingue was notably badly defended by its white settlers. The Acadians of Nova Scotia were unusual, in being both successful farmers and, though loyally French, accused by their rulers of being 'seditious republicans'. Most protests by colonists, however, arose from attempts by France to raise taxes in various ways: the government tried several times to levy a tax on the numbers of slaves held by plantation-owners and on the licences to trade with the colonies of other countries. In St. Domingue and Martinique in the 1720s the colonial councils tried to turn themselves into elected bodies, on the British model, and claimed the right to approve legislation and regulations. As the colonies rejected the control of the India Company, their demands were more or less conceded and their councils became legislative bodies representing the (white) colonists. This was not revolutionary change exactly, but it indicated that if the central authorities of the French state wanted to gain the co-operation of the colonies they had, at the least, to consult with them and to concede that colonies needed the political processes of representation in order to express their wishes to royal ministers in Versailles. The 'absolute' French state had found its limitations in its far-flung colonies (Pritchard, 2004: 254–260).

The British, too, could not count on the unconditional acquiescence of their colonies. Much depended on the character and policies of individual governors and on the internal relationships between rich and poor whites in each colony. In New England, religious sensibilities were always a potential source of opposition until the early eighteenth century at least, and, elsewhere, polices towards land and natives could cause tension, given the hunger for new lands as well as the need for adequate protection from native reprisals. In many areas, particularly in the early period of the mid-seventeenth century, the Irish formed a potentially dissident white population. We have seen (Chapter 4) how the Irish in Montserrat switched their loyalties to the invading French when it was convenient to do so, and the Irish of St. Kitts are reported to have used the outbreak of war between England and France in 1666 to evict 800 English settlers, repeating this assault in 1689 at the accession of William of Orange. Tensions between Catholics and Protestants were found elsewhere and lay behind much local conflict (Doan, 2006).

More threatening politically were those conflicts from within the white community that challenged the governors and were directed at political changes of regime. These arose particularly in times of political change in the home country, and largely affected British colonies in the seventeenth century. The most challenging were Nathaniel Bacon's Rebellion in Virginia (1676), the attempted coup by Jacob Leisler (1688) in New York, action against Governor Andros in Boston, Massachusetts, and disturbances in Maryland (1689) – all political conflicts with both local and British dimensions, to some degree mirroring conflicting ideologies arising from British seventeenth-century politics in the years after the restoration of the monarchy in 1660, culminating in the Glorious Revolution of 1688. It would, however, be a misreading to attribute the colonial conflicts entirely to the unfinished business of the civil wars, to conflicts under Charles II and James II about the comparative powers of the monarchy and Parliament. But the highly charged atmosphere of political conflicts in London in the 1670s and 1680s had parallels in some of the northern colonies. Wherever royal governors acted in an exclusive way, restricting voting rights (the franchise) to the more propertied who they deployed as a narrow band of influence or 'clique' around them, the outsiders formed opposing groups, petitioned and protested, and campaigned for what they considered their rights as Englishmen (Lovejoy, 1972). Their weapons usually were printed protestations and proclamations, but as matters became more tense there were threats leading to armed uprisings. Most of these were also significantly *social* movements, gathering the relatively poor in different colonies together: only in Massachusetts, perhaps, did anxiety about their religious and political independence bind all classes together (Middleton, 1992: 138–157).

Nathaniel Bacon's Rebellion in Virginia 1676 began with him leading a bloody raid on the Native American Susquehannocks in alleged reprisal for their depredations. Governor Sir William Berkeley regarded this as a usurpation of the authority of himself and the colonial council and declared Bacon a traitor and rebel. Bacon himself, a well-connected migrant with relatives in the colony, consequently came to represent the grievances of the more remote counties in Virginia such as Henrico, where there were many complaints about taxes on the movement of goods between the colonies, the general costs of colonial government, and the authorities' refusal to take action against the Indians. Bacon's proclamation complained of the 'cabal' of 'grandees' running the colony in their own interest (see Document

5.2). His movement produced a large band of armed men who marched on the colonial capital, Jamestown, forcing Berkeley to escape to the eastern shore of the **Chesapeake**, leaving his estate to be ransacked by the rebels. With Bacon's death in October, Berkeley was able to react and successfully arrested many men, sentencing and executing 23 of them despite a royal pardon being given to all the rebels except Bacon. The protests reflected serious divisions within the white community and the extent to which Berkeley – who had been governor under Charles I, and returned to his post in 1660 under Charles II – had managed to alienate large numbers of the more vulnerable settlers. Some have seen Bacon as a precursor of those American opponents of royal powers a century later who declared independence, but that would be to give him greater significance than he deserves. His actions were in some ways reflective of increasing divisions among whites in many colonies but also of Virginia's economic problems. In his rhetoric, though, Bacon, speaking 'in the name of the people', touched on the whole issue of the rights of Englishmen and their hold over their own government (Thompson, 2006; Billings, 1970).

Jacob Leisler in New York had believed that a letter from William III, on his assuming the throne, gave him the right to assert the power of the Dutch and, more generally, the Protestants of New York against the officials appointed by James II and their governor. The governor himself, Francis Nicholson, had defended James II's regime in the Monmouth Rebellion of 1685 as a young officer, and at the age of 33 was unclear where his duty lay in 1689. James had rejected the charter as well as the colonial assembly and its laws in 1686, and the Dutch were almost completely excluded from the colonial council that advised the governor. Leisler himself was German but had joined the Dutch Reformed congregation on his arrival in New York. New York was thus a divided city at this time. There was widespread political dissent produced by a factious politics in what was supposed to be an 'English' city. Since the city's surrender to the British in 1664 local society was divided in several ways: between white Dutch – the majority for a long period – and the English newcomers; between white and Indian; and between white and black. Many of the political and social upheavals of the first 80 years of British rule derived from the authorities' attempts to Anglicise the culture of the Dutch population and place English Protestantism at the centre of society. Leisler's supporters, with the militia under his command, took control of the forts and the instruments of power, arresting their opponents, but soon came up against British forces sent to accompany a new governor. Several people were killed before Leisler surrendered, and in the subsequent trials eight men were sentenced to death for treason, including his son-in-law, Jacob Milbourne. Only Leisler and Milbourne were executed, in 1691, with the grim ritual of being half-hanged, then being cut down and beheaded. Leisler was regarded as a martyr by many and, in fact, Parliament gave him a posthumous pardon in 1695 (Voorhees, 1994). His legacy remained controversial in the city, as an apparently ardent supporter destroyed by royalist forces; the conflicting views remained unreconciled for more than 20 years (there was a pamphlet war between the warring parties in the 1690s and after).

Maryland also saw disturbances in 1689. In its essence, Maryland's constitution was a personal proprietorship, with Lord Baltimore, as proprietor, having the authority to make the key appointments to the colony, including the governor. There were no mechanisms for appeal in the case of disputes between colonists and their proprietor, who had the power to refuse and annul legislation passed by the colonial assembly. By the 1670s the Calvert family, Lord Baltimore among them, were dominant in most areas – there was an act passed against 'divulgers of falce news' which 'was extended so as to mean any reports about the justices of the Provincial or the county courts. This act was bound to prove of great service to the Proprietary government in suppressing any kind of disorder, and, with such a government, would certainly be used in a manner to awaken resentment' (Sparks, 1896: 522). In parallel with Bacon's Rebellion in 1676 there were moves of protest in Maryland against the richer planter and proprietor interests, but these died away. Men who spoke against the government were arrested for sedition, some of them old enemies of the restored proprietorship going back to the 1650s. Though the disturbances in 1689 were called a rebellion, it seems from the complaints made in the assembly and the formation of an armed association to defend Protestantism that religious differences between Catholic proprietors and a large proportion of white settlers had finally erupted. Letters to Leisler seem to have contained a long account of Protestant fears and protests, as well as grievances which included the corrupt levying of taxes, the oppressive use of laws suppressing free speech, and even murder (McAnear, 1942). There were allegations that Catholics were conspiring with Native Americans to invade the colony. It seems that rumours of the accession of William and Mary had reached the colony, and that local officials had tried to suppress the news. In this context, something close to anarchy and civil war was developing. The leaders of the campaign against 'slavery and popery' took control and expressed their loyalty to William III and Queen Mary. Their position was validated by the decision of the London government to strip Lord Baltimore of his powers, in effect bringing to an end 70 years of private proprietorship.

Massachusetts had, perhaps, the easiest time in 1688–1689. The governor, Sir Edmund Andros, another military veteran loyal to James II, had caused great offence in previous years by enforcing taxation laws and flouting what the New Englanders regarded as their rights. The absence of orders from London left Andros in a quandary, and, when the council expressed support for William and Mary and crowds more or less imprisoned him in his residence, he gave up. Colonists in Massachusetts were negotiating for a new charter underpinning their independent rights, and their commitment to the new monarchs would stand them in good stead. The 1688 Glorious Revolution thus had profound implications for the colonies in North America.

The issue of basic legal rights, the accountability of governments, and the Protestant character of 'English' freedoms were entrenched in American consciousness, to be revived even more passionately in the revolutionary period of the 1760s and 1770s.

5.6 Revolutions

The 'age of revolutions' once seemed a simple enough summary of the period 1770–1848 for teachers of history, but in fact there was little in common across all the different upheavals of the time. The two 'revolutions' that shook the British and French empires in the Atlantic, the War for Independence that led to the creation of the United States, and the slave revolt in Haiti could not have been more different in terms of their origins and participants. They shared only the experience of a long and bitter period of warfare before eventual success against colonial powers. Yet the radical implications of the American Revolution in 1776–1783 and of the Haitian Revolution were not obvious when the conflicts began. Both raised the questions of freedom, of rights, and of accountability of government to those who are ruled by it. Some of these were old questions repeatedly raised in the colonies, particularly, as we have seen, in the contest with elements of royal absolutism at the end of the seventeenth century. There was no discussion of the rights of slaves at that time, but both France and Britain had come to the legal conclusion that there could be no slaves in the home countries, although things were different in the colonies (see Chapter 3). The constitutional aspects of the conflicts prior to the declaration of independence in 1776 have led many historians to conclude that the final war between Britain and 13 of its colonies was a struggle over constitutional rights of those colonies, concentrating on their refusal to be taxed where there was not representation (in Parliament) and their recognition as independent jurisdictions from which offenders could not be taken to be tried in England. Yet both Britain and America shared a political background on these issues: to the Americans, the problem was persuading the British to live up to their own standards of liberty and rights. This is not the whole story: the Seven Years' War had shown Americans the limitations of the British state in terms of military competence. The seamen of the American ports had also learned to hate the Royal Navy and its press gangs. The need for land drove many settlers to oppose British policy restricting expansion into Indian territory. Above all, the attempts by the British to introduce new taxes, partly to pay off the huge debts of the war, drove many colonists to instinctive opposition to British policies of any kind or, at the least, deep mistrust of them. The British politicians, for their part, were mostly doubtful of any assertions of colonial rights, given the sacrifices in men and money the colonies had cost them in years of war. Yet in practical terms the colonies had been autonomous in many areas, with legislatures passing their own laws and courts and officials locally chosen to enforce them.

The supervising power in London (the Board of Trade) occasionally struck down laws on various grounds but could not determine from the outside and in great detail the legal needs of so many different colonies. Historians are therefore in a quandary, acknowledging the way that the transatlantic British colonies participated in a wider, even global, empire and its economy, while also emphasising 'the special character of the American experience' (Greene, 1993: 3). American *exceptionalism* was for a long time treated as almost a sufficient explanation for the American Revolution. The USA's founders' reliance, though, on very British notions of rights rather undermines the idea of their originality or uniqueness. Before the fighting started, the opposition to the two main British attempts to impose taxes, the 1764 Sugar Act and the 1765 Stamp Act (on newspapers and official documents), was led, significantly, by organisations called the 'Sons of Liberty'. In addition the 13 colonies had formed societies of correspondence as a means to exchange information and co-ordinate action, and had in 1774 formed a representative body, the Continental Congress, which became a *de facto* government.

Most commentators agree that the American Revolution was not an inevitable outcome of the preceding 200 years (Roper, 2009: 4), yet the seeds of the conflict can be detected in the many forms of colonial resistance to British controls and some of the collective rebellions outlined above. The complexities of nearly eight years of fighting need not concern us, as there are many excellent guides to the events and processes that led to British defeat (see Conway, 2013). There are, though, profound questions about the British state and its American colonies bound up with that narrative. That a group of colonies should come together in what sympathetic philosopher Richard Price called 'a revolution in favour of liberty' (Greene, 1993: 182) was remarkable and unprecedented. The kind of rebellion that the British had faced only 30 years earlier, the Jacobite rising in Scotland and the north of England in 1745–1746, had been a simple dispute over which branch of the royal family should sit on the throne. A war of political principles had not occurred since the civil wars of the seventeenth century, and the American Revolution echoed some of those challenges to royal absolutism in its rejection of the edicts of a non-representative body such as the British Parliament. The Americans spent 1764 to 1775 in conflict with London over what they regarded as unconstitutional impositions of taxes and commercial penalties. Their resistance challenged the very economic and political basis of the 'first British empire'.

Neither side could be sure of their position, since both faced internal opposition and critical rejection of their policies. In Britain there was the continual sniping from radicals such as John Wilkes and from the more measured – and famously eloquent – Edmund Burke. The debates in print by 1775 had aired the issue of the rights of the colonial peoples, and there were widespread feelings of sympathy with the colonists' cause. There was also the problem of a lack of popular support for the war during which, as it wore on, the British public showed increasing respect for George Washington. Scepticism about the war in America was reinforced by the entry of France into the conflict in 1778 and, later, Spain: these were the traditional enemies of Britain. In America it soon became clear that the Canadians would not support the bid for independence, and in most of the 13 colonies a large minority of the population, known as 'Tories', would remain loyal to Britain. These loyalists became one of the early casualties of the conflict and would remain a financial burden on the British government, who had to meet their claims for compensation. London absorbed many of those driven from America (Jasanoff, 2012). Yet the British authorities always thought that these people would form the basis of an army against the 'patriots' of the American cause, and it is true that some regiments were formed from among them to help in the fighting. But there was never a general rising on behalf of British rule, and the British notion that the American people were deluded by a clever leadership into claiming independence – and that they would soon see their mistake – lasted almost to the end of the war. The British faced other problems. Though they drove Washington out of New York, and later seized Charleston (South Carolina), they never established secure bases further inland. As a naval power, these ports were seen as essential, but the occupation of Philadelphia in 1777 had to be given up. The result was that a world power with thousands more troops than their opponents found it almost impossible to bring their enemies to a decisive battle. In the South in 1780 and 1781, for example, every defeat of the Americans in open battle proved so costly in British casualties that Lord Cornwallis's campaign in the Carolinas, which had started triumphantly at the Battle of Camden in 1780, was continued with repeated retreats after each victory. It was also difficult to sustain a war when the supply lines across North and South Carolina were so long and vulnerable to attack by increasingly confident patriot irregulars. Here there was a real civil war, with atrocities committed by both patriots and loyalists as bitter divisions produced rival militias which concentrated on attacking civilians (Lee, 2001). The two big strategic errors of the British campaign – the strike from the North which resulted in surrender at Saratoga in 1777, and the attempt to cut the American territory in half by seizing Virginia in 1781 – both failed because of the problems of supply lines. In the second, the poor performance of the Royal Navy off the Chesapeake allowed the French to land thousands of troops and, importantly, heavy artillery which were deployed to besiege Cornwallis at Yorktown and force his surrender. In one clear sense the Americans under both Washington and, in the South, Nathanael Greene showed a better grasp of strategy than their opponents: by keeping an army in the field, and close enough to threaten their enemies while avoiding serious defeat, they ensured the survival of the United States. Both craved a decisive victory – neither in fact defeated the British army in a conventional battle – yet they won the war (O'Shaughnessy, 2013, for the personalities of the British commanders who 'lost' America).

The American side also face extraordinary difficulties, derived in part from the embryonic character of the state and its financial and administrative apparatuses. There were no professional soldiers under American command in 1775, when the British attacked Boston, and the formation of the Continental Army, a professional army on European lines that Washington wanted, was continually undermined by shortages of funds and equipment. Recruitment had to be induced or forced to some degree, as individual states were given quotas to fill for the army: this was supposed to be by lottery, so everyone was in theory liable to serve. Forcible conscription, or draft, was carefully avoided, but few states met their quota (Ward, 1999: 111–112). Training was another problem, and though the army issued its own training manuals for officers to follow, derived from British models, there were few who had previous experience of how to implement them. A handful of professionals such as Baron von Steuben proved vital in providing the basic drills and even the guidance on the layout of army camps. The other military force, the militias, was less disciplined, had more variable weaponry (though it did bring some rifles), and served for a shorter period in the field than the 'Line' regiments of the Continental Army. Both Washington and Greene regarded the militia as being of limited use, though their reputation grew after the war. Above all, the problems of the fledgling United States were financial: there was little currency and there were only rudimentary systems of tax collection, few of them administered centrally by the Congress. The complaints of the army concerning basic clothing and equipment persisted to the end of the war. The assistance of the French was sought from the beginning, but they did not enter the war until 1778, when the British surrender at Saratoga suggested an easy victory for the America side. In fact it took another three years of fighting, and the French dedicated significant numbers of ships and men to the cause. Supplies of gunpowder and muskets came in from them and suppliers such as the Dutch, and a considerable official effort was made by the Americans to organise smuggling lines (for a concise guide to the war, see Marston, 2002).

Relationships between the two sides depended on conflicting notions of the right and proper way to treat enemies in war. For the British authorities, 'rebels' could not count on the proper treatment afforded to prisoners of war taken from a legitimate rival great power. Their treatment of American prisoners of war in New York was a shocking mixture of starvation and disease, yet Americans brought to be imprisoned in Britain found a popular organisation raising money for their support. Opponents of the war kept a careful eye on the treatment of Americans. The British policy was short-sighted, as, from the defeat by Washington in Trenton, New Jersey, in Christmas 1776 to the end of the war, there were always more British army prisoners in American hands than the reverse. Moreover, those conducting the war against America were forced to acknowledge, as General Thomas Gage admitted after the costly British victory at Bunker's Hill outside Boston in 1775, that their enemies were more than mere rebels: 'these tryals we have show that the Rebels are not the despicable rabble too many have supposed them to be' (Marston, 2002: 29). In 1777 Edmund Burke noted the contradiction in the British position, organising paroles and the exchange of prisoners as though with a foreign power while officially regarding the Americans as rebels and traitors. In practice, by the end of the war the British were treating the Americans as equals in a conventional conflict, even though there were breaches of the laws of war being committed on both sides – in the Carolinas, for example, as mentioned above. A second factor undermining British credibility was their deployment of Indian allies in the North, which resulted in many accusations of atrocities. The 'law of war' was rudimentary in some ways, but decent behaviour towards each other's wounded and captured personnel was fundamentally understood to be essential. In this regard, Washington was always a stickler for the proprieties and threatened to take reprisals for the mistreatment of Americans in British hands, though he rarely carried this out. In the end, for the first (but not the last) time, the British empire had to acknowledge the rights of its 'subjects' to self-determination.

The loss of America did not provoke a revolution in Britain, though the Tory government fell. This left the Whig opposition to take over the negotiations that led to the Peace of Paris in 1783, accepting the independence of the United States. The British government found itself paying large sums of money in compensating the losses of loyalists, and their claims spilled over into other colonies. In the Bahamas, land was allotted to loyalists from America, and the arrival of 1,600 white settlers with 5,700 black slaves more than trebled the population of the island. Equally important the 114 land grants were turned into the first cotton plantations there, their owners taking advantage of the increasing demand from the industrialising industry in Britain in the 1780s and 1790s. In other places, too, loyalists had a decisive influence, particularly in Canada, which became even more emphatically 'British'. For France, the consequences proved more drastic. The economic burdens as a result of the war (made worse by the Americans refusing to pay their debts) were one of the key factors behind the French Revolution of 1789. Soon after, in 1791, Haiti exploded into open conflict with the French authorities, starting a 13-year war against both French and British forces before a new nation could be proclaimed in 1804. This violent uprising by both the free and enslaved in France's most profitable colony was a shock to the new republican regime and to the old monarchical powers such as Britain who opposed it.

> The revolution began as a challenge to French imperial authority by colonial whites, but it soon became a battle over racial inequality, and then over the existence of slavery itself. The slaves who revolted in 1791 organized themselves into a daunting military and political force, one ultimately embraced by French Republic officials. Facing enemies inside and outside the colony, these Republicans allied themselves with the

insurgent slaves in 1793. They offered freedom in return for military support, which quickly led to the abolition of slavery in the colony. The decision made in Saint-Domingue was ratified in Paris in 1794: the slaves of all the French colonies became citizens of the French Republic. These events represented the most radical political transformation of the "Age of Revolution" that stretched from the 1770s to the 1830s.

(Dubois, 2005: 3)

The slaveowners were largely concerned with autonomy from France, while the slave insurgents were increasingly engaged in the abolition of slavery itself. The impact of the Declaration of the Rights of Man and the Citizen (approved on 26 August 1789 by the National Assembly) was strong, even if the exclusion of women, servants, and the poor meant that this had limited universal application. 'Men are born and remain free and equal in rights. Social distinctions may be founded only upon the general good,' went the first clause, written by the Abbé Sieyès and Marquis de Lafayette – and he did mean *men* ('les droits de l'homme'), without any elaboration. There were American influences on this document, as Thomas Jefferson, the United States' ambassador to France, is generally credited with having assisted in its drafting. From the first, the conflict involved terrible levels of violence, both by the invading armies of France and Britain and the insurgent slaves, and later by the black officers of troops who eventually won Haitian independence (Dubois, 2005: 5). Though this was a uniquely successful rising, it was not the first act of resistance by the slaves: there had been many examples of *marronage* in the previous 150 years, and many of the military tactics used by maroons to defend their strongholds were adopted in the 1790s with great success (Dubois, 2005: 52–55).

Haiti's revolt suggested to many that rebellion *was* revolution in these panicky times, particularly as far as the British in the Caribbean were concerned. Trouble soon followed, most of it blamed on the French, and the British authorities found themselves involved in serious fighting on several islands. The most striking aspect of the rebellions in British colonies in the 1790s was the role of the free, mostly French-speaking, smallholders in framing the grievances and leading the resistance. Many were also of mixed African and European ancestry. Though the English-speaking planters were convinced their opponents were stirred up and led by agents of the French Republic, with predictable revolutionary aims, it is equally likely that the marginalisation of the French language and the Catholic Church over many years lay behind the initial disaffection. These men were not rich and were often engaged in producing commodities such as coffee rather than sugar. Another factor was that these men were frequently of mixed European and African ancestry and represented an anomalous category for the richer plantation owners and the British authorities, who ideally preferred a racial social structure simply divided into white and black. As in other colonies, the mixed race and freed black population were increasingly regarded as deserving lesser status and fewer legal or civil rights (Craton, 1982: 180–202). The role of slaves is rather more problematic: many clearly ran from the larger plantations to the rebel areas, but their places of work were being destroyed in the rebellion. White planters had left their estates to trustworthy slaves and others, and these people were vulnerable in the fighting. Some have suggested that slaves formed a key part of the fighting force in places such as Grenada and St. Lucia (Candlin, 2018).

> The most remarkable episode . . . was the rebellion led by the coloured planter Julien Fédon, which paralysed Grenada for almost two years. More than 7,000 slaves were actively involved, half of the island total, but the leaders were undoubtedly the 150 or more French-speaking coffee planters and smallholders who, like Fédon, felt oppressed by the British regime and looked to the French Revolution for redress and revenge.
>
> (Craton, 1982: 183)

When Fédon's emissaries, Joachim (or Joachin) Phillip and Charles Nogues, met the president and Privy Council of the island in March 1795 to demand the British surrender, they had already killed a number of whites in two areas and taken 40 prisoners, including Lieutenant-Governor Ninian Home, held on Fédon's family estate. The two emissaries were themselves from relatively affluent backgrounds, like Fédon himself, Phillip in particular coming from a family with extensive holdings in land and slaves. They impressed by their appearance in blue French uniforms with the tricolour sash of the revolution around their waists (Candlin, 2012; Cox, 1982). In their pronouncements to the council they pointed to the demands of the French government agent, Victor Hugues, who had been decisive in defeating the British forces in Guadaloupe, that the British surrender their possession in the Caribbean. Yet, although this sounds like a traditional military move by the French against the British in the region, masquerading as a wave of revolutionary activity, there were complex social and historical factors behind the insurgency in Grenada.

Anderson (2010) agrees:

> The island, until recently a French possession, had crisscrossing fault lines dividing Catholic and Protestant; French-speaking and Anglophone; slave and free; black, white, and mixed-race. These groups clashed repeatedly over the questions of who was to enjoy the rights of a British subject, and who was to shoulder its obligations. In 1795, slave and free coloured resistance incited by the French and Haitian Revolutions combined with simmering Anglo-French resentment on Grenada in Fédon's Rebellion, a 16-month uprising that at its height boasted an estimated 7,200 adherents—black, white, slave and free—and

controlled nearly all the island before its suppression in the summer of 1796.

(Anderson, 2010: 202)

She raises the question of the concept of citizenship and rights in this ferment of contrasting identities. The 'French' had had 'Britishness' forced on them by conquest some years earlier. Yet discrimination and a frustrated economic position saw them become insurgents. Convinced that they faced a major threat to both British control and slavery itself, the authorities declared martial law, which provoked from Fédon both indignation and a threat to execute hostages. As the British mustered troops and began to intrude into rebel areas, Fédon carried out his threat to execute 48 of the 51 hostages, including Governor Home. The British attacks were not initially successful, while Fédon's strategy of menacing the large slave plantations forced most of the Anglophone white planters to abandon their estates and seek refuge in the island's capital. The British had to import more than 1,000 troops and, in June 1796, 15 months after the rebellion began, decisively defeated the rebels.

Hundreds of prisoners were taken at the end of the fighting, including Fédon – the surviving list of those held by the authorities has more than 400 names (Court of Oyer and Terminer, 1796). The legal proceedings in Grenada were unorthodox, with suspects named following the legislature passing an Act of Attainder, which was a form of conviction by the legislative body (such as the British Parliament), and reduced subsequent legal proceedings to the identification of those named in the Act and a choice of sentence in most cases – chosen by the decision of a panel of judges. This replaced the formal adversarial trial by jury with legal representation on both sides, as specified under the 1696 Treason Act which was supposed to enforce due processes in these essentially political trials. At least 100 of the accused were sentenced to death and others order to be transported out of the colony (Court of Oyer and Terminer, 1796). One contemporary writer, Turnbull (1795: 161, 210), thought the rebels were 'fellow-subjects' who had committed treason, though a number may have been French: most were of local origin, though he noted that four 'execrable traitors' were born of British parents. Contemporary accounts of the Grenada fighting were largely from the viewpoint of those whom Craton calls the 'plantocracy', such as Gordon Turnbull's *A Narrative of the Revolt and Insurrection of the French Inhabitants of Grenada, by an Eye-Witness* (1795), for example, and other narratives by British people from the island. None had any doubts about the threat and the treachery of the accused. Most were charged with treason – in the words of the accusations, 'not only of subverting His Majesty's Government but of totally extirpating His Loyal Subjects of this Island', and many others with either murder or manslaughter. There were few doubts about the main participants' guilt, but some of the accused made the only objection or defence available to them and asserted that they were not the people named in the Act of Attainder. Nearly all these were dismissed. Those who were accused of manslaughter, if convicted, were branded on their hands, while others were fined for committing assaults. Even if not convicted, a handful of the accused were only released from jail on condition of their 'shipping themselves off the Island'. The racial pattern of punishment was striking. As Cox (1982: 16) has observed:

> Of the guilty, most of those condemned to death and actually executed were free coloureds, while the whites were reprieved. Those guilty free coloureds who were not executed, together with whites who were reprieved, were shipped to non-British territories along the coast of Honduras. The feeling was that under no circumstances should such 'dangerous persons' remain in the island, and when in May, 1797, some female relatives attempted to reenter the island from Trinidad, the public outcry against them was so loud that Governor Charles Green accepted Council's advice in refusing them permission to land.

With attainder and conviction went the seizure of the convicts' properties, and this brought hundreds of Grenadan slaves into ownership by the Crown. When the uprising began, some slaves took part, and at least one slave was listed among the 'traitors'. This raised questions of them having duties as citizens or subjects, above those due to masters; that is, loyalty to the state or crown as though they were free. Prosecuting them in this way suggested their freedom, acting as citizens or subjects, not chattels. This had been an issue in revolutionary Virginia in the War for Independence, when one slave fighting in the Royal Navy was seized as a traitor by the Virginia authorities. Advisedly, Thomas Jefferson, then the Governor of Virginia, decided against prosecution on the grounds that this would have treated the slave as a free, if offending, citizen (Anderson, 2010). There were limits to British rights.

The reactions of the British authorities in 1795–1796 were vigorous but ineffective military invasions of rebel territories. Troops were rushed to Barbados and thence allocated to the different troublespots. In St. Lucia the promising career of John Moore (famous for his retreat to Corunna 15 years later) was almost stifled by his inability to bring the 'brigands' or rebels to a decisive battle. In St Vincent, the 'Black Caribs' (a term which the British authorities used to designate African slaves and runaways, while the relatively few 'Yellow Caribs' were regarded as genuine indigenous people) almost overran the capital of the island, and the situation was saved only by heroic defence and, eventually, by a level of savagery that British participants thought unprecedented (Craton, 1982: 192). As in Grenada and St. Lucia, the alliance with French smallholders, equally disaffected by British rule, provided the Black Caribs with crucial intelligence as well as military support. In political ideals, too, there were elements of French republican rhetoric, but the key factor was the British determination to abolish a zone of freedom, into which it was believed French government agents were infiltrating, and suppress a group who did not acknowledge British authority or legitimacy. The Second Carib War was therefore aimed at the removal of an entire people.

As the fighting progressed, the 'inhabitants' (white, Anglophone settlers) petitioned the authorities:

> In various instances the Cultivation of the lands has been greatly retarded by the Negroes inhabiting the Windward Coasts of this Island, a Race of People who have been vulgarly and most improperly stiled Charibs; but who are really and strictly nothing but Negroes and Intruders into this Country.
>
> (Grenada Petition, 1795)

Alleging terrible crimes committed by these supposed Caribs, they pointed out that 'hundreds' of British people had been transported to the colonies for less serious crimes, and pleaded for the complete removal of 'these merciless and faithless Savages' (Grenada Petition, 1795). The colony's governor and military commander, General Ralph Abercrombie, explored the possibilities for more than 4,700 people, suggesting that 'if there is a Spanish War, send them to Rattan, or any of the part of the Main considerably to Leeward. If there is not, land them upon St. Domingo when the Spaniards have given it up – perhaps the Island of Samana ... The yellow Charibs who are few in number, and innocent of the late War, may safely and properly be allowed to remain. They are the origines of the island' (Abercrombie, 1795). For the Black Caribs, 'Rattan', more properly Roatán, an island off what is now Honduras, was chosen. At least 1,300 of the Black Caribs died before arriving in Latin America as they were moved from one waterless island to another: apart from the removal of the Acadians from Nova Scotia in 1755, this was the worst instance of ethnic cleansing since Cromwell's policies in Ireland in the 1650s. Like the 'cajuns', though, these people – the Garifuna – have survived, with their own language (in part derived from Arawak, one of the native Carib languages) and their own distinctive style of music, both in central America and as a diaspora culture in places such as New York (Taylor, 2012; Thompson, 2006).

At the same time, on Jamaica, the Second Maroon War saw the authorities turn on the Trelawny maroons who had observed the peace settlement of 1739 without any real breaches. They were one of two towns – the other was Accompong – which had made an agreement at the end of the First Maroon War and generally lived peacefully alongside Jamaica's slave society. In the 1790s, though, there were again allegations of serious depredations and crimes committed by the maroons, and the same policy of deportation was adopted. One longstanding grievance of the slaveowners was that the maroons had not fulfilled the agreement to recapture and return runaway slaves. This was despite repeated severe legislation making the harbouring of runaways punishable by transportation (which in fact meant re-enslavement for a maroon, being sold outside the colony). As one contemporary author put it, 'that the Maroons had proved themselves a useful body, cannot be denied. Besides their utility in preventing assemblages of fugitives, they had been active in the suppression of rebellions' (Dallas, 1804: I, 97, 101). By the 1790s, however, the mutual trust and practical coexistence of maroon and slave societies had broken down. With the dominant white plantation owners hostile to them, and under increasing pressure from the authorities, the maroons in effect declared war in 1795 after a nasty incident in which two of their members had been flogged for pig-stealing, and began raiding white properties. In one view, the maroons had:

> flagrantly reneged and encroached on the treaty arrangements, resulting in the second Maroon War (1795–1796), in which the Trelawny Maroons (the largest group . . .) declared war on the British. The Trelawny Maroons went on a bloody rampage of killing, plundering, and burning that resulted in the death of many people and farm animals, and the destruction of a large number of farms . . . Quite apprehensive, Alexander Lindsay, the Duke of Balcarres, the Governor of Jamaica in 1796, was determined to save the island from the Maroons' destructiveness; his prescription for this was a simple one: it was to deport the Trelawny Town Maroons, in spite of the fact that they had laid down their arms under pledge that they would not be deported from the colony.
>
> (Lockett, 1999: 9)

This was very much the view of the other major account at the time by Edwards (1801), who included his Jamaica story in a more condemnatory account of Haiti and revolutionary activity in the Caribbean and who had few doubts about their threat to disorder and violence. It is clear from both Dallas and Edwards that one problem for the white authorities was the mobility of these maroons, who moved out of their area for economic and social reasons, wandering from estate to estate. Their freedom contrasted with the restrictions imposed on slaves who could not leave a plantation without a pass signed by their owner or his overseer. The maroons were in some ways an anomaly in a highly controlled slave society. Exactly how many were in Trelawny Town and involved in the deportation is not entirely clear: the population was estimated at 1,400 in 1788 (Dallas, 1804: 120). They were sent to Nova Scotia, to the surprise of the governor who published his protesting correspondence on the subject, and proved expensive to maintain there. After three years suffering Canadian winters, 538 were sent to Sierra Leone from Nova Scotia, of perhaps 600 who had been sent from Jamaica (Lockett, 1999: 12; Edwards, 1801: 355). Return to Jamaica was impossible; a 1796 Act made it a hanging offence to return or even to *receive* a returner – even if the maroons had been able to arrange it (Dallas,

1804: II, 249). The second group, the Accompong maroons, remained uninvolved and have survived the subsequent two centuries.

White troops in these conflicts were vulnerable to disease and, moreover, remarkably ineffective in straightforward military terms in the fighting, so the British cabinet in 1795 authorised the recruitment of the first West Indian regiments. There had been efforts on individual islands, such as Jamaica in the 1760s, to recruit black troops as a more effective force compared with the local militias, but this was the first plan to copy the French pattern of creating Caribbean regiments in the regular army. Many of the 'recruits' were in fact slaves, and at least 12,000 were bought for this purpose in following decades. They mostly proved trustworthy, though in 1808 the Second West India Regiment mutinied in Jamaica and plotted to seize Kingston (Craton, 1982: 336). The formation of what were in effect units of slave soldiers is a kind of backhanded compliment to the effectiveness of the rebellions of the 1790s. Yet the aims of these various insurgencies are by no means clear: they are not identical, though all have similar roots. In Grenada, where the leader Fédon wrote and published more statements, there seems to have been conventional republican ambitions, since he talks of 'citizens' and himself as 'the President': the French influence is obvious. As in Haiti itself, the Grenadan rebels were not a single group, but French revolutionaries and slaves mixed together. They were certainly rebels against British rule, but less clearly against slavery itself. The latter seems improbable, despite the participation of many slaves. Elsewhere the fighting was largely instigated by the British authorities on grounds that seem specious and invented. In St. Vincent and Jamaica the attack on inconvenient minorities, and the cruelty of their deportations, arose from the long-term campaigning by owners of big plantations and the acquiescence of the British state to their demands. These policies were, in effect, ethnic cleansing at the command of the local rich landowners.

6 Conclusion

This book has attempted to analyse the processes of European discovery, exploration, and settlement, together with the native reactions and conflict, that characterised the two empires of Britain and France. Above all, these processes took place in a context of imperial rivalry and violent war between the two powers on an increasingly global scale. These wars eventually embraced the Caribbean and North America, and their peoples, and provided a spur to their development in many ways while also underpinning the violent removal of native peoples from many areas. Despite the unfamiliarity of the new environment, peoples from Europe and Africa made new forms of society across the Atlantic. These new societies created in North America and the Caribbean were unlike anything in Europe, but they – or their leaders – often claimed a common heritage as well as a language and culture. The core of this in the British colonies was made up of the laws and the rights established in the seventeenth century, which were in formation when most of the colonies were being established. This was not exactly a process of co-creation, but of a shared culture of law and legalism that shaped both Britain and its colonies. In the French colonies, laws tended to be laid down from the centre and there were few bodies making laws specifically for the circumstances of the transatlantic societies. Yet, however the transfer was effected, little remained untouched or entirely the same in the move across the Atlantic, and far more had to be invented from scratch there. New social relations such as slavery or **indentured servitude** required new laws and forms of legal regulation, and, as land was acquired, new forms of land law – much simpler than those of ancient European forms – had to be created.

When the two countries set out to create their empires they had little idea that this kind of adaptation and invention would be required. They intended to rival the Spanish empire and dreamed of easy wealth in gold or silver. They were continually disappointed. New forms of wealth took generations to create, and great efforts in conflict against native resistance – or against each other – were required. The native societies with which they interacted in the Americas were seriously affected, and many destroyed. Through the slave trade the two empires corrupted and disrupted African societies and their leadership and created a lasting legacy of bitterness and division that shapes the black experience in the Caribbean and North America to this day. For white settlers their lives were not more secure or safe than they might have been in Europe. Continually engaged in conflict with both natives and rival empires, the 'westward enterprise' was continually in danger of foundering in the face of violence and economic disaster. Yet there was land to be claimed and farmed, and, for a rich few, opportunities for a relatively quick seizure of wealthy plantations that could yield extravagant profits.

These were not formally 'free' societies, given the prevalence of slavery and servitude, in the sense that most migrants were forced, or volunteered, to be in legal subjection. The short-term servitude of servants did not necessarily lead to a prosperous future, and, in places as different as Barbados and North American colonies such as Pennsylvania and New York, class differences among whites emerged and were entrenched. In the slave or plantation societies these inequalities were there from the beginning and the forms of racial stratification forced on the more powerful white elites a changing politics of class and race. Uniting the white 'race' in the face of a growing population of African slaves became a problem of integration across some of those class differences, and this was not always successful; unless the smaller planters and farmers, and the artisans and shopkeepers in the towns, felt equally threatened and, importantly, were willing to serve in the local armed militias against slave risings and other forms of resistance. For the most exploited, such as Jamaican slaves, life was hard and short, while in other contexts, including parts of North America such as Virginia, slaves were at least able to have a semblance of a family life. Nevertheless, both slaves and servants ran away from their work whenever they could and in the British colonies such as Virginia and Maryland established a long-lasting tradition of running to the towns of the North. In all the slave societies there was a tense situation of potential conflict and rebellion, accompanied by a wariness and alert surveillance of the subordinated population. Internal conflict and resistance were always latent and sometimes broke out into violent opposition.

Throughout the period the vaguely defined 'frontier' between settled and native was a confusing zone of both trade and violence. From some islands in the Caribbean, where the French in particular confronted **Carib** resistance, to the far north in Canada, a contradictory process of both collaboration and conflict was carried on in unstable circumstances that were easily disrupted further by wars between Britain and France. Some white settlers lived relatively amicably and peacefully alongside natives, while others were in perpetual fear of raids and violence. Fear and even hatred were fuelled by stories of native cruelty and captivity, both among Jesuit missionaries in Canada and white settlers everywhere up against the frontier. The native peoples were often clever in negotiating alliances and, being deployed by both imperial powers in war, were often able to exploit violent situations to their own advantage. They became losers in several contexts, where they had supported the defeated side in an imperial war or, in the case of those who supported the British in the American Revolution, when an empire was itself defeated by its former subjects. In the British North American colonies, in particular, the rising settler populations in need of land produced a continual pressure to expand into Indian country, and restrictions on this provided one of the causes of tension between Americans and their British authorities in the 1760s and early 1770s. The ethnic cleansing of natives from their territories was a result of this pressure, exercised intermittently throughout the period.

There were also internal threats as well as those from outside. Internal rebellion by Africans was a threat in the slave colonies, and conflicts between poorer and richer whites over land and rights could produce major threats to the authorities, as in Bacon's Rebellion in Virginia. These new societies were therefore neither stable nor secure in either their internal or their external relations but were always in danger of disruption, if not complete breakdown. The recurrent wars, either with natives or between empires, took a terrible toll in material damage and lives lost, unevenly inflicted on some communities. Throughout the period, Massachusetts maintained the largest militia and suffered among the heaviest casualties in losses of both civilian and military lives. If rebellion was a permanent danger during the colonial period, revolution was more unexpected. Revolution in the 13 North American colonies shattered the achievements of the British empire – know often as the 'first empire' because of the break caused by the American Revolution – and forced a gradual development of an expanded empire in India and Africa. For France, the loss of territories in the Seven Years' War was one level of shock, but the Haitian revolution was more than a challenge to the hegemony of the French. The threat to slavery as an institution produced an international fear that slaves were about to abolish their own slavery and undermine 200 years of economic security and wealth for European powers.

The cultural development of the British and French colonies, though, created a permanent springboard for later patterns, particularly the location of English- and French-speaking communities in the Americas. French survives and flourishes from the Caribbean, in places such as Guadaloupe and Martinique (technically still part of France), to Quebec in Canada. English is, however, overwhelmingly dominant, as is to be expected given the large number of migrants, both before 1800 and since, over such a large territory. In that sense the conquests of 1759 cemented English as a global language, and Britain as a global power. The consequences of that transformation, as much cultural as political, are still with us.

Documents

Chapter 2

Document 2.1

Itinerary of Régis du Roullet April to August 1732, from Mobile to the Choctaw nation and down the Pearl river, with detailed map, as discussed on pages 20–21.

I passed the great cypress swamp of Mobile on the edge of which is very fine bayou[1], which is as wide as the *Bayou du Moulin* (Mill Bayou), but not so deep, sandy bottom. The Indians call it *Boukouma*, that is to say 'Red Bayou'. In this part of my way I went five quarter-leagues[2] NNW. The great cypress swamp is about half a quarter of a league in width; the passage is very dangerous for horses; it is full of huge roots and moving earth in which horses sink extraordinarily; in heavy rains this place is inundated, the Indians can scarcely pass through it. Some of the Choctaws told me that one can avoid this passage by making a day's detour.

Without great expense this cypress swamp could be made passable by building a levée with trees and faggots, a ditch to carry the water into the bayou, and it would be highly useful. After having passed this cypress swamp I went to pass the night at Kalé, that is to say, the 'Spring', which lies one league distant on the route to the north-west.

One league from my sleeping place I passed [29 April] Bouk Tchakalé, which means 'Nine Bayous'. Before reaching it one pass a low stretch of quaking ground full of routes, nearly as wide as the great cypress swamp but less dangerous; this bayou has a sandy bottom, eight feet wide and four in depth. [137–138]

[2 May] I went half a league to the NW, another half-league to the NNW, a half-league further to the NW, still another half-league to the N. Then I went to *Bouk janaché founiatcha*, which means the 'Bayou of Buffalo Bones'. One cannot cross this bayou at all, but leaves it on one's left hand.

---

1 A 'bayou' is usually a flat, swampy stretch of water.
2 A French league was 10,000 feet, or about 2.5–3 English miles.

The Indians have given this bayou its name because the Indians formerly killed buffalos there whose bones are still visible [139–140]

[He reaches Yowanis, 22 May]

The Yowanis is a Choctaw village where I established a post in the year 1729. After having received a visit of several chiefs of the Choctaw nation and set in order the fort of the Yowanis where I left Mr. De Chambellan, an officer and the son of Mr. Périer, Governor of the Province, and with him only four Frenchmen, I took up my march towards the village of *Bouk fouka*, which is to the Pearl River, which is only five leagues from that village, and which I have to explore. [143]

[28 May] I shall say that the village of *Boucfouca* is the one of those of the Choctaw nation, whose cabins are the most separated one from the other. This village is divided into three hamlets, each hamlet at a quarter of a league from the others, and all three surrounded by bayous. Lastly this village is at least twenty leagues in circumference.

I had no sooner arrived at this village than the warriors and the Honoured Men came to see me at the house of their chief where I had council with them, and asked of them some people to protect me in the places where I shall work to build my pirogue[3], which are exposed to the Chickasaws with whom we are at war. [145–146]

[12 July he finished his pirogue on the banks of the Pearl river, and set out.]

[14 July] I set out on my way to New Orleans, At the point of embarkation, the river runs NNW and SSW, and is about seven to eight fathoms wide and nine feet deep, but this distance is only one hundred and fifty fathoms. Such was the amount of water before it rained, and rain having fallen for two days, it caused the river to rise three feet. But for that I should not have been able to get round the trees that had fallen and lay across the river, and at several other places sand-banks had been formed which are visible at low water.

[10 August] I reached the foot of St. John's Bayou at eleven o'clock and New Orleans at four o'clock in the afternoon.

End of my journey [148–149]

> Source: *Mississippi Provincial Archives, 1729–1740: French Dominion* Vol.1 (Jackson Mississippi: Mississippi Department of Archives and History, 1927), pp. 139–140.

Document 2.2

This expedition by Henry Bouquet, as discussed on page 16, was conducted at the end of the Seven Years' War, in an attempt (among several) to find viable routes between Pennsylvania and the newly-acquired Canadian colonies.

---

3 A pirogue was a long canoe, often made from a single tree trunk hollowed by fire and axe.

Journal of our March from Fort Pitt, to Wenango . . . and thence to Presque Isle [Col. Henry Bouquet]. Extracts:

Left Fort Pitt 7th July 1760 about half an hour past 3 o'clock pm; marched four miles and a half, the first half of the way through a rich fertile Bottom and the other through a dry gully between two hills, at the end of which we encamped on the side of an hill, where were several good springs.

[8 July] Decamped early in the morning and marched 16 miles. About 7 miles from Fort Pitt found two or three very small runs almost dry; three miles further a sharp descent to a small creek, then crossed a meadow three hundred yards over and went up another hill the ascent of which is not difficult: here you see many hundreds of acres of clear land or barrens, the soil of which is bad excepting only the meadows; from this creek we found no water till within half a mile of our encampment. This whole march is upon high ridges with very small intermissions. The soil, except on the berrens, is tolerably good and indifferently timbered with small black and white oaks. Very little water, but an abundance of pea vine and other food. The woods are open and free from under wood. Course to the eastward of North.

[11 July] After ascending the rising ground on the north side of the brook we entered a very narrow rich meadow, which soon brought us upon flat level open woods that continued two miles when we came upon the 7th branch of Beaver Creek, a shallow, rapid rocky stream 60 yards over; passing which, and a thick shrubby bottom on the other side, we came on the same kind of open flat woods as before, which continued this days march (14 miles), interrupted every two or three miles by a small run and a thick bottom. The soil and timber still continue bad and the food grows worse.

[15 July] Marched through low grounds upon or near the banks of French Creek almost all this day; runs at the end of one, two or three miles, and at four miles a creek 12 yards wide. Seven miles from camp we came upon a high sidling hill opposite to Custalogas Town, which is situated on the south-west side of French Creek. Two miles further are three Mingo[4] huts a mile beyond which we met with the richest meadows I ever saw, quite clear, more than two miles in length and a half mile broad; at the north end of these meadows are three more Mingo huts near which we encamped having marched 13 miles. Course: N, W: Excellent food, fine open woods but no timber.

[17 July] This days march was two miles open dry woods near Presque Isle, and one mile at the other end excepted. A continued chestnut bottom or swamp near nine miles of which are laid with logs, but much out of repair. Marched this day 14 miles, our course North.

From Fort Pitt to Wenango	81½
From Wenango to Le Beuf	46

---

4 The Mingo and the Seneca had attacked and taken Fort Venango earlier in the war.

From Le Beuf to Presque Isle 15
[Total: 10 days]   142½ Miles

Source: S.K. Stephens and D.H. Kent (1941) *Wilderness Chronicles of Northwestern Pennsylvania*, eds Sylvester K. Stevens and Donald H. Kent (Harrisburg, PA: Pennsylvania Historical Commission, 1941) originally BL Add. MSS 21638, f.103, pp.175–179.

Chapter 3

Document 3.1

William Moraley

Moraley, from north-east England, had begun his service in Philadelphia in 1729 and moved north later, returning to England (Newcastle upon Tyne) in 1734. At this point in his story he is living a wandering life, and the editors' notes refer to New Jersey laws, since Moraley had transferred there by this time in his narrative, but slavery was more common further south, where he had observed it. On his return to England he waited almost ten years before publishing this memoir in 1743. See pages 51, 53–4.

The Condition of the Negroes is very bad, by reason of the Severity of the Laws, there being no Laws made in Favour of these unhappy Wretches: For the least Trespass, they undergo the severest Punishment; but their Masters make them some amends, by suffering them to marry, which makes them easier, and often prevents their running away. The Consequence of their marrying is, all their Posterity are Slaves without Redemption; and it is vain to attempt an Escape, tho' they often endeavour it; for the Laws against them are so severe, that being caught after running away, they are unmercifully whipped; and if they die under the Discipline, the Masters suffer no Punishment, there being no Law against murdering them. So if one Man kills another's Slave, he is obliged to pay his Value to the Master, besides Damages that may accrue for the Loss of him in his Business.

The Masters generally allow them a Piece of Ground, with Materials for improving it. The Time of working for themselves, is *Sundays*, when they raise on their own Account, divers Sorts of Corn and Grain, and sell it to the Markets. They buy with the Money Cloaths for themselves and their Wives; as for the Children, they belong to the Wives Master, who bring them up; so the Negro need fear no Expense, his Business being to get them for his Master's use, who is as tender of them as his own Children. On *Sundays* in the evening they converse with their Wives, and drink Rum, or Bumbo, and smoak Tobacco, and the next Morning return to their Master's Labour.

They are seldom made free, for fear of being burthensome to the Provinces, there being a Law, that no Master shall manumise them, unless he give Security they shall not be thrown upon the Province, by settling Land on them for Support . . .

The Condition of bought Servants is very hard, notwithstanding their indentures are made in *England*, wherein it is expressly stipulated, they shall have at their Arrival, all the Necessaries specified in those Indentures, to be given 'em by their future Masters, such as Clothes, Meat, Drink; yet upon Complaint made to a Magistrate for Nonperformance, the Master is generally heard before the Servant, and it is ten to one if he does not get his Licks for his Pains, as I have experienced upon the like Occasion, to my Cost.

If they endeavour to escape, which is next to impossible, their being a Reward for taking up any Person who travels without a Pass, which is extended all over the *British* Colonies, their Masters immediately issue out a Reward for the apprehending them, from Thirty Shillings to Five Pound, as they think proper, and this generally brings them back again. Printed and Written Advertisements are also set up against the Trees and Publick Places in the Town, besides those in the News-papers. Nothwithstanding these Difficulties, they are perpetually running away, but seldom escape; for a hot Pursuit being made, brings them back, when a Justice settles the Expences, and the Servant is oblig'd to serve a longer time.

Source: S.E. Klepp and B.G. Smith (eds.) (1992), *The Infortunate: The Voyage and Adventures of William Moraley, an Indentured Servant* (University Park, PA: Pennsylvania State University Press: 58–61.

Document 3.2

Father Mosley

Father Mosley worked on the Eastern Shore of the Chesapeake and provides one of the few descriptions of the fate of the indentured servant; he was trying to dissuade people from migrating in this way, in a letter to his sister in 1772. See pages 51 and 56.

I must give you an insight of the nature of an imported servant, indented servant here to be sold.

1. An indented servant must be vice publickly sold for a slave, for the term of years signed in his indentures, which brings him for that term of years on a footing with our negroes slaves.
2. They have no choise of masters, but the highest bidder at publick sale carrys them off to be used at his mercy, without any redress at law.
3. These masters (as they are chiefly accustomed to negroes, a stubborn dull set of mortals, that do nothing but by driving) are in general cruel, barbarous, and unmerciful, some worse than others.
4. The servant's labour is chiefly in the field with an ox, plough, or hoe, with an overseer by them, armed with a cudgel, to drive them on with their work.
5. Their diet is mean and poor, chiefly some composition of our Indian corn, which at best is very strong and ill-savoured to an European taste, and I think more fit for horses and hogs than Christians, although in my mission I have made many a hearty meal of it.

Lastly, and what is the worst of all for Roman C—th—ks [Catholics], by the law of Maryland every indented servant must take the oath on landing, or the Captains of ships pay £5 for each recusant. A law invented to hinder the importation of C—th—k servants. The Captains of ships before landing use the utmost rigour with them to drive them to it. Many have told me that they have for trifling faults been severely whipt to bring them to that one point. Most are brought to it by threats and promises before they come to anchor. I beg of you to use all your interest to hinder any of your acquaintance, especially of our persuasion, from shipping themselves to America; they will bitterly repent it when it is too late. Masters of ships may sing them fine Canterbery stories of this wild country; but as a friend they may believe me, as being an eye-witness of what I say and advance. It has been a fine poor man's country; but now it is well peopled; the lands are all secured; and the harvest for such is now all over. The lands are mostly worked by the landlords' negroes; and, of consequence, white servants, after their term of bondage is out, are stroling about the country without bread.

Source: Thomas Hughes (1908), *The History of the Society of Jesus in North America, Colonial and Federal*, Vol. 1 (New York: Columbia University and Longmans, Green and Co.): 342.

Document 3.3

This document was copied to London in response to a questionnaire concerning the rights of slaves in 1788. It seems to have been a deliberate attempt to provide some reassurances about slaves at a forthcoming debate in Parliament about the slave trade and slavery (CO 101/28/161). The argument hinges on the humanity of slaves rather than their legal status, and, by extension of mediaeval law in Magna Carta, the prohibition against lords killing their unfree subordinates, the villeins of the manorial system. See page 48.

Extract from the Minutes of the Court of Kings Bench and Grand Sessions of the Peace holden for the Island of Grenada

Friday September 8th 1775
Present
The Honorable Thomas Martin President
Roumel de St Laurent
Alexander Lymson
Richard Worsley Cormick
Alexander Midleton
Peter Francis Laurent
Samuel Sandbach
John Peschier
Thomas Goodhall   Esquires

The Reverend James McKinzie

The Court being called and proclamation made the Justices who did not attend yesterday took the usual oaths and qualified themselves as members of the court agreeable to law and then Mr Justice McKinzie withdrew.

The Indictment which had been found by the Grand Jury against Richard Brigstock otherwise called Richard Preston for the murder of Anna Ritta was then called and the prisoner being brought to the Bar was arraigned with the Indictment and pleaded thereto – Not Guilty. Whereupon the following Gentlemen were impannelled and sworn as petty jurors to try the Issue viz.

John Alexander Foreman
Andrew Orr   Simon Nugent
Robert Patterson   Samuel Hall
James Wilkinson   George English
Patrick Hewley   Duncan Forbes
James Munro   John Bodkin

The evidence on behalf of the Crown being called and gone through, the prisoner having no witnesses to examine, the Attorney General observed upon the Evidence and His Honor the President having delivered the Charge to the Jury they withdrew and soon after returning were called over and all appearing they found their verdict Guilty which was to be recorded and the prisoner remanded to gaol.

Saturday September 9th 1775

The Court being called and proclamation made Richard Brigstock otherwise called Richard Preston who had been yesterday found guilty of murder was brought to the Bar and the Court being about to pass Sentence of Death upon the Prisoner, Mr Staunton moved in arrest of Judgment and having spoke fully in support of the Motion was answered by Mr Attorney General on behalf of the Crown and after debate of the matter, and hearing what could be urged on both sides, the Court were pleased to take time until Tuesday next to give their opinion.

Tuesday September 12th 1775

The Court being called and proclamation made Richard Brigstock otherwise called Richard Preston was brought to the Bar and his Honor the President delivered the Opinion of the Court as followeth vizt., The Court having taken into their mature deliberation the arguments offered in support of the motion of arrest of judgment against Richard Brigstock alias Preston the prisoner at the bar on the ground that by law no ffree man ought to suffer Death for the murder of a slave, are unanimously of opinion that judgment ought to pass. Because by my Lord Coke's definition murder is, when a man of sound memory and of the age of discretion unlawfully killeth any reasonable creature in rerum natura under the King's Peace, with malice aforethought – and his Lordship afterwards explained who he means by a reasonable creature in rerum natura, in the following terms, as man, woman, child, subject born [126v/127] alien,

118   Documents

persons outlawed or otherwise attainted of Treason Felony or Premunire, Christian, Jew, Heathen, Turk or other Infidel being under the King's Peace. And that the murder of slaves was comprehended under the Doctrine evidently appears from the following passage in his Treatise on Villeinage (Book 2 Lect 172) "And it was ordained for the cruelty of some Lords that none should kill them, that is to say, villeins or slaves, as well as of ffree men were in the hands and protection of the King, and that he that killeth his villeins or slaves should have the same Judgment as he that killeth a freeman", by which it evidently appears that the Laws of England made no distinction betwixt the Murder of a ffree man and the Murder of a Slave.

Then Proclamation was made for persons to keep silent whilst Judgment was passing against the Prisoner and Execution according to Law.

The Court then proceeded to give Judgment and sentenced the prisoner to be hanged by the Neck until he is Dead.

Then the Court ordered the Clerk of the Crown to prepare a warrant for the Execution of the Prisoner on Thursday next the fourteenth instant between the Hours of Ten and Twelve O'Clock in the public Market Place of the town of Saint George and the Clerk of the Crown having accordingly prepared the said warrant it was signed by all the Justices present and delivered to the Provost Marshall.

These are also to certify that the Return of the Deputy Provost Marshall made upon the back of the Warrant abovementioned it appears that the Sentence of the Court was Carried into execution and the said Richard Brigstock alias Preston [was] executed on the day and at the time and place therein mentioned.

Certified by me this Twelfth day of April 1788
      Ben Webster
      Clerk of the Common Peace

Note: (PR)
(1) All underlinings are in the original.
(2) This seems to have been sent in reply to a request to the colonies for reports on the rights of slaves in 1788, probably in response to anti-slave trade legislation being proposed in Parliament.
      Source: The National Archives, TNA CO 101/28/126-7

Document 3.4

This is one of the few population censuses from this period in any of the colonies, and is striking because it includes both gender and race, slave and free. See the discussion on pages 55–6.

Number of Inhabitants in Maryland. 261

Mr URBAN,

Herewith I send you a distinct Account of the Number of Inhabitants, white and black, bond and free, which were in the Province of Maryland in the Year 1755. Many Observations, political and commercial, may be drawn from these Tables; but I shall only beg room for one of another Kind. It hath been always alleged that more than two thirds of the Female, white and black, band and free, have arrived in this Colony; how comes it to pass that the Number of Males and Females, white and black, whether above or under sixteen Years of age, should at this Time bear so near a Proportion of the Sexes, and likewise the Number of feasible Men, to the Proportion in old and settled Countries. What say the Sceptics to this? Is this Chance? or is there a ruling Providence? I am, &c. NUMBER.

Maryland, Nov. 20, 1763.

An Account of the Number of Souls in the Province of MARYLAND, in the Year 1755.

Name of the county.	Taxable Persons sixteen Years of Age.						Persons not taxable.							Persons under sixteen Years of Age.									
	Whites.			Mulattoes.		Blacks		Whites				Mul.		Black		Whites.				Mulattoes.			Blacks	
	Free. Men	Servants. Men hired, or indented	Men convicts.	Free. Men	Slaves. Women	Free. Men	Slaves. Men Women	Free Clergy	Men poor.	Women	Servants hired or indented.	Convicts women.	Free Slaves	Free Slaves	Free Boys Girls	Servts hired or indented Boys Girls	Servts convicts Boys Girls	Free Boys Girls	Slaves Boys Girls	Free Boys Girls	Slaves Boys Girls
Baltimore	1639	595	472	36	21	25	16	2	2	1144	833	4	58	1587	200	87	14	9	47	3115	2951	126	49	6	63	62	28	43	3	954	1041
Ann Arundell	1534	438	184	16	23	25	11	8	4	1472	1060	3	64	1539	92	51	15	6	92	2923	1705	82	26	16	28	35	31	23	5	1314	1321
Calvert	629	124	...	24	8	...	4	...	...	550	519	3	20	639	61	27	2	8	39	261	745	46	12	1	30	31	17	17	...	671	645
Prince George	1515	255	79	17	21	37	43	3	...	1278	151	2	44	1680	55	27	8	7	30	1840	1674	80	46	10	41	46	19	55	3	1340	1239
Frederick	4775	216	94	33	4	10	24	...	3	437	314	...	45	2223	265	34	8	7	13	3346	3105	238	13	4	32	39	19	26	3	465	473
Charles	1029	173	205	60	36	48	33	16	1	1196	950	4	51	1777	205	78	8	4	32	2681	1799	238	41	6	69	57	52	51	7	1145	1197
St Mary's	1361	194	99	16	17	38	97	16	1	882	761	8	61	1806	164	13	16	4	49	1845	1764	194	29	6	57	13	53	96	13	862	839
Worcester	1768	45	1	31	32	3	7	...	3	401	359	1	57	1964	37	13	7	...	24	2067	2083	18	24	5	24	96	7	81	1	561	511
Somerset	2348	31	...	23	16	15	15	2	2	637	571	...	61	1446	37	2	1	1	27	1330	1333	12	...	...	34	19	7	12	1	8..	8..
Dorset	1950	172	6	9	7	15	23	4	...	634	514	9	44	2097	136	17	2	...	41	2347	2322	54	17	...	12	23	35	32	6	875	811
Talbot	1233	204	25	24	18	72	63	12	3	547	595	3	34	1216	160	51	8	2	44	1312	1297	57	9	3	39	29	81	74	6	666	681
Queen Anne's	1745	284	287	18	20	33	33	9	...	443	572	1	31	1246	259	73	10	4	30	2037	1864	57	44	9	32	39	24	57	4	579	657
Kent	1454	365	82	8	13	7	18	...	6	691	523	2	31	1491	285	7	4	...	36	1577	1423	134	76	1	31	19	39	20	3	611	...
Cecil	1345	390	47	3	12	7	86	...	10	286	216	...	33	1186	286	32	2	9	13	1506	1372	55	30	1	16	49	...	30	5	650	613
Total	23326	3576	1507	307	247	433	392	119	69	10826	8938	35	655	21242	1849	588	95	59	593	26637	24414	1423	367	59	493	577	378	708	57	10505	10063

Chapter 4

Document 4.1

The successful attack and seizure of Port Royal (now Annapolis), Nova Scotia, was the main achievement of British forces in the north during the War of the Spanish Succession/Queen Anne's War. The place had been taken from the French three times before, in the seventeenth century, and each time returned. This time it was treated as a reprisal for the Deerfield atrocity of 1704. See discussion on page 63.

Articles of Capitulation, 12 October 1710 pp.19–21.
At Port Royal, 12 Oct. N. S. 1710.
Articles of capitulation agreed for the reduction of Port Royal Fort in L'Acadie, between Mr. Daniel Auger DeSubercase, Esqr. of the military order of St. Louis, Governor under his most Sacred, most Christian Majesty, &c. and Mrs. [Sic'] Francis Nicholson, General and Commander in Chief of the troops belonging to her sacred majesty Anne, Queen of Great Britain.

1. That the Garrison shall go out with arms and baggage, beating the drum, and colours flying.
2. That we shall have good vessels, with sufficient provision to carry us to Rochel or to Rochfort by the nearest way, where the said vessels shall receive a good passport for their returning home.
3. That I shall have liberty to take six pieces of cannon, to my choice, with two mortars, to my choice also.
4. That the officers shall carry away all their effects, of what nature they may be; or they shall have liberty to sell them to the best advantage; the payment thereof shall be made faithfully.
5. That the inhabitants within cannon shot of the fort may stay upon their estates, and enjoy their grain, vessels and immoveables, for the space of two years, if they do not choose to go before that time; and that those that shall be willing to stay, shall have liberty so to do, provided, that they shall take the oath of fidelity to her sacred majesty of Great Britain.
6. That the privateers belonging to the West Indies shall have one vessel to carry them home.
7. That those that shall be willing to retire themselves to Placentia in Newfoundland, shall have the liberty by the nearest way.
8. That the Canadians and others that have a mind to go to Canada, may go in the space of one year.
9. That the effects, ornaments and utensils belonging to the Chapel shall be returned to the Chaplain, with the rest belonging to the hospital.
10. I promise to deliver the fort of Port Royal into the hands of Francis Nicholson, for the Queen of Great Britain, three days after the

ratification of these presents and agreement, with all the effects belonging to the king, viz: cannons mortars, bombs, bullets, powder and small arms.
11. I shall faithfully discover all the mines and underground works.

All the articles of the present agreement shall be faithfully fulfilled, and without difficulty, and signed on both sides.
Given at Port Royal, this 13th of October, 1710, N. S. Nicholson; Subercase
> Source: Journal of Rev. Thomas Buckingham, from *Roll and Service of Connecticut Service in Queen Anne's War, 1710–1711* (for the Acorn Club, The Tuttle, Morehouse and Taylor, 1916).

Document 4.2

This petition from Massachusetts in 1708 was a heartfelt plea emphasising the sufferings of the people of the colony, and their contribution to the war effort. See the discussion on page 67.

Thee State of the Province of Massachusetts Bay in New England to Queene
Anne [during Queen Anne's War] by Thomas Oliver
Boston, Massachusetts, October 20, 1708.
Address of the Council and Assembly of the Massachusetts Bay to the Queen. Oct. 20, 1708. It's nothing short of 20 years that your Majesties good subjects of this Province have been wasting under the calamitys of a distressing and expensive war, taking the commencement thereof from the rebellion and eruption of the Eastern Indians in 1688, save only the intervention of 3 or 4 years cessation after the Peace of Reyswick, during the continuance whereof they forbore to commit their bloody villanies and outrages. The French not daring then openly to avow, assist and protect them therein, yet in those years we were put to a very considerable charge in keeping constant guards and espyals over them to prevent surprisals by their perfidy and treacheries. And very soon upon the new declaration of war with France, they broke out again in open rebellion and hostility, committing divers barbarous murthers, just after a repeated and fresh recognition of their duty and allegience to your Majesty. We have been sharers in common with other our fellow subjects to a great degree in losses both of men and estate at home and at sea, both in the former and the present war, our trade is greatly diminished and we are very much exhausted, our yearly expence for our necessary defence, and to prevent the incursions of the enemy, is vastly great. But by the good Providence of God, in the early advice from time to time given of the motions of the enemy, and the prudent methods taken by your Majesty's Captain General to observe them, and preparations made for their reception in their descents upon us, has prevented those impressions which probably we might otherwise have felt, and they have

been forced to return back ashamed, not without loss on their part. But we have no prospect of the end of these troubles and of being eased of our heavy and insupportable charge and burthen, whilst we can act only defensively, and have to doe with enemys and rebells within our very bowells, who like beasts of prey, seek their living by rapine and spoil, and are such monsters that their barbaritys and crueltys are horrendous to humane nature, and they are animated and encouraged to such barbaritys by the French setting the heads of your Majesty's subjects at a price upon bringing in their scalps, and they kill many in cold blood after they have received them to quarter; they have the advantage of retiring for shelter to the obscure recesses of a vast rude wilderness, full of woods, lakes, rivers, ponds, swamps, rocks and mountains, whereto they make an easy and quick passage by means of their wherries, or birch canoes of great swiftness and light of carriage, the matter whereof they are made being to be found almost everywhere, and their skill and dexterity for the making and using of them is very extraordinary, which renders our tiresome marches after them inaffectual. These rebels have no fixed settlement, but are ambulatory and make frequent removes, having no other houses but tents, or hutts made of bark or rinds of trees, matts, etc., which they soon provide in all places where they come, so that it is impracticable to pursue or follow them with any body of regular troops; they are supported and encouraged by the French who make them yearly presents gratis of cloathing, armes and ammunition, besides the supplys they afford them for the beaver and furrs which they take in hunting, and constantly keep their priests and emissaries among them to steady them in their interests, and the bigoteries they have instiled into them. The French also oftimes join them in their marches on our frontiers. We humbly conceive, with submission, that the most probable method of doing execution upon them and reducing of them, is by men of their own colour, way and manner of living. And if your Majesty shall be graciously pleased to command the service of the Mohawks and Nations of the Western Indians, that are in friendship and covenant with your Majesty's several Governments, against these Eastern Indian rebels, for which they express themselves to stand ready, and to whom they are a terrour, they would, with the blessing of God, in short time, extirpate or reclaim them, and prevent the incursions made upon us from Canada, or the East. The force of the Enemy is chiefly bent against this your Majesty's Province and Province of New Hampshire, whilst we are a barrier to ye others. A letter from Monsieur Vaudreuil, Governour of Canada, to Mr. Brouillan, late Governour of Port Royal, was sometime since happily intercepted, and came to our Governour's hand, wherein he writes thus, namely, that he endeavours to keep all quiet on the side of Orange (or Albany) having command from the King his Master not to have any quarrel with your Majesty's subjects on that side, or with the Mohawks, which he hath strictly observed, and they are in a profound peace, having met with little or no loss on the land side, either in men or estates this warr, which has proved so very chargeable and grievous to us, in respect of both, which we made bold humbly to represent to your Majesty in 1704 *etc*. In the former war, when your Majesties subjects of Albany with their dependant Indians acted offensively against the enemy by partys frequently issuing forth into the woods, they greatly distressed the French and the Indians in their interests, made considerable spoils upon them, and prevented the descents from Canada upon these Plantations, which now are frequent. We pray leave in most humble manner further to offer to your Royal consideration the very great disadvantage this your Majesty's Province is at all times under, more especially in time of warr, by reason of Port Royal remaining in the hands of the French, which was originally a Scotts Colony granted and begun, and is included in the Royal Charter, or Letters Patent of this Province granted by their late Majestys King William and Queen Mary; the situation whereof makes it a Dunkirk to us with respect to navigation, it lying so apt and commodious for the intercepting of all shipping coming to, or going from hence to the eastward, and is a fit receptacle for privateers, who can soon issue out thence, and are near hand to send in their prizes, as also to annoy our Fishery, whereof we have had frequent experience, to the very great hurt of the trade of our Nation, and the diminution of your Majesty's Revenue. If your Majesty shall be graciously pleased, during the continuance of the present war, by your Royal Armes to reduce that Countrey and take it by force out of the French hands, or if by the blessing of God the just armes of your Majesty and your Allies be followed with repeated glorious successes, as of late they have been, so that the French King find himself under a necessity of suing for peace, and a treaty be thereupon negotiated, and your Majesty in your princely wisdom shall think fit, that place may have a consideration in that Treaty to be restored to your Majesties obedience, and setled by your Majesty's British subjects. It will be of the last importance to your Majesties. good subject, trading to and from these Provinces, and a general security to them, and also of singular benefit and advantage for the providing of masts for the use of your Majesty's Royal Navy, whereof that Countrey affords great plenty, which are now grown scarce nearer hand, and prevent the French King of that yearly supply he has from thence of Naval Stores. *Signed by Order*, Isa. Addington, Secrey. Council; Thomas Oliver, Speaker. *2 closely written pp.* [*C.O. 5, 865, Nos. 16, 16. i.; and 5, 913. pp. 66–74.*]

Source: *Calendar of State Papers Colonial, America and West Indies: Volume 24, 1708–1709*, ed. Cecil Headlam (London, 1922), pp. 314–317.

Chapter 5

Document 5.1

Advertisements for runaway slaves and servants were a common feature of colonial newspapers, particularly in Virginia, Maryland and Pennsylvania, from the 1730s. These are both convict servants, that is, criminals convicted in Britain and sentenced to be indentured servants in the North American colonies. See the discussion on pages 78–80.

RUN away from the Schooner Billy, at Hobb's Hole, on Monday the 15th Instant, a Convict Servant Man named Timothy Carpenter, about five Feet nine Inches high, is young, slim made, fair Hair, and has the Mark of the Irons he wore in Goal on one of his Ancles; had on a Cotton Jacket and Breeches, brown Linen Shirt and Trowsers, Felt Hat, Shoes and Stockings. He was imported last Winter in the Hodgson, Capt. Pajer. As it is probable he will offer himself as a Soldier or a Sailor, all Recruiting-Officers and Masters of Vessels are desired to take Notice of the said Servant. Any person who apprehends him and conveys him to the Iron-Works, in Prince-William County, shall receive Forty Shillings Reward, besides what the Law allows, from the Agent there, on Account of the Honorable John Tayloe, Esq;
Virginia Gazette (Purdie & Dixon), Williamsburg, April 5, 1770.

Thirteen Pounds Reward. RUN away, on Saturday the 10th instant, from the subscribers, living in Baltimore town, Maryland, the following servants, viz. JOHN CHAMBERS, an English convict servant man, about 21 years of age, 5 feet 7 or 8 inches high, of a pale complexion, gray eyes, and bandy legs; had on and took with him sundry suits of clothes, nine ruffled shirts, a brown bush wig, a pair of single channel boots, a blue cloth great coat, and 150 l. cash, which he robbed his masters house of on the night of his elopement. MARGARET GRANT, a mulatto, about 20 years of age, 5 feet 1 or 2 inches high; had on and took with her sundry women's apparel, but has since disguised herself in a suit of mens blue cloth clothes, attending as waiting boy on the above John Chambers. She is an artful hussy, can read and write, has been in Barbados, Antigua, the Grenades, Philadelphia, and says she was born in Carolina. Whoever apprehends the said servants, and secures them and the money, so that their masters may have them again, shall have the above reward, and reasonable charges, if brought home, paid by
HENRY JAMES. MORDECAI GIST. March 14, 1770.
Runaway Servant: *Virginia Gazette* (Rind), Williamsburg, June 2, 1774.

Ten Pounds Reward. RUN away, on the 8th of May, from the subscriber, living in Annapolis, two convict servant men, viz. Charles Sawyer, about 20 years of age, 5 feet 4 or 5 inches high, wears his own short black hair, looks bold, thin visaged, has been lately whipped for running away, and the marks are still to be seen; he is a Londoner. James Scarborough, about 5 feet 8 or 9 inches high, 25 years old, wears his own dark hair, dark eyebrows, came from the north of England, and speaks much in that dialect, is very talkative, and knock-kneed. Both these servants are bricklayers. They stole, and took with them, one Bath surtout coat, a blue cloth ditto, two pair of buckskin breeches, one new castor hat, bound with velvet ribband, three white shirts, two oznabrig ditto, and trousers, together with many other cloaths, the quality unknown. Whoever takes up and secures said servants, so that their masters may get them, shall receive the above reward, with reasonable charges, if brought home.

Thomas Price,
Thomas Michum.

     Source: *Virginia Gazette* (Hunter), Williamsburg, September 2, 1757.

N.B. The *Virginia Gazette* is obtainable through the Colonial Williamsburg portal, at http://research.history.org/DigitalLibrary/va-gazettes/, and all the runaway advertisements – both slaves and servants – are indexed and searchable online at Virginia Runaways Project, at http://www2.vcdh.virginia.edu/gos/index.html.

Document 5.2

Declaration of Nathaniel Bacon, Virginia, 1676. This is one of several documents Bacon produced during his brief control of affairs.

THE DECLARATION OF THE PEOPLE.

For having upon specious pretences of Publick works raised unjust Taxes upon the Commonalty for the advancement of private Favourits and other sinnister ends but noe visible effects in any measure adequate.

For not having dureing the long time of his Government in any measure advanced this hopefull Colony either by Fortification, Townes or Trade.

For having abused and rendered Contemptible the Majesty of Justice, of advancing to places of judicature scandalous and Ignorant favourits.

For having wronged his Majesty's Prerogative and Interest by assuming the monopoley of the Beaver Trade.

By having in that unjust gaine Bartered and sould his Mat Country and the lives of his Loyal Subjects to the Barbarous Heathen.

For haveing protected favoured and Imboldened the Indians against his Mat most Loyall subjects never contriveing requireing or appointing any due or proper meanes of satisfaction for their many Invasions Murthers and Robberies Committed upon us.

For having when the Army of the English was Just upon the Track of the Indians, which now in all places Burne Spoyle and Murder, and when wee might with ease have destroyed them who then were in open Hostility for having expresly Countermanded and sent back our Army by passing his word for the peaceable demeanour of the said Indians, who imediately prosecuted their evill Intentions Committing horrid Murders and Robberies in all places being protected by the said Engagement and word pass'd of him the said S'r William Berkley having ruined and made desolate a great part of his Majesty's Country, have now drawne themselves into such obscure and remote places and are by their successes soe imboldened and confirmed and by their Confederacy soe strengthened that the cryes of Bloud are in all places and the Terrour and consternation of the People soe great, that they are now become not only a difficult, but a very formidable Enemy who might with Ease have been destroyed &c. When upon the Loud Outcries of

126   Documents

Blood the Assembly had with all care raised and framed an Army for the prevention of future Mischiefs and safeguard of his Majesty's Colony. . . .

Of these the aforesaid Articles wee accuse Sir William Berkely, as guilty of each and every one of the same, and as one, who hath Traiterously attempted, violated and Injured his Ma[jesty's] Interest here, by the losse of a great Part of his Colony, and many of his Faithfull and Loyall subjects by him betrayed, and in a barbarous and shamefull manner exposed to the Incursions and murthers of the Heathen.

And we further declare these the Ensueing Persons in this

List, to have been his wicked, and pernitious Councellors, Aiders and Assisters against the Commonalty in these our Cruell Commotions [List follows]

> Source: 'Proclamations of Nathaniel Bacon', *The Virginia Magazine of History and Biography*, 1 (1) (July, 1893), pp. 55–63, 59–60.
> See the account and discussion on pages 92–93.

Document 5.3

This is one of several reports to arrive from Antigua, found in many editions in both the North American and London newspapers. The punctuation has been slightly amended, and superfluous capital letters reduced to lower case. See discussion on pages 85–86.

The Following is an Extract of another Letter from Antigua.
St.John's in Antigua, Oct. 24 1736

SIR,

There has been a general stop to all business, occasioned by the happy discovery of an accursed Negro Plot, which should have been perpetrated on the 11th Instant, which was the Anniversary of the King's Coronation, on which day the General usually gives a handsome ball to the Gentlemen and Ladies of the whole island but was postponed till the 30th Instant, upon the account of the death of the General's son at St.Christopher's some little time ago. This was the only preservative to all their lives. The plot was thus, *viz.*, One Court, a Negro man belonging to Thomas Kerby Esq, was the chief person in this affair. Tomboy, a Negro man belonging to Mr Thomas Hanson, Hercules, a Negro man belonging to Mr John Christophers: these two was to have been at this King Court's head Generals, and wile the Gentlemen and ladies were diverting themselves at the ball, which was to have been held at Mr Christopher Dunbar's new house, they were to convey a great quantity into the cellar and blow the house up, at the same time this King Court, Tomboy and Hercules was to head a party of four hundred men each, one from the East of the town, one from Otter's Pasture, and one from Morgan's Pasture, all armed with cutlasses, and to fall on the whites in the town, men, women and children without reserve, at the same time the House blew up, which was to be a general signal to the other parts of the island, for they were to place themselves (or at least a look-out) on several eminencies which, with a false fire they were to make at each place, was to convey the signal through the island. Then the Negroes of each plantation was to raise and destroy all the whites in their respective districts, and so have made themselves sole masters of the whole island. How this happy discovery was made is hardly to be accounted for, but some kind hand of providence induced the magistrates to enquire more strictly into their proceedings than usually they had done for playing dice etc., which was contrary to the wholesome laws of this island. They still discovered more and more, 'till at lat this Court, Tomboy and Hercules, being suspected for former crimes and high misdemeanors, was taken up, and after some struct examination found sufficient cause to commit them, and still more and more evidences against them, they were at length convicted.

On the 19th Instant at night being last Tuesday, the day following King Court was brought to the place of execution, there was laid extended on a wheel, seized by wrists and ankles, and so laid basking in the sun for the space of an hour and a quarter or more, when he begged leave to plead, the Justices gave their assent, when he acknowledged every thig that was alleged against him, and what his General Tomboy had confessed in prison the same morning when he was assured his time drew near for execution. At last about noon Mr King Court (for so they had actually made him, and bowed the knee to him at some great feast they had a little before the day they intended to prosecute their accursed design) was broke on the wheel, and his kingly cap and canopy was found in some Negro's possession, since which Tomboy was broke on the wheel on the Thursday, and on Friday Hercules, their bones were broke, and after, their heads cut off and stuck up on a pole of some considerable height, and four more of these honest Gentlemen were burnt the same day in Otter's Pasture, and tomorrow will be seven more, and so many as they can find leading men into this plot. This is all I can say to the affair at present, only that it puts us all into the utmost confusion, and all our people are under arms, and 'tis believed will continue so 'till after Christmas.

Source: *New York Weekly Journal*, 6 December 1736.

Glossary

Artificers: craftsmen or women, artisans whose employment conditions were governed by the English 1563 Statute of Artificers.
Black Caribs: a people of St. Vincent, described as such by the British authorities, who fought against them twice in the late eighteenth century, because of their mixed African and Carib descent. They were distinguished from the 'Yellow Caribs' who were regarded as the more authentic descendants of the native peoples.
Bridewell: generic word for prison or lock-up, named after the institution in London that from the late sixteenth century was used as a reformatory for many kinds of offenders.
Caribs or **Kalinago**, or **Island Caribs:** the native peoples of islands such St. Vincent and Dominica. They gave their name to the West Indian islands as a whole, though they spoke a language entirely different from that of the Tainos of the northern islands, and from that of the Arawak who they drove out of some of the islands before the arrival of Christopher Columbus in 1492.
Chesapeake, or **'The Chesapeake':** the bay off the coast of Virginia and Maryland, often used to designate those two colonies.
Convict servant: British or Irish criminal, transported to the colonies as a judicial sentence for petty crimes or as a reprieve from a death sentence.
Encomienda: Spanish system of forced or enslaved labour directed at Native Americans.
Habeas corpus: both a court order to release a prisoner and the English 1679 Act guaranteeing rights against arbitrary imprisonment and removal outside the jurisdiction.
Indentured servitude, indenture servant: British worker contracted for a fixed term to work in the colonies, whose voyage there was often paid for by the employer in advance, or undertaken by the captain of the ship who would recover costs by selling the contract on arrival. Equivalent to the French system for *les engagés*.
Les engagés: French colonial servants under contract or indenture, equivalent to British 'indentured servants'.

Mardi Gras: literally 'far Tuesday', the last Tuesday before Lent in the Christian calendar, or Shrove Tuesday in England, a time of final feasting and pleasure before the period of fasting.

Maroon: runaway or free slave, usually of African descent.

***Nouvelle France*:** the French colonies of North America, known in many British publications as New France.

Poor Law: English welfare system established in 1601 whereby every Church of England parish had an obligation to provide assistance for local people in need.

***Terra nullius*:** literally 'nobody's land' in Latin, which allowed a claim by European occupation in the absence of native peoples with a title to it.

Further reading

Chapter 1

Debates about how to approach the Atlantic and its complex history of imperial conquest and settlement, and the transatlantic relations of exchange and trade that were created, are best covered by Bernard Bailyn (2005), *Atlantic History: Concepts and Contours* (Cambridge, MA: Harvard University Press). A brief and interesting critical review can be found in P. A. Coclanis (2006), 'Atlantic World or Atlantic/World?' (WMQ 3rd. Ser. 63 (4), pp. 725–742). A key collection of essays exploring the possibilities and problems can be found in J.P. Greene and P.D. Morgan (eds.) (2009), *Atlantic History: A Critical Appraisal* (Oxford: Oxford University Press).

Chapter 2

Exploration tended to be heroic histories, and some of the original accounts of French explorers in L.P. Kellogg (1917), *Early Narratives of the Northwest, 1634–1699* (New York: Charles Scribner and Sons), still impress with tales of determination and hardiness. The conflicts about territorial claims and maps are well analysed by J.R. Short (2009), *Cartographic Encounters: Indigenous People and Exploration of the New World* (London: Reaktion Books).

Chapter 3

T. Benjamin (2009), *The Atlantic World: Europeans, Africans, Indians and their Shared History, 1400–1900* (Cambridge: Cambridge University Press), provides the most detailed and sweeping overview of exploration and settlement within the context of Atlantic relations, while providing a comparative context for the growth of the British and French empires. J. Pritchard (2004), *In Search of Empire: The French in the Americas, 1670–1730* (Cambridge: Cambridge University Press), has the best overall account of the French empire and its colonies in the Americas. P.N. Moogk (2000), *La Nouvelle France: The Making of French Canada: A Cultural History* (East

Lansing, MI: Michigan State University Press), provides a vivid historical account of the northern colonies.

On general patterns of development and settlement, Philip D. Morgan (ed.) (1993), *Diversity and Unity in Early North America* (London: Routledge), covers a great deal of ground, while useful syntheses can be found in Eric Nellis (2010), *An Empire of Regions: A Brief History of Colonial British America* (University of Toronto Press), and Alan Taylor (2002), *American Colonies: The Settling of North America* (Harmondsworth, Middlesex: Penguin).

Chapter 4

The general context of the wars can be gathered, along with more detailed accounts, from A. Gallay (2015), *Colonial Wars of North America, 1512–1763: An Encyclopedia* (London: Routledge), and D.F. Marley (2008), *Wars of the Americas: A Chronology of Armed Conflict in the Western Hemisphere*, 2nd ed. (Santa Barbara CA: ABC/CIO). Individual wars are studied by M.S. Anderson (1995/2014), *The War of the Austrian Succession, 1740–1748* (London: Routledge), and, in perhaps the best study of its kind, F. Anderson (2000), *Crucible of War: The Seven Years' War and the Fate of Empire in British North America, 1754–1766* (New York: Vintage/Random House). Overviews such as B. Simms (2007), *Three Victories and a Defeat: The Rise and Fall of the First British Empire,1714–1783* (New York: Basic Books), on the British Empire, J. Grenier (2005), *The First Way of War: American War Making on the Frontier, 1607–1814* (Cambridge University Press), on the American forms of warfare, and J. Axtell (1985), *The Invasion Within: The Contest of Cultures in Colonial North America* (New York: Oxford University Press), on cultural conflicts, give broader sweeps of warfare in the period.

Chapter 5

M. Craton (1982), *Testing the Chains: Resistance to Slavery in the British West Indies* (Ithaca NY: Cornell University Press), is one of the key studies of slave resistance; C. Taylor (2012), *The Black Carib Wars: Freedom, Survival and the Making of the Garifuna* (Oxford: Signal Books), is excellent on the wars against the Black Caribs. For servants and slaves, there are online sources such as the Virginia Runaways Project, at http://www2.vcdh.virginia.edu/gos/index.html, which allows a search of the runaway advertisements in the Virginia Gazette, and studies such as G. Morgan and P. Rushton (2004), *Eighteenth-Century Criminal Transportation: the Formation of the Criminal Atlantic* (Basingstoke: Palgrave), which provide the context of criminal transportation from Britain and the forms of running away and returning. The literature on the American and Haitian revolutions is huge. For the long-term background to the American Revolution there is J.P. Greene (1998), 'Empire and identity from the Glorious Revolution to the American Revolution', in P.J. Marshall (ed.) *The Oxford History of the British Empire vol.2: The Eighteenth Century* (Oxford University Press, pp. 208–230), while the story of the fighting is covered by S. Conway (2013), *A Short History of the American Revolutionary War* (London: I.B. Tauris), and A. O'Shaughnessy (2013), *The Men who Lost America: British Command during the Revolutionary War and the Preservation of Empire* (London: Oneworld Publications). Gwenda Morgan (2007), *The Debate on the American Revolution* (Manchester University Press), examines the way that the American Revolution has been interpreted, from its first historians who lived through it to the present day.

On Haiti, L. DuBois (2005), *Avengers of the New World: The Story of the Haitian Revolution* (Cambridge, MA: the Belknap Press of Harvard University), is one of the best accounts, and makes an interesting contrast with contemporary accounts, such as that by B. Edwards (1801), *An Historical Survey of the Island of Saint Domingo, together with an Account of the Maroon Negroes of the Island of Jamaica* (London: John Stockdale).

References

Manuscript sources

Court of Oyer and Terminer (Grenada), 1796, transcribed, Lawrence Brown, EAP295/2/6/1 Court of Oyer and Terminer for Trial of Attained Traitors record book [1796], transcription, online at https://eap.bl.uk/sites/default/files/legacy-eap/downloads/eap295_2_6_1_transcription.pdf [accessed 9 August, 2018].

National Archives, WO 1/82/423–6 Petition of the inhabitants of St. Vincent, 11 September, 1795; 583–586, R. Abercrombie's report and recommendations about the Black Caribs.

The National Archives, TNA CO 101/28.

Primary printed sources

Boston, Patience (1738a), *Faithful Narrative of the Wicked Life and Remarkable Conversion of Patience Boston alias Samson*, with a supplement by Samuel Moody and Joseph Moody and others. Boston: S. Kneeland and T. Green, online at http://xroads.virginia.edu/~ma05/peltier/conversion/boston.html [accessed 17 August, 2017].

—— (1738b), *The Confession, Declaration, Dying Warning and Advice of Patience Boston alias Samson*. Boston: S. Kneeland and T. Green.

Buckingham, T. (1916), Journal of Rev. Thomas Buckingham, from *Roll and Service of Connecticut Service in Queen Anne's War, 1710–1711* (for the Acorn Club, The Tuttle, Morehouse and Taylor).

Caillot, M.-A. (2016), A Company Man: The Remarkable French-Atlantic Voyage of a Clerk for the Company of the Indies, ed. E.M. Greenwald . New Orleans, LO: The Historic New Orleans Collection.

Callaghan, E.B. (ed.) (1885), *Documents Relative to the Colonial History of the State of New York*. Vol. V. Albany, NY: Weed, Parsons and Company.

Carleton, M. (1673a), *The Memoires of Mary Carleton, commonly stiled the German Princess, being a Narrative of her Life and Death*. London: Nathaniel Brooks.

—— (1673b), *The Counterfeit Lady Unveiled, being a Full Account of the Birth, Life, most remarkable Actions and untimely Death of Mary Carleton, Known by the Name of the German Princess*. London: Peter Parker.

Crouch, N. /Burton, R. (1685), *The English Empire in America, from Newfoundland to the Caribbean*. London: Nathaniel Crouch.

Dallas, R.C. (1804), *A History of the Maroons*. London: A. Strahan.

de La Salle, R. (1677), 'Memoir of Robert Cavelier de la Salle, On the Necessity of Fitting Out an Expedition to Take Possession of Louisiana', from B.F. French (ed)

Historical Collections of Louisiana (1846), Vol. 1, pp 25–34. New York: Wiley and Putnam.

de Rochefort, C. (1666), *History of the Caribby Islands* 2 Vols, trans. John Davies. London: Thomas Dring and Thomas Starkey.

Dumont, L. (2012), *The Memoir of Lieutenant Dumont, 1715–1747: A Sojourner in the French Atlantic. Jean-Francois-Benjamin Dumont de Montigny*, translated by Gordon M. Sayre, ed. by Gordon M. Sayre and Carla Zecher. Omuhundro IEAHC, University of North Carolina Press.

du Pratz, A.S. Le Page (1763), *The History of Louisiana, or of the Western Parts of Virginia and Carolina: Containing a Description of the Countries that Lie on Both Sides of the River Mississippi: with an Account of the Settlements, Inhabitants, Soil, Climate, and Products* 2 Vols. London: T. Beckett and P.A. de Hondt.

Edwards, B. (1801), *An Historical Survey of the Island of Saint Domingo, together with an Account of the Maroon Negroes of the Island of Jamaica*. London: John Stockdale.

Hennepin, L. (1699), *A New Discovery of a Vast Country in America . . . between New France and New Mexico* London: Henry Bonwicke.

Horsmanden, D. (1744), *The New York Conspiracy, or a History of the Negro Plot, with the Journal of the Proceedings against the Conspirators at New-York in the Years 1741–1742*. New York: Southwick and Pelsue, 1810.

Hughes, T. (1908), *The History of the Society of Jesus in North America, Colonial and Federal*, Vol. 1. New York: Columbia University and Longmans, Green and Co.

Joutel, M. (1714), *A Journal of the Last Voyage performed by Ms. De la Sale, to the Gulph of Mexico to the Mouth of the Mississippi River . . . translated from the Edition just Published at Paris.*

Kellogg, L.P. (1917), *Early Narratives of the Northwest, 1634–1699*. New York: Charles Scribner and Sons.

Kephart, H. (ed.) (2005), *The Captivity of Mary Rowlandson and other Indian Captivity Narratives*. Mideoloa, NY: Dover Publishing.

Klepp, S.E. and Smith, B.G. (eds.) (1992), *The Infortunate: The Voyage and Adventures of William Moraley, an Indentured Servant*. University Park, PA: Pennsylvania State University Press.

Ligon, R. (1657), *A True and Exact History of the Island of Barbados*. London: Humphrey Moseley.

Long, E. (1774), *The History of Jamaica*, 3 Vols, Vol. 2. London: T. Landes.

Mississippi Provincial Archives, 1729–1740: French Dominion Vol. 1. Jackson, MS: Mississippi Department of Archives and History, 1927.

Oldmixon, J. (1708), *The British Empire in America, containing . . . the History of all the British colonies on the Continent and Islands of America* 2 Vols. London: John Nicholson.

Stephens, S.K. and Kent, D.H. (eds.) (1941), *Wilderness Chronicles of Northwestern Pennsylvania*. Harrisburg, PA: Pennsylvania Historical Commission, 1941.

Turnbull, G. (1795), *A Narrative of the Revolt and Insurrection of the French Inhabitants of Grenada, by an Eye-Witness*. Edinburgh, UK: Constable.

Vaughan, T. and Clark, E.W. (eds.) (1981), *Puritans among the Indians: Accounts of Captivity and Redemption, 1676–1724*. Cambridge. MA: Belknap Press.

von Uchteritz, H. (1970), 'A German Indentured Servant in Barbados in 1652: The Account of Heinrich von Uchteritz'. Edited and translated by Alexander Gunkel and Jerome S. Handler, *Journal of the Barbados Museum and Historical Society* 33: 91–100. http://www.jeromehandler.org/wp-content/uploads/2009/07/Uchteritz-70.pdf

Yeardley, G. to Sir Henry Peyton, 10 November 1610, *Records of the Virginia Company* Vol. 3: 30. Washington, DC: Library of Congress, 1933.

Secondary sources

N.B. Where the university press and the city are identical, the publisher alone has been provided; e.g., Cambridge University Press. *The William and Mary Quarterly* has been shortened to *WMQ*.

Adams, C. and Pleck, E.H. (2010), *Love of Freedom: Black Women in Colonial and Revolutionary New England*. New York, NY: Oxford University Press.

Anderson, C. (2010), 'Old subjects, new subjects and non-subjects: silences and subjecthood in Fédon's Rebellion, Grenada, 1795–96', in R. Bessel and N. Guyatt (eds.), *War, Empire and Slavery, 1770–1830* (pp. 201–217). Basingstoke, UK: Palgrave Macmillan.

—— (2016), 'Rediscovering native North America: settlements, maps and empires in the Eastern Woodlands', *Early American Studies*, 14 (3), pp. 479–505.

Anderson, F. (2000), *Crucible of War: The Seven Years' War and the Fate of Empire in British North America, 1754–1766*. New York, NY: Vintage/Random House.

Anderson, M.S. (2014, originally 1995), *The War of the Austrian Succession, 1740–1748*. London: Routledge.

Ardener, E. (1968), 'Belief and the problem of women', in S. Ardener (ed.), *Perceiving Women* (pp. 1–27). London: Malaby Press.

Armitage, D. (2000), *The Ideological Origins of the British Empire*. Cambridge University Press.

Aubert, G. (2004), 'The Blood of France: race and purity of blood in the French Atlantic World', *WMQ*, 3rd Series, 61 (3), pp. 439–478.

Axtell, J. (1985), *The Invasion Within: The Contest of Cultures in Colonial North America*. New York, NY: Oxford University Press.

Bailyn, B. (2005), *Atlantic History: Concepts and Contours*. Cambridge, MA: Harvard University Press.

—— (2012), *The Barbarous Years. The Peopling of British North America: The Conflict of Civilizations, 1600–1675*. New York, NY: Random House/Vintage Books.

Bailyn, B. and Denaults, P.L (eds.) (2009), *Soundings in Atlantic History: Latent Structures and Intellectual Currents, 1500–1830*. Cambridge, MA: Harvard University Press.

Bannett, E.T. (ed.) (2011), *Transatlantic Stories and the History of Reading, 1720–1820*. Cambridge University Press.

Baugh, D. (2011), *The Global Seven Years War: Britain and France in a Great Power Contest*. London: Routledge.

Beckles, H.McD. (1985), 'Plantation production and white "proto-slavery": white indentured servants and the colonisation of the English West Indies, 1624–1645', *The Americas*, 41 (3), pp. 21–45.

—— (1990), '"A riotous and unruly lot": Irish indentured servants and freemen in the English West Indies, 1644–1713', *WMQ*, 47 (4), pp. 503–522.

Benjamin, T. (2009), *The Atlantic World: Europeans, Africans, Indians and their Shared History, 1400–1900*. Cambridge University Press.

Bentley, J.H. (1997), 'Revisiting the expansion of Europe: a review article', *The Sixteenth Century Journal*, 28 (2), pp. 503–510.

Berlin, I. (1993), 'Time, space, and the evolution of Afro-American society on British Mainland North America', in P.D. Morgan (ed.), *Diversity and Unity in Early North America* (pp. 81–104). London, Routledge.

Berson, J.S. (2009), 'How the Stono rebels learned of Britain's war with Spain', *The South Carolina Historical Magazine*, 110 (1–2), pp. 53–68.

Bialuschewski, A. (2011), 'Jacobite pirates?', *Histoire Social/Social History*, 44 (87), pp. 147–164.

Bickham, T.O. (2007), *Savages within the Empire: Representations of American Indians in Eighteenth-Century Britain*. New York, NY: Oxford University Press.

Billings, W.M. (1970), 'The causes of Bacon's Rebellion: some suggestions', *The Virginia Magazine of History and Biography*, 78 (4), pp. 409–435.

Bly, A.T. (1998), 'Crossing the lake of fire: slave resistance during the middle passage, 1720–1842', *Journal of Negro History* 83 (3), pp. 178–186.

Boorstin, D.J. (1958), *Americans: The Colonial Experience*. New York, NY: Random House.

Boucher, P.P. (1992), *Cannibal Encounters: Europeans and Island Caribs, 1492–176*. Baltimore, MD: The Johns Hopkins University Press.

Bowen, H.V., Mancke, E. and Reid, J.G. (eds.) (2012), *Britain's Oceanic Empire: Atlantic and Indian Ocean Worlds, c. 1550–1850*. Cambridge University Press.

Bromley, J.S. (1987), *Corsairs and Navies, 1600–1760*. London: The Hambledon Press.

Calloway, C.G. (1992), *North Country Captives: Selected Narratives of Indian Captivity from Vermont and New Hampshire*. Hanover, NH: University Press of New England.

—— (2013), *Ink and Pen Witchcraft: Treaties and Treaty Making in Native American History*. Oxford University Press.

Candlin, K. (2012), *The Last Caribbean Frontier, 1795–1815*. Basingstoke, UK: Palgrave Macmillan.

—— (2018), 'The Role of the enslaved in the "Fédon Rebellion" of 1795', *Slavery and Abolition*, published online April 2018.

Canny, N. (1978), 'The permissive frontier: the problem of social control in English settlements in Ireland and Virginia, 1550–1650', in K.R. Andrews, N.P. Canny and F.E.H. Hair (eds.), *The Westward Enterprise: English Activities in Ireland, the Atlantic and America, 1480–1650* (pp. 17–44). Liverpool, UK: Liverpool University Press.

—— (1994), 'English Migration into and across the Atlantic during the Seventeenth and Eighteenth Centuries', in Nicholas Canny (ed.), *Europeans on the Move: Studies on European Migration, 1500–1800* (pp. 64–75). Oxford, UK: Clarendon Press.

Clark, G. (1954), 'The character of the Nine Years' War, 1688–1697', *Cambridge History Journal*, 11 (2), pp. 168–182.

—— (1970), 'The Nine Years' War, 1688–1697', in J.S. Bromley (ed.), *New Cambridge Modern History, Vol. 6: The Rise of Great Britain and Russia, 1688–1715/25* (Chapter 7, pp. 223–253). Cambridge University Press.

Coclanis, P. A. (2006), 'Atlantic World or Atlantic/World?', *WMQ 3rd* Ser. 63 (4), pp. 725–742.
Coffman, D., Leonard, A. and O'Reilly, W (eds.) (2015), *The Atlantic World*. London: Routledge.
Colley, L. (1992), *Britons: Forging the Nation, 1707–1737*. New Haven, CT: Yale University Press.
—— (2002), *Captives: Britain, Empire and the World*. New York/London: Random House.
Conway, S. (2013), *A Short History of the American Revolutionary War*. London: I.B. Tauris.
Corrucini, R.S., Handler, J.S., Mutaw, R.J. and Lange, F.W. (1982), 'Osteology of a Slave Burial Population from Barbados, West Indies', *American Journal of Physical Anthropology*, 59, pp. 443–459.
Cox, E.L. (1982), 'Fédon's Rebellion 1795–1796: causes and consequences', *The Journal of Negro History*, 67 (1), pp. 7–19.
Crane, V.W. (1919), 'The Southern Frontier in Queen Anne's War', *American Historical Review*, 24 (3), pp. 379–395.
Craton, M. (1982), *Testing the Chains: Resistance to Slavery in the British West Indies*. Ithaca, NY: Cornell University Press.
Daniels, C. (2001), ' "Liberty to Complaine": servant petitions in Maryland, 1652–1797', in C.L. Tomlins and B.H. Mann (eds.), *The Many Legalities of Early America* (pp. 219–249). University of North Carolina Press/Omohundro Institute of Early American History and Culture.
Davies, K.G. (1974), *The North Atlantic World in the Seventeenth Century*. St. Paul, MN: University of Minnesota Press.
Dawdy, S.L. (2008), *Building the Devil's Empire: French Colonial New Orleans*. Chicago, IL: University of Chicago Press.
Debien, G. (1952), 'Engagés pour le Canada au XVIIe siècle vus de La Rochelle', *Revue d'histoire de l'Amérique française*, 6 (2) (1952), pp. 177–233.
Delbourgo, J. and Dew, N. (eds) (2008), *Science and Empire in the Atlantic World*. New York, NY: Routledge.
de Vorsey, L. (1992), 'Silent witnesses: Native American maps', *The Georgia Review*, 46 (4), pp. 709–726.
Doake, R.S. (2006), *Slave Rebellions*. New York: Chelsea Publishing (volume in the series *Slavery in the Americas*, general editor Philip Schwartz).
Doan, J.E. (2006), 'The Irish in the Caribbean', *ABEI Newsletter: Associação Brasileira de Estudos Irlandeses*, 8, pp. 105–116.
Drake, S.A. (1897), *The Border Wars of New England Commonly Called King William's and Queen Anne's Wars*. New York, NY: Charles Scribner's and Sons.
DuBois, L. (2005), *Avengers of the New World: The Story of the Haitian Revolution*. Cambridge, MA: The Belknap Press of Harvard University.
—— (2009), 'The French Atlantic', in J.P. Greene and P.D. Morgan (eds.), *Atlantic History: A Critical Appraisal* (pp. 137–162). Oxford University Press.
Duindam, J. (2010), 'Early Modern Europe: beyond the strictures of modernization and national historiography', *European History Quarterly*, 40(4), pp. 606–623.
Dunn, R.S. (1984), 'Servants and slaves: the recruitment and employment of labour', in J.P. Greene and J.R. Pole (eds.), *Colonial British America: Essays in the New History of the Early Modern Era*. Baltimore, MD: Johns Hopkins University Press.
—— (2014), *A Tale of Two Plantations: Slave Life and Labor in Jamaica and Virginia*. Cambridge, MA: Harvard University Press.

DuPlessis, R.S. (2016), *The Material Atlantic: Clothing, Commerce and Colonization in the Atlantic World, 1650–1800*. Cambridge University Press.

Eloranta, J. and Land, J. (2011), 'Hollow victory? Britain's public debt and the Seven Years' War', *Essays in Economic & Business History*, 29, pp. 101–117.

Falola, T. and Roberts, K.D. (eds.) (2008), *The Atlantic World, 1450–2000*. Bloomington, ID: Indiana University Press, part of the series *Blacks in the Diaspora*.

Farnsworth, P. (2000), 'Brutality or Benevolence in Plantation Archaeology', *International Journal of Historical Archaeology*, 4 (2), pp. 145–158.

Fauquez, A.C. (2015), 'Otherness and English identity in the colony of New York in the seventeenth century', in V. Alayrac-Fielding and C. Dubois (eds.), *The Foreigness of Foreigners: Cultural Representation of the Other in the British Isles, Seventeenth to Twentieth Centuries* (pp. 2–15). Newcastle, UK: Cambridge Scholars Publishing.

Fearnow, M. (1996), 'Theatre for an angry god: public burnings and hangings in colonial New York, 1741', *The Drama Review*, 40 (2), pp. 15–36.

Fitzpatrick, T. (1991), 'The figure of captivity: the cultural work of the puritan captivity narrative', *American Literary History*, 3 (1), pp. 1–26.

Foote, T.W. (2004), *Black and White in Manhattan: The History of Racial Formation in Colonial New York City*. New York, NY: Oxford University Press.

Franklin, J.H. and Schweninger, L. (1999), *Runaway Slaves: Rebels on the Plantation*. Oxford University Press.

Gallay, A. (2002), *The Rise of the English Empire in the American South, 1670–1717*. New Haven, CT: Yale University Press.

—— (2015), *Colonial Wars of North America, 1512–1763: An Encyclopedia*. London: Routledge.

Games, A. (1997), 'The English Atlantic world: a view from London', *Pennsylvania History: A Journal of Mid–Atlantic Studies*, 64, special edition, Empire, Society and Labour: Essays in Honor of Richard S. Dunn, pp. 46–72.

Gaspar, D.B. (1978), 'The Antigua slave conspiracy of 1736: a case study of the origins of collective resistance', *WMQ* 35 (2), pp. 308–323.

Gaspar, D.G. and Geggus, D.P. (eds.) (1997), *A Turbulent Time: The French Revolution and the Greater Caribbean*. Bloomington, IN: Indiana University Press.

Gaucher, M., Delafosse, M. and et Debien, G. (1959), 'Les engagés pour le Canada au XVIIIe siècle (suite)', *Revue d'histoire de l'Amérique française*, 13 (3), pp. 402–421.

—— (1961), 'Les engagés pour le Canada au XVIIIe siècle (suite et fin)', *Revue d'histoire de l'Amérique française*, 14 (4), pp. 583–602.

Gilroy, P. (1993), *Black Atlantic: Modernity and Double Consciousness*. London: Verso.

Gould, E.H. (2003), 'Zones of law, zones of violence: The legal geography of the British Atlantic, circa 1772', *WMQ*, 60 (3), pp. 471–510.

Grant-Costa, P. and Mancke, E. (2012), 'Anglo–Amerindian commercial relations', in H. V. Bowen, E. Mancke and J.G. Reid (eds.), *Britain's Oceanic Empire: Atlantic and Indian Ocean Worlds, c. 1550–1850* (pp. 370–406). Cambridge University Press.

Grave Matters: The Preservation of African-American Cemeteries (1996) anon, Columbia, SC: Chicora Foundation.

Greene, J.P. (1993), *The Intellectual Construction of America: Exceptionalism and Identity From 1492 to 1800*. Chapel Hill, NC: University of North Carolina Press.

—— (1993), 'Convergence: development of an American society', in P.D. Morgan (ed.), *Diversity and Unity in Early North America* (pp. 31–52). London: Routledge.

—— (1998), 'Empire and identity from the Glorious Revolution to the American Revolution', in P.J. Marshall (ed.), *The Oxford History of the British Empire* Vol. 2: The Eighteenth Century (pp. 208–230). Oxford University Press.

Greene, J.P. and Morgan, P.D. (eds.) (2009), *Atlantic History: A Critical Appraisal*. Oxford University Press.

Grenier, J. (2005), *The First Way of War: American War Making on the Frontier, 1607–1814*. Cambridge University Press.

Haffenden, P.S (1970), 'France and England in North America, 1789–1713', in J.S. Bromley (ed.), *New Cambridge Modern History, Vol. 6: The Rise of Great Britain and Russia, 1688–1715/25* (Chapter 9, pp. 480–508). Cambridge University Press.

Handler, J.S. (1995), 'An African-Type Burial, Newton Plantation', *African Diaspora Archaeology Newsletter*, 2 (3), Article 1, pp. 1–4.

—— (1996), 'A Prone Burial from a Plantation Slave Cemetery in Barbados, West Indies: Possible Evidence for an African-type Witch or Other Negatively Viewed Person', *Historical Archaeology*, 1996, 30 (3) pp. 76–86.

Handler, J.S. and Corrucini, R.S. (1983), 'Plantation Slave Life in Barbados: A Physical Anthropological Analysis', *Journal of Interdisciplinary History*, 14 (1), pp. 65–90.

Handler, J.S. and Reilly, M.C. (2017), 'Contesting "white slavery" in the Caribbean: enslaved Africans and European indentured servants in seventeenth-century Barbados', *New West Indian Guide*, 91, pp. 30–55.

Harrigan, M. (2012), 'Mobility and language in the Early Modern Antilles', *Seventeenth-Century French Studies*, 34 (2), pp. 115–132.

Hay, D. and Craven, P. (eds.) (2004), *Masters, Servants, and Magistrates in Britain and the Empire*. Chapel Hill, NC: University of North Carolina Press.

Higman, B.W. (2005), *Plantation Jamaica, 1750–1850: Capital and Control in a Colonial Economy*. Jamaica: University of the West Indies Press.

Hinderaker, E. (2012), 'Diplomacy between Britons and Native Americans, c. 1600–1830', in H.V. Bowen, E. Mancke and J.G. Reid (eds.), *Britain's Oceanic Empire: Atlantic and Indian Ocean Worlds, c. 1550–1850* (pp. 218–248). Cambridge University Press.

Hitchcock, D. (2016), *Vagrancy in English Culture and Society, 1650–1750*. London: Bloomsbury.

Hodson, C. (2012), *The Acadian Diaspora: An Eighteenth-Century History*. Oxford University Press.

Hoffer, P.C. (2003), *The Great New York Conspiracy of 1741*. Lawrence, KS: University Press of Kansas.

Holloway, J.E. (2005), *Africanisms in American Culture* (2nd ed.). Bloomington, IN: Indiana University Press.

Jamieson, R.W. (1995), 'Material Culture and Social Death: African-American Burial Practices', *Historical Archaeology*, 1995, 29 (4), pp. 39–58.

Jasanoff, M. (2012), *Liberty's Exiles: American Loyalists in a Revolutionary World*. New York, NY: Random House.

Kessel W.B. and Wooster, R. (eds.) (2005), *Encyclopedia of Native Americans Wars and Warfare*. New York, NY: Facts on File.

Kivelson, V. (2007), 'Claiming Siberia: Colonial Possession and Property Holding in the Seventeenth and Early Eighteenth Centuries', in N. B. Breyfogle, A. Schrader and W. Sunderland (eds.), *Peopling the Russian Periphery: Borderland Colonization in Eurasian History* (pp. 21–41). London: Routledge.

Klein, H.S. (1986), *African Slavery in Latin America and the Caribbean*. New York, NY: Oxford University Press.

Kopytoff, B.K. (1978), 'The early political development of Jamaican Maroon societies', *WMQ*, 35 (2), pp. 287–307.

—— (1979), 'Colonial treaty as sacred charter of the Jamaican Maroons', *Ethnohistory*, 26 (1), pp. 45–64.

Kupperman, K.O. (2012), *The Atlantic in World History*. Oxford University Press.

Lauber, A.W. (1913), *Slavery in Colonial Times within the Present Limits of the United States*. New York, NY: Columbia University/Longmans Green and Co.

Lee, W. (2001), *Crowds and Soldiers in Revolutionary North Carolina: The Culture of Violence in Riot and War*. Gainesville, FL: University Press of Florida.

Le Pelley, J. (1944), 'The Jacobite privateers of James II', *The Mariner's Mirror*, 30 (4), pp. 185–193.

Lepore, J. (2005), *New York Burning: Liberty, Slavery, and Conspiracy in Eighteenth-Century Manhattan*. New York, NY: Alfred A. Knopf.

Lewis, G.M. (1987), 'Misinterpretation of Amerindian Information as a Source of Error on Euro-American Maps', *Annals of the Association of American Geographers*, 77 (4), pp. 542–563.

Linebaugh, P. and Rediker, M. (2000), *The Many-Headed Hydra: Sailors, Slaves, Commoners, and the Hidden History of the Revolutionary Atlantic*. Boston, MA: Beacon Press.

Lockett, J.D. (1999), 'The deportation of the Maroons of Trelawny Town to Nova Scotia and then back to Africa', *Journal of Black Studies*, 30 (1), pp. 5–14.

Lockley, T. (2005), 'Rural poor relief in colonial South Carolina', *Historical Journal*, 48 (4), pp. 955–976.

Lockridge, K. (1970), *A New England Town: Dedham Massachusetts*. New York, NY: Norton and Co.

Lovejoy, D.S. (1972), *The Glorious Revolution in America*. New York, NY: Harper and Row.

Macinnes, A.I. (2007), *Union and Empire: The Making of the United Kingdom in 1707*. Cambridge University Press.

Mackey, H. (1965), 'The operation of the English Old Poor Law in colonial Virginia', *The Virginia Magazine of History and Biography*, 73(1), pp. 29–40.

Marley, D.F. (2008), *Wars of the Americas: A Chronology of Armed Conflict in the Western Hemisphere* (2nd ed). Santa Barbara, CA: ABC/CIO.

Marshall, P.J. and Low, A. (eds.) (1998), *The Oxford History of the British Empire Vol. II. The Eighteenth Century*. Oxford University Press.

Marston, D. (2002), *The American Revolution, 1774–1783*. Osceola, WI: Osprey.

McAnear, B. (1942), 'Mariland's Grevances Wiy the Have Taken Op Arms', *The Journal of Southern History*, 8 (3), pp. 392–409.

McCleskey, T. (1990), 'Rich land, poor prospects: real estate and the formation of a social elite in Augusta County, Virginia, 1738–1770', *Virginia Magazine of History and Biography*, 98 (3), pp. 449–486.

Meaders, D. (1975), 'South Carolina fugitives as viewed through local colonial newspapers, with emphasis on runaway notices, 1732–1800', *Journal of Negro History*, 60, pp. 288–319.

Meinig, D.W. (1986), *The Shaping of America: A Geographical Perspective on 500 Years of History. Vol. 1: Atlantic America, 1492–1800*. New Haven, CT: Yale University Press.

Middleton, R. (1992), *Colonial America: A History, 1607–1760*. Cambridge, MA: Blackwell.
Moogk, P.N. (2000), *La Nouvelle France: The Making of French Canada: A Cultural History*. East Lansing, MI: Michigan State University Press.
Moore, B.L., Higman, B.W., Campbell, C. and Bryan, P. (eds.) (2001), *Slavery, Freedom and Gender: The Dynamics of Caribbean Society*. Kingston, Jamaica: University of West Indies Press.
Morgan, E.S. (1975), *American Slavery, American Freedom: The Ordeal of Colonial Virginia*. New York, NY: W. Norton.
Morgan, G. (1984), 'Sold into slavery in retribution against the Nanziattico Indians', *Virginia Cavalcade*, 33 (4), pp. 168–173.
Morgan, G. and Rushton, P. (2004), *Eighteenth-Century Criminal Transportation: the Formation of the Criminal Atlantic*. Basingstoke, UK: Palgrave.
—— (2005), 'Visible bodies: power, subordination and identity in the eighteenth-century Atlantic world', *Journal of Social History*, 39 (1), pp. 39–64.
—— (2011), 'Fraud and Freedom: Gender, Identity and Narratives of Deception among Female Convicts in Colonial America', *Journal for Eighteenth-Century Studies*, 34 (3), pp. 335–355.
—— (2013), *Banishment in the Early Atlantic World: Convicts, Rebels and Slaves*. London: Bloomsbury Academic.
Morgan, K. (1989), 'Convict Runaways in Maryland', *Journal of American Studies* 23, pp. 253–268.
—— (2007), *Slavery and the British Empire: from Africa to America*. Oxford University Press.
Morgan, P.D. (1985), 'Colonial South Carolina runaways: their significance for slave culture', *Slavery and Abolition*, 6, pp. 57–78.
—— (1993), 'Bound labour: The British and Dutch colonies', in J. E. Cooke (ed.), *Encyclopaedia of the North American Colonies*. New York, NY: Charles Scribner's Sons.
—— (1999), *Slave Counterpoint: Black Culture in the Eighteenth-Century Chesapeake Low Country*. Chapel Hill, NC: University of North Carolina Press.
Morgan, P.D. (ed.) (1993), *Diversity and Unity in Early North America* (particularly Ira Berlin, 'Time, Space, and the Evolution of Afro-American society'). London: Routledge.
Mullin, G.W. (1972), *Flight and Rebellion: Slave Resistance in Eighteenth-Century Virginia*. Oxford University Press.
Murphy, T. (2018), 'A Reassertion of rights: Fédon's Rebellion, Grenada, 1795–96', *La Révolution française*. Online since 18 June 2018, connection on 20 June 2018. URL: http://journals.openedition.org/lrf/2017; DOI: 10.4000/lrf.2017
Nellis, E. (2010), *An Empire of Regions: A Brief History of Colonial British America*. Toronto: University of Toronto Press.
Nelson, L.H. and Alder, H.C. (eds.) (2002), *A History of Jonathan Alder, His Captivity and Life with the Indians,* transcribed by D. H. Davison. Akron, OH: University of Akron Press.
Newell, M.E. (2015), *Brethren by Nature: New England Indians, Colonists, and the Origins of American Slavery*. Ithaca, NY: Cornell University Press.
Newman, S.P. (2013), *A New World of Labour: The Development of Plantation Slavery in the British Atlantic*. Philadelphia, PA: University of Pennsylvania Press.
Njoh, A.J. (2016), 'French urbanism in North America', in A.J. Njoh (ed.), *French Urbanism in Foreign Lands* (pp. 17–46). New York, NY: Springer International.

O'Brien, J. (1997), *Dispossession by Degrees: Indian Land and Identity in Natick, Massachusetts, 1650–1790.* Cambridge University Press.

Ogborn, M. (2008), *Global Lives: Britain and the World.* Cambridge University Press.

O'Shaughnessy, A. (2013), *The Men who Lost America: British Command during the Revolutionary War and the Preservation of Empire.* London: Oneworld Publications.

Pagden, A. (1990), *Lords of All the World: Ideologies of Empire in Spain, Britain and France, c.1500–1800.* New Haven, CT: Yale University Press.

Paton, D. (2017), 'Maternal struggles and the politics of childlessness under pronatalist Caribbean slavery', *Slavery and Abolition*, 38 (2), pp. 251–268.

Patterson, O. (1970), 'Slavery and slave revolts: a socio-historical analysis of the First Maroon War. Jamaica, 1655–1740', *Social and Economic Studies*, 19 (3), pp. 289–325.

—— (1982), *Slavery and Social Death: A Comparative Study.* Cambridge, MA: Harvard University Press.

Perreault, M. (2006), '"To Fear and to Love Us": intercultural violence in the English Atlantic', *J. World Hist.*, 17 (1), pp. 71–93.

Pestana, C.G. (2009), *Protestant Empire: Religion and the Making of the British Atlantic World.* Pennsylvania, PA: University of Pennsylvania Press.

Pierre, M. (2017), *Le temps des bagnes, 1748–1953.* Paris: Éditions Tallandier.

Plank, G. (2001), *An Unsettled Conquest: The British Campaigns against the Peoples of Acadia.* Philadelphia, PA: University of Pennsylvania Press.

Powell, S.C. (1963), *Puritan Village: The Formation of a New England Town.* Hanover, NH: Wesleyan University Press.

Pritchard, J. (2002), 'The French West Indies During the Nine Years' War, 1688: 1697: A Review and Reappraisal', *French Colonial History*, 2, pp. 45–59.

Pritchard, P. (2004), *In Search of Empire: The French in the Americas, 1670–1730.* Cambridge University Press.

Prude, J. (1991), 'To Look upon the "Lower Sort": runaway ads and the appearance of unfree laborers in America, 1750–1800', *Journal of American History*, 78, pp. 124–159.

Rabin, D. (2012), 'In a Country of Liberty?: slavery, villeinage and the making of whiteness', *History Workshop Journal*, 72 (1), pp. 5–29.

Reid, J.G. et al. (2004), *The 'Conquest' of Acadia, 1710. Imperial, Colonial and Aboriginal Constructions.* Toronto: University of Toronto Press.

Richardson, R. (2001), 'Shipboard revolts, African authority and the Atlantic slave trade', *WMQ*, 58 (1), pp. 69–92.

Roper, L.H. (2009), *The English Empire in America, 1607–1658: Beyond Jamestown.* London: Pickering and Chatto.

Roper, L.H. and Van Ruymbeke, B. (2007), *Constructing Early Modern Empires: Proprietary Ventures in the Atlantic World, 1500–1750.* Leiden and Boston, MA: Brill.

Rushforth, B. (2012), *Bonds of Alliance: Indigenous and Atlantic Slaveries in New France.* Omuhundro IEAH/Chapel Hill, NC: University of NC Press.

Sandberg, B. (2006), 'Beyond encounters: religion, ethnicity, and violence in the early modern Atlantic World, 1492–1700', *Journal of World History*, 17 (1), pp. 1–25.

Schiebinger, L. (2004), *Plants and Empire: Colonial Bioprospecting in the Atlantic World.* Cambridge, MA: Harvard University Press.

Scott, J.C. (1990), *Domination and the Arts of Resistance: Hidden Transcripts*. New Haven, CT: Yale University Press.
Seed, P. (1995), *Ceremonies of Possession in Europe's Conquest of the New World, 1492–1640*. Cambridge University Press.
Shoemaker, N. (2004), *A Strange Likeness: Becoming Red and White in Eighteenth-Century North America*. Oxford University Press.
Short, J.R. (2009), *Cartographic Encounters: Indigenous People and Exploration of the New World*. London: Reaktion Books.
Sieminski, G. (1990), 'The Puritan captivity narrative and the politics of the American Revolution', *American Quarterly*, 42 (1), pp. 35–56.
Simms, B. (2007), *Three Victories and a Defeat: The Rise and Fall of the First British Empire, 1714–1783*. New York, NY: Basic Books.
Skidmore-Hess, C. (2013), 'Njinga of Matamba and the politics of Catholicism', in E. Clark and M. Laven (eds.), *Women and Religion in the Atlantic Age, 1550–1900* (pp. 123–140). Farnham, UK: Ashgate.
Smith, B.G. and Wojtowicz, R. (1989), *Blacks Who Stole Themselves: Advertisements for Runaways in the Pennsylvania Gazette, 1728–1790*. Philadelphia, PA: University of Pennsylvania Press.
Sparks, F.E. (1896), *Causes of the Maryland Revolution of 1689*. Baltimore, MD: Johns Hopkins University Press.
Stanwood, O. (2011), *The Empire Reformed: English America in the Age of the Glorious Revolution*. Philadelphia, PA: University of Pennsylvania Press.
Starkey, A. (1998), *European and Native American Warfare, 1675–1815*. London: Taylor and Francis/UCL Press.
Steele, I.K. (1980), 'The Empire and provincial elites: an interpretation of some recent writings on the English Atlantic, 1675–1740', in P. Marshall and G. Williams (eds.), *The British Atlantic Empire before the American Revolution* (pp. 1–32). London: Frank Cass and Co.
—— (1986), *The English Atlantic, 1675–1740: An Exploration of Communication and Community*. New York, NY: Oxford University Press.
Strong, P.T. (1999), *Captive Selves, Captivating Others: The Politics and Poetics of Colonial American Captivity Narratives*. Boulder, CO: Westview Press.
Szasz, F. (1967), 'The New York slave revolt of 1741: a re-examination', *New York History* 48 (3), pp. 215–230.
Taylor, A. (2002), *American Colonies: The Settling of North America*. Harmondsworth, UK: Penguin Books.
Taylor, C. (2012), *The Black Carib Wars: Freedom, Survival and the Making of the Garifuna*. Oxford, UK: Signal Books.
Thompson, A.O. (2006), *Flight to Freedom: African Runaways and Maroons in the Americas*. Jamaica: University of the West Indies Press.
Thompson, P. (2006), 'The thief, the householder, and the commons: languages of class in seventeenth-century Virginia', *WMQ*, 3rd Series, 63 (2), pp. 253–280.
Thornton, J.K. (1991), 'African dimensions of the Stono Rebellion', *The American Historical Review*, 96 (4), pp. 1101–1113.
Tomlins, C. (2010), *Freedom Bound: Law, Labour and Civic Identity in Colonising English America, 1580–1865*. Cambridge University Press.
Trattner, W. I. (1999), *From Poor Law to Welfare State: A History of Social Welfare in America*, 6th edition. New York, NY: The Free Press.

Usner, D.H. (1987), 'The frontier exchange economy of the Lower Mississippi Valley', *WM Q* 3rd ser., 44 (2), pp. 165–193
—— (1992), *Indians, Settlers and Slaves in a Frontier Exchange Economy: the Lower Mississippi*. Omohundro Institute of Early American History and Culture. Chapel Hill, NC: University of North Carolina Press.
Voorhees, D.W. (1994), 'The "Fervent Zeale" of Jacob Leisler', *WMQ*, 51 (3), pp. 447–472.
Wahrman, D. (2004), The Making of the Modern Self: Identity and Culture in Eighteenth-Century England. New Haven, CT: Yale University Press.
Waldstreicher, D. (1999), 'Reading the runaways: self-fashioning, print culture, and confidence in slavery in the Eighteenth-Century Mid-Atlantic', *WMQ*, 3rd ser, 56(2) (1999), pp. 243–272.
Ward, G. (2011), 'Nowhere is perfect: British naval centres on the Leeward Island Station during the Eighteenth Century', *Caribbean Connections*, 1 (1), unpaginated, online, [accessed 11 July, 2018].
Ward. H.M. (1999), *The War for Independence and the Transformation of American Society*. London: Taylor and Francis/UCL Press.
Wareing, J. (2017), *Indentured Migration and the Servant Trade from London to America, 1618–1718. 'There is Great Want of Servants'*. Oxford University Press.
Watson, K.L. (2015), *Insatiable Appetites: Imperial Encounters with Cannibals in the North Atlantic World*. New York, NY: University Press.
Watters, D.R. (1994), 'Mortuary Patterns at the Harney Site Slave Cemetery, Caribbean Montserrat, in Perspective', *Historical Archaeology*, 28 (3), pp. 56–73.
Watts, C. (2007), *The Cultural Work of Empire: The Imagining of the Shandean State*. Edinburgh University Press.
Weddle, R.S. (1991), *The French Thorn: Rival Explorers in the Spanish Sea, 1682–1762*. College Station, TX: Texas A&M University Press.
White, S. (2011), 'Geographies of slave consumption: French colonial Louisiana and a world of goods', *Winterthur Portfolio*, 45 (2/3), pp. 229–247.
—— (2013), 'Massacre, Mardi Gras, and torture in early New Orleans', *The WMQ* 3rd ser. 70 (3), pp. 497–538.
Wilson, K. (2009), 'The performance of freedom: Maroons and the colonial order in Eighteenth-Century Jamaica and the Atlantic Sound', *WMQ*, 3rd ser. 66 (1), pp. 45–86.
Wolf, E.R. (2010), *Europe and the People Without History*. Oakland, CA: (originally 1982). University of California Press.
Zacek, N. (2009), '"A People so subtle": Sephardic Jewish pioneers of the English West Indies', in C.A. Williams (ed.), *Bridging the Early Modern Atlantic World: People, Products and Practices on the Move* (pp. 97–112). Farnham, UK: Ashgate.
—— (2010), *Settler Society in the English Leeward Isles, 1670–1775*. Cambridge University Press.
Zimmerman, J.F. (1999), *The New England Town Meeting: Democracy in Action*. Westport, CT: Praeger.

Index

Abercrombie, General Ralph 104, 132
Acadia (Nova Scotia), Acadians 26–7, 67, 69–71, 91, 104
Accompong Town (Jamaica) 104, 106
Adams, C. 42
Advertisements (Newspapers) 2, 12, 43, 78–80, 115, 130, 142
Africans ix, 1, 3–4, 7, 12, 20, 22, 27, 29, 34, 36, 39, 46–7, 50, 54–5, 57, 77–8, 82, 86, 103, 108, 128
Aix-la-Chappelle, Treaty of 69
Akan 82, 90
Amazon, The 15
Amherst, Lord Jeffery 72–3
Anderson, C. (2010) 102
Anderson, F. 71, 73
Anderson, M.S. 68–9
Andros, Governor Sir William (Massachusetts) 92, 94
Anguilla 68
Annapolis Royal, Nova Scotia 119, 123
Antigua viii, 13, 29, 46, 63, 84–5, 125, 137
Antilles 11, 29
Apalachee (Native Americans) 67
Arawaks 29
Ardener, E. 78
Armitage, D. 14
Atlantic, The Atlantic World 5, 30, 47, 67, 129
Atlantic, The Black 5
Atlantic, The Criminal 5 130
Atlantic, The Green 5
Atlantic, The Material Atlantic 5
Atlantic, The Red 5
Attainder, Act of 102–3
Aubert, G. 34
Axtell, J. 61–2, 69

Bacon, Nathaniel 64, 92–3, 109, 124
Bahamas 99
Bailyn, B. 4, 5
Baltimore Company 56
Baltimore, Lord 94
Barbados 12–13, 23, 29, 49, 53–5, 84, 108, 133–4, 138
'Barbadosed' 23
Battle of Camden 97
Battle of the Saintes (1782) 74
Baugh, D. 72–3
Bay of Fundy 70
Beckles, H.McD. 24, 84
Behn, Aphra 9, 13
Belle Île-en-Mer (Brittany) 70
Benjamin, T. 3, 12, 26, 32
Berkeley, Sir William 92–3
Berlin, I. 39
Berson, J.S. 87
Bickham, T.O. 14
Bideford (Devon, England) 11
Bly, A.T. 84
Board of Trade (London) 96
Boorstin, D.J. 41, 62
Boston (Massachusetts) 42, 92, 98
Boston Evening Post 86, 89
Boston Gazette 83
Boston Weekly Newsletter 85
Boston, Patience 33
Boucher, P.P. 34
Bouquet, Henry 21, 112
Braddock, General Edward 70–1
Brest 57, 74
Bridewell 41, 127
Bristol 24, 70
British Honduras 90
Bromley, J.S. 65
Buccaneers 63–4, 66
Buckinghan, Rev. Thomas 119

Burke, Edmund 96, 99
Burton, Richard 14

Caillot, M.-A. 57
Callaghan, E.B. 88
Calloway, C.G. 37, 62
Canada 9, 16, 26–7, 31, 57, 60, 64, 70, 72–3, 81, 99, 108, 119, 121–2
Candlin, K. 101
Canny, N. 4, 26
Cap Français 89
Cape Verde 12
Captive narratives 34–7
Captives (war) 23, 33, 63
Caribbean 1, 3, 11–12, 22, 25–7, 29, 34, 40, 50, 50–1, 57–8, 60, 64, 66, 68–9, 73–5, 81, 100, 105, 107
Caribbean Regiments 106
Caribs 104
Caribs, Black 29, 73–4, 127
Caribs, Yellow 84, 103
Carleton, Mary 13
Carolina, North 11
Carolina, South 23, 33, 39, 50, 67, 70, 84, 86, 97
Cartagena 68
Carter Grove Plantation (Virginia) 49
Catholic Church 28, 100
Catholics 27, 66, 71, 87, 94, 115
Cayenne 63
Charleston (Charlestown), South Carolina 45, 67, 86, 97
Chesapeake 53, 74, 93, 97, 115, 127
Chickasaws 20, 112
Choctaw 20, 111
Church of England 38, 41, 45
Clark, E.W. 35, 37
Coclanis, P.A. 6
Code Noire (French Law Code for African slaves) 44, 47
Coffman, D. 7
Colden, Lt. Governor Cadwallader 88
Colley, L. 36–7, 60
Continental Army (of the USA) 98
Continental Congress 96
Conway, S. 96
Cooke, Ebenezer 14
Cornwallis, Charles 74
Coromantee (or Coromantin, Akan-speaking people) 82, 85, 90
Corrucini, R.S. 50
Corunna/Coruña 103
Cox, E.L. 101, 103
Craton, M. 101–3, 106

Craven, P. 52
Creek (Native Americans) 67
Cromwell, Oliver 23, 71, 104
Crouch, N., See Burton, Richard
Cudjo (maroon) 83
Cuffee (maroon) 83
Curaçao 89

Dahomey 82
Dallas, R.C. 105
Dauphine Island (Mobile) 20
Davies, K.G. 26–7, 29, 57
Dawdy, S.L. 44
De Grasse, François-Joseph Paul, Admiral 74
De La Salle, René Robert Cavalier Sieur 16
De Menonville, Thierry 17
De Rochefort, C. 11, 14, 28
De Vorsey, L. 18–19
Death, Mortality Rates 25, 28, 50
Debien, G. 22
Dedham (Massachusetts) 41–2
Deerfield (Massachusetts) 67
Defoe, D. 9, 13, 36
Delbourgo, J. 17
Denaults, P.L. 5
Dew, N. 17
Dickenson, Jonathan 36
Disease 4, 25, 28–9, 41, 44–5, 56, 64–9, 114, 122
Doake, R.S. 86
Doan, J.E. 92
Dominica 13, 29, 73
Drake, Francis 81
Du Pratz, A.S. Le Page 16
Du Roullet, Régis 20–1
Dubois, L. 26–7, 100
Dumont, Lieutenant 19, 23–4, 34
Dunn, R.S. 26, 48–50
DuPlessis, R.S. 5, 7, 80
Dutch 8, 25, 60, 63–4, 66, 74, 93, 98

East Indies 24
Edwards, B. 105
Eloranta, J. 73
Empire, British 1–2, 14, 58, 96, 99, 109
Empire, French 1, 3, 28, 44, 76, 95
Empire, Mugha 41
Empire, The Ottoman 4
Encomienda 7, 31
Engagés (French indentured servants) 22, 27, 57, 78

Index 147

England, Expansion of 2, 4
Ethnic cleansing 31, 58, 71, 104, 106, 109

Falola, T. 6
Farnsworth, P. 50
Fearnow, M. 89
Fédon, Julien 101–2, 106
First Carnatic War (India) 68
Florida 36, 67, 69, 86
Foot Guards (British) 64
Ford, John 35
Fort Duquesne 70–2
Fort Necessity 70
Fort Pitt 72, 112
Fort William Henry 71
France, French Republic 48, 99–100, 103

Gallay, A. 53
Games, A. 9
Garifuna 104
Gaspar, D.B. 85
Gaucher, M. 22
George I 65
Georgia 51, 68–9
Germany/German 13, 26, 65, 86, 93
Ghana (see also Akan, Coromantee) 82, 90
Gilroy, P. 5
Glorious Revolution (1688) 64, 92, 94
Gold Grove Plantation (Jamaica) 48
Gould, E.H. 47
Grant-Costa, P. 32
Great Lakes 16
Greene, J.P. 6, 14, 45–6, 96
Grenada 47, 73–4, 101–4, 106, 111
Grenier, J. 62
Guadaloupe 29, 66, 72, 74–5, 101, 109
Gullah culture (South Carolina) 50

Habeas Corpus 44
Haffenden, P.S. 65
Haiti 48, 74–5, 84, 90, 95, 99–101, 105–6, 109
Hakluyt, Richard 38
Hammon, Briton 36
Handler, J.S. 23, 49–51, 53, 55
Harrigan, M. 12
Hay, D. 52
Heights of Abraham 63, 72
Hennepin, Louis 16
Higman, B.W. 48
Hispaniola 89
Hitchcock, D. 45

Home, Lt. Governor Ninian 101
Horsmanden, Daniel 88–9
Hudson River 3
Hughes, T. 56
Huguenot 26, 57
Hugues, Victor 101
Hunter, Governor Robert 87–8
Huron 32, 34, 62

Indians, see Native Americans
Ireland 38 53, 64, 71, 104
Irish xii, 26, 55, 63, 66, 77, 79, 84, 86, 92
Ironworks 56
Iroquois 32, 34, 62, 65–6

James (Stuart), the 'Old Pretender' 65
James II 65, 92–4
Jamieson, R.W. 50
Jasanoff, M. 97
Jefferson, Thomas 100, 103
Jesuit Relations See Jesuits
Jesuits 9, 15–16, 34–5, 56, 108
Jews 25, 27, 117
Joutel, Henri 16

Kellogg, L.P. 16
Kent, D.H. 21, 112
Kessel, W.B. 66–7
King William III 64, 66, 93–4
Kingston (Jamaica) 106
Kivelson, V. 3
Knowles, Admiral Charles 69
Kongo 87
Kopytoff, B.K. 83
Kupperman, K.O. 7–8, 24–5, 33, 57–8

Labour, forced 7, 31
Lachine (Canada) 65
Land, J. 73
Lauber, A.W. 32–3
Lawrence, Lt.Gov. Charles (Nova Scotia) 70
Le Pelley, J. 65
Lee, Charles 21
Leeward Islands 47, 49, 82–3
Leisler, Jacob 92–4
Lepore, J. 85, 89
Les Filles de roi (French female indentured servants) 58
Lescarbot, Marc 11
Lewis, G.M. 19
Ligon, Richard 12–13, 54–5
Linebaugh, P. 5

Lockett, J.D. 105
Lockley, T. 45
Lockridge, K. 41–2
Long, Edward 90
Louis XIV (of France) 19, 44, 47, 63, 65
'Louis', slave 47
Louisbourg 69, 72
Louisiana 16–17, 19–20, 24, 26, 28, 32, 43–4, 57, 70, 73
Lovejoy, D.S. 64, 92
Loyalists 97, 99

Macinnes, A.I. 14
Mackey, H. 45
Madeira 12, 89
Magna Carta 47, 116
Maine 33
Mancke, E. 32
Mansfield, Lord Chief Justice James 47
Mardi Gras (Shrove Tuesday) 80–1
Marley, D.F. 63–4, 69, 72
Maroons 82–4, 104–5
marronage 81, 100 see also maroons
Marston, D 98–9.
Martinique 29, 66, 74, 91, 109
Maryland 19, 22, 38, 53, 55–6, 79, 81, 92, 94, 108, 115, 118
Maryland Gazette 79
Maryland, population survey of (1764) 118
Massachusetts 14, 23, 31–3, 35, 38, 41–2, 67, 69, 88, 92, 94, 109, 120
McAnear, B. 94
McCleskey, T. 58
Meinig, D.W. 29–31, 34, 44
Micmac (Native Americans) 69
Middleton, R. 92
Migration, forced 8, 23
Milbourne, Jacob 93
Ministry of Marine (France) 8, 17, 23, 64
Minorca 71
Mississippi, River 16, 18–19, 21, 111
Mitchell, John 18
Mobile 17, 20, 24, 111
Mohawks 65, 121
Moll Flanders, see Defoe
Monmouth, Duke of 13, 53, 93
Montcalm, Marquis de 71–2
Montreal 21, 65, 73
Montserrat 50, 63, 92
Moogk, P.N. 28
Moore, B.L. 51
Moore, James (Governor of South Carolina) 67

Moore, John 103
Moraley, William 51, 53–4, 114
Morgan, E.S. 53–4
Morgan, G. 13, 23–4, 26, 31, 53, 71, 78–80
Morgan, K. 51
Morgan, P. 6, 26, 38–9, 49
Mosley, Father 51, 56, 115
Mount Airy Plantation (Virginia) 48
Munro, Colonel George 71
Murrin, J.M. 38

'Nanny' (Jamaica maroon), Nanny Town 82–3
Natchez 20, 57
Native Americans 4–5, 7, 11, 18, 24–5, 29–32, 35, 37, 39, 61–3, 65–7, 69, 71, 92, 94
Negro Act, South Carolina 1740 87
Nellis, E. 38
Nevis 66
New England 1, 9, 23, 25, 27, 29–30, 32–3, 35–6, 38, 40–2, 45, 69–70, 81, 83, 91, 94
New England Weekly Journal 83
New France/Nouvelle France 15, 27, 34–5
New Hampshire 37
New Orleans 15–17, 20–1, 43, 58, 78, 80, 112
New York, Slave 'conspiracy' 1741 46–8, 90
Newell, M.E. 32
Newfoundland 11, 14, 39, 66–7, 73
Newman, S.P. 23, 54
Newspapers, runaway advertisements 43, 78–81, 84
Newtown Plantation (Barbados) 49
Niagara 21
Nicholson, Governor Francis (New York) 93, 119–120
Njoh, A.J. 43
Nova Scotia 43, 45–6, 63, 66–7, 69–71, 74, 91, 104–5, 119

O'Shaugnessy, A. 97
Obeah 83, 90
O'Brien, J. 33
Ogborn, M. 47
Oglethorpe, Governor James (Georgia) 68–9
Ohio, River 17, 25
Oldmixon, John 14
Oyer and Terminer, Court of 102

Pagden, A. 2
Palatinate (Rhineland) 20
Paton, D. 24, 51
Patriarchy 77
Patterson, O. 50, 82–3
Peace of Paris (1783) 99
Pennsylvania 21–2, 33, 55, 58, 70, 79, 97, 108
Pepperell, William 69
Pestana, C.G. 64
Philadelphia 45, 53, 58, 78–9, 97
Philippines 61
Pierre, M. 57
Pitt, William (the Elder) 60, 70–2
Pittsburgh 21, 72
Plank, G. 71
Plantation (economy) 7–8, 12, 22, 24, 32, 34, 39, 41–3
Plantation, Golden Grove (Jamaica) 48
Plantation, Mount Airy (Virginia) 48–9
'Plantocracy' 102
Pleck, E.H. 42
Poor Law (British North America) 44–5
Poor Law (England) 41
Porto Bello 68
Portugal/The Portuguese 15, 20, 23–4, 29, 89
Powell, S.C. 41
Pownall, Thomas 18
Price, Richard 96
Prisoners of war 33, 98
Pritchard, J. 65–6
Pritchard, P. 27–9, 57, 91
Privateers 44, 64–5, 75, 119, 122
Prude, J. 78
Punishment 24, 33, 43, 46, 50, 52–3, 57, 85–7, 88, 90, 103, 105, 114
Puritan 12, 23, 25, 34, 38, 41–2

Quakers 23
Quebec 43, 63, 66, 72–3, 109
Quiberon Bay (Brittany) 72

Rebellion, definition 76–7
Rediker, M. 5
Reilly, M.C. 23, 51, 53
Resistance, definition 76–7
Revolution, definition 77
Rhodes, John 36–7
Richardson, R. 84
Rights of Man, Declaration 100
Roanoke (North Carolina) 11
Roatán Island 104
Roberts, K.D. 22

Rodney, Admiral George 74
Roper, L.H. 8, 61, 96
Rowlandson, Mary White 35
Royal Navy (British) 39, 64, 73–4, 95, 97, 103, 122
Runaways 13, 43, 78–81
Rushforth, B. 34, 46–7
Rushton, P. 13, 23–4, 26, 53, 71, 78–80

Salem (Massachusetts) 88
Sandberg, B. 30–1
Santiago de Cuba 68
Schiebinger, L. 17
Scott, J.C. 78, 80
Seed, P. 2
Seeley, J.R. 2
Senegal Company 91
Servants, see Indentured Servants
Shakespeare, W. 13
Shirley, Governor William (Massachusetts) 31, 69
Shoemaker, N. 18
Short, J.R. 18–9
Siberia 2
Simms, B. 75
Skidmore-Hess, C. 7
Slave Graveyards 49–50
Slave Trade 1, 3, 5, 45, 47–8, 51, 75, 107, 116
Slavery – Slave Societies 1, 42, 46–51
Slaves, revolts 74, 77, 84–91
Smith, B.G. 78–9
Smith, John 39
Somerset, James 47
Southampton 70
Spain/the Spanish 3–5, 7–8, 11, 15–17, 25, 28–9, 31, 33, 36–8, 59, 63–4, 66–8, 73–5, 81, 86, 97, 104, 107
Sparks, F.E. 94
St. Augustine, Florida 67, 69, 86
St. Domingue 17, 29, 86, 91, 104
St. Eustatius 74, 89
St. John's, Newfoundland 67, 89
St. Kitts (St. Catherine's) 63, 66, 92
St. Lawrence (River) 16, 72
St. Lucia 29, 74, 82, 101, 103
St. Vincent 29, 73–4, 84, 106
Stanwood, O. 64
Starkey, A. 33, 66
State Papers Colonial 2
Steele, I.K. 25–6
Stephens, S.K. 21, 112
Stockwell, Quentin 37

Strong, P.T. 35–6
Surinam 11, 63
Susquehannocks (Native Americans) 92
Szasz, F. 88

Tacky's Rebellion, Jamaica 80
Taylor, C. 104
Terra Nullius 30
Thompson, A.O. 93, 104
Ticonderoga (Fort Carillion) 72
Tobago 73
Tomlins, C. 25
Toulon 74
Trafalgar 75
Transportation (of Criminals) 86, 105
Transportation Act 1718 23, 57
Trattner, W.I. 45
Treaty of Paris (1763) see Paris
Treaty of Utrecht (1713) 67
Trelawny Town (Jamaica) 104–5
Trenton (New Jersey) 98
Trinidad 74, 103
Turnbull, Gordon 102

United States, Constitution 62
Ury, John 89
Usner, D.H. 32

Van Ruymbeke, B. 8
Vattel, E. de 63
Vaughan, T. 35, 37
Venango or Wenango Trail 21, 113
Vermont 37
Vernon, Admiral Edward 68
Versailles 91
Virginia 9, 12–13, 19, 22, 27, 31, 38–42, 45, 48–9, 51–5, 61, 64, 68, 70, 74, 79, 81, 92–3, 97, 103, 108–9
Von Steuben, Baron 98
Von Uchteritz, Heinrich 55
Voodoo 90
Voorhees, D.W. 93

Wahrman, D. 78
Waldstreicher, D. 78–80
War, First Maroon 83
War, Second Maroon 84, 104–5
War, for American Independence (1776–83) 22, 56, 62, 65, 95, 103

War, King Philip's (1675–6) 32–3, 35, 37, 67, 81
War, Laws of 63, 99
War, Nine Years' (King William's War) (1688–97) 64–6
War, of Jenkin's Ear (1739–42) 67–8
War, of the Austrian Succession (1742–48) 68–9
War, of the Spanish Succession (Queen Anne's) (1702–1713) 66–7
War, Pequot 32
War, Second Anglo-Dutch (1665–7) 63–4
War, Second Carib 104
War, The Seven Years' (French and Indian War) (1756–1763) 69–73
Ward, G. 64
Ward, H.M. 98
Wareing, J. 23
Watson, K.I. 34–5
Watters, D.R. 50
Watts, C. 61
Weddle, R.S. 16
Wenango, See Venango
Wentworth, Admiral 68
West, Benjamin 73
Whipping, See Punishment
White, John 13
White, S. 20, 79–81
Williamsburg (Virginia) 42, 45
William III and Queen Mary 64, 66, 93–4
Williams, John 37
Williamson, Peter 23, 36
Windwards 83
Winslow, Edward 41
Wojtowicz, R. 78
Wolf, E.R. 9
Wolfe, General James 72
Wooster, R. 66–7
Worcester, Battle of 55

Yamasee (Native Americans) 67
Yeardley, Sir George 39
Yorktown (Virginia) 74, 97

Zacek, N. 25, 49
Zimmerman, J.F. 41